"Donald Kraybill penetrates the rhetoric of the arms race and gives Christians the help we need in understanding what is going on, and what God thinks about the nuclear madness. I believe *Facing Nuclear War* has the potential for doing for the Christian community what Jonathan Schell's *The Fate of the Earth* is accomplishing in the larger public."—John Kenyon, associate editor, *Christian Herald.*

*   *   *

"Kraybill's book is the best introduction to the problems of nuclear war that I have read. It says what needs to be said—but without being hysterical or rude to those who disagree. It's excellent—ideal for adult discussion groups, Sunday schools, or to give to someone you're encouraging to grapple with the issue."—John Alexander, coeditor, *The Other Side.*

*   *   *

"For the Christian who may read only one book on nuclear weapons, that book should be Donald Kraybill's *Facing Nuclear War.* It is an ingenious combination of distilled facts and analyses with an uncompromising evangelical faith. The subtitle, "A Plea for Christian Witness," indicates the consistent faith orientation. But the significant surprise in reading the book is how complex matters such as nuclear strategy are simplified without being simplistic. The book also excels in exposing the many myths that prevail in the heated debate about nuclear weapons. The writer has a welcome gift of separating out the multiple strands of moral arguments in a way that invites dialogue and further thought. If nuclear weapons confront Christians with the most urgent ethical problem of our time, every Christian should read this book."—Edgar Metzler, National Coordinator, New Call to Peacemaking.

*   *   *

"Donald Kraybill's *Facing Nuclear War* (1) is well-researched, but written in such a way as to make statistics and technical data easily understandable; (2) combines in each chapter some facet of the nuclear threat with biblical material that points to alternatives; (3) is an excellent study resource for youth and adult groups in local churches; and (4) will be useful for lay persons who are concerned about nuclear escalation and wish to be more conversant on the issues."—Earle W. Fike, Jr., moderator of the Church of the Brethren Annual Conference.

*   *   *

"*Facing Nuclear War* moves on a deeper level than discussions of pessimism and optimism. It looks despair in the eye and gives a reason for hope. It shows Jesus Christ coming and restoring wholeness to God's creation—coming in the past, present, and the future. For this reason, the book has a contribution to make to the renewal of the church as well as to the avoidance of nuclear holocaust. Everyone who is waging peace, or thinking about it, should read this book."—John K. Stoner, executive secretary of the Mennonite Central Committee (MCC) U.S. Peace Section.

FACING
NUCLEAR
WAR

FACING NUCLEAR WAR

A Plea for Christian Witness

Donald B. Kraybill

A Christian Peace Shelf Selection

HERALD PRESS
Scottdale, Pennsylvania
Kitchener, Ontario
1982

Library of Congress Cataloging in Publication Data

Kraybill, Donald B.
   Facing nuclear war.

   Bibliography: p.
      1. Atomic warfare.   2. Atomic warfare—Religious
aspects—Christianity.   I. Title.
UF767.K72   1982   261.8'73   82-11765
ISBN 0-8361-3312-9 (pbk.)

UF
767
. K72
1982

Unless otherwise indicated, Scripture quotations are from the
Revised Standard Version of the Bible, copyrighted 1946, 1952,
© 1971, 1973. References marked NEB are from *The New English
Bible.* © The Delegates of the Oxford University Press and The
Syndics of the Camridge University Press, 1961, 1970. Reprinted by
permission.

FACING NUCLEAR WAR
Copyright © 1982 by Herald Press, Scottdale, Pa. 15683
   Published simultaneously in Canada by Herald Press,
   Kitchener, Ont. N2G 4M5
Library of Congress Catalog Card Number: 82-11765
International Standard Book Number: 0-8361-3312-9
Printed in the United States of America
Design by Alice B. Shetler

82 83 84 85 86 12 11 10 9 8 7 6 5 4 3 2 1

Contents

Author's Preface

Nuclear war has emerged as the chief moral issue of our time. It's not easy or pleasant to face up to such an awful threat. We'd all prefer to avoid it. For too long, as Christians we have passed by on the other side of the road that leads by nuclear war. But now the time has come when we must face the issue squarely. Christian faith does not allow us the luxury of apathy, resignation, or even ignorance. We must ask whether Christians can support the manufacture, possession, and use of nuclear weapons?

If you are already familiar with the issues surrounding nuclear war, you'll find little new in these pages. I have written for those who are newcomers to nuclear war and for those who haven't thought much about how their Christian faith relates to this urgent moral question.

I've attempted to cut through the foggy technical jargon of nuclear war and to say things in a down-to-earth manner. I wove together many strands of fact and faith as I tried to integrate the technical issues with the Christian perspectives. So you will find numbers as well as Bible verses. I played the role of prophet and of priest. You will find words of danger here; the threat is real. But there are also words of hope and comfort. There are harsh words of criticism for the forces that propel the deadly nuclear race forward, and there are words of affirmation for those who courageously drop out of the race. You will find words of admonition and warning, terror and consolation, and most importantly words of hope and promise.

Although I am trained in the social sciences, I wrote this primarily as a Christian pacifist. However, I'm not a dogmatic dove; I realize there aren't easy answers to many of the thorny questions revolving around Christian faith and military force. In these pages I simply plead for God's children to come halfway from wherever they are and at least agree on nuclear pacifism. You will find an urgent plea for Christian witness threading its way through all the chapters. I contend that those who say and do nothing not only encourage the arms race, but forfeit their stewardship of the gospel of Jesus Christ as well.

It's easy to sensationalize and exaggerate the threat of nuclear war with verbal overkill. For example, estimates of the number of tons of explosive TNT per person in the world range anywhere from two to fifteen tons. Such calculations are more emotional than helpful, since bombs and people are not ever likely to be spread evenly around the world. In a nuclear exchange it's more likely that people near targets would get killed hundreds of times and those in remote areas would never be touched. I have tried to avoid the extreme. I have used the more conservative estimates and have been cautious in making sweeping generalizations. Even conservative predictions are bad enough to convince most skeptics in this business. Many of the facts I report are widely accepted in the public domain. I have provided documented sources only in the cases of the more obscure ones.

An irony of nuclear war is that precision doesn't matter much in this technical field. Does it really matter whether there are 47,000 or 49,000 nuclear bombs, when several hundred would be more than enough to devastate the United States or the USSR? What difference does it make whether the defense budget is 1.5 or 1.6 billion dollars over the next five years? I have tried to handle the numbers carefully, yet there's a sense in which accuracy doesn't make a whole lot of difference in this ball game.

Hopefully you will find much of the book to be provocative. It's not intended to be the last word on the subject. I hope that it stimulates vigorous discussion among God's people so that together under the guidance of the Holy Spirit we can come to grips and face up to this ultimate moral issue of our time.

My debts are many and great. Numerous persons have contributed to the final product. From beginning to end, Stan Godshall and John Stoner provided all sorts of support, ideas, and most importantly encouragement. John P. Ranck, my colleague at Elizabethtown College, convinced me that the issue was urgent and provided the collegial affirmation I needed in the early stages. Dale Aukerman's *Darkening Valley: A Biblical Perspective on Nuclear War* laid the groundwork for my theological analysis. His ideas have influenced my thinking a great deal. He kindly made suggestions for improving the manuscript.

Through personal correspondence and the exchange of papers, Ted Koontz was immensely helpful in clarifying my ideas and in reminding me that the ethical issues surrounding nuclear war are quite complicated and paradoxical. His influence pervades these pages. Many others thoughtfully reacted to a draft copy of the manuscript with useful suggestions: Salvatore V. Zangari, Mable Hershey, Duane Brown, Ron Flickinger, and Curtis Heisey. J. Kenneth Kreider and Bill Puffenberger shared helpful comments on chapters 4 and 5 respectively. Many other thoughtful colleagues at Elizabethtown College contributed ideas, support, and information. Elizabethtown College provided generous library resources and computing facilities. Paul M. Schrock, editor at Herald Press, and the other support personnel there were simply amazing! All of these have so graciously contributed their time and ideas.

And to my family, thanks for so patiently waiting.

Donald B. Kraybill
Elizabethtown, Pennsylvania

FACING
NUCLEAR
WAR

1
WHY IT'S URGENT NOW

THE FRONT DOOR

There are two ways of facing up to nuclear war. We can open the front door in our modern house and view the growing danger. Or we can open the back door and search for spiritual resources in the Scripture and in our Christian faith. Looking out the front door, we see that the threatening cloud of nuclear war hangs heavy over the horizon. We hear rumors of war rumbling down the valley. It's a frightening view as the billowing clouds grow darker and darker. Looking out the back door, we find the helpful record of Scripture and the teachings of the church. This approach anchors our response in the church's witness down through the centuries.

We must open both doors, but where do we begin? Starting with the back door makes more sense, but if we don't open the front door first, we may never get to the back door. Before we can hear what the Scripture has to say about this nuclear woods, we must know where we are in it. So in this chapter we'll begin by looking out the front door. That view will send us scurrying out the back door in search of spiritual resources.

Now I know that looking at the scary threat and effects of nuclear war is not a pleasant way to begin a book. No one enjoys a nightmare. But that *is* what nuclear war is all about, and we probably won't face up to it until we look it straight in

15

the eye and know exactly what it involves. So at the risk of frightening you away, we'll begin by cautiously opening the front door.

Big words and technical terms clutter most discussions of nuclear war. The strange jargon of ICBM, SLBM, megaton, MIRVing, and counterforce is meaningless to average people and makes it difficult for us to deal with nuclear war. The special language prevents us from understanding clearly what's going on and gives us a good excuse for avoiding the subject.

We'll begin this chapter by scanning some of the technical aspects of our nuclear predicament. We'll cut through the verbiage and translate it into understandable, eveyday language. I hesitate to begin with a boring technical overview, yet we do need a common grasp of where we are in this nuclear woods before we can grapple with the faith issues. First of all, we'll look at why the nuclear threat is especially urgent today. Then we'll consider some emotional responses to the danger, and end by reflecting on the spiritual meaning of all of this. So, brace yourself for a few pages of technical orientation.

DEADLY CHANGES

We've lived with nuclear weapons for a long time. It's almost forty years since the first nuclear bombs were exploded over Hiroshima and Nagasaki. Even though nuclear bombs have been around for a while, most of us haven't thought much about them. They quietly found their niche along with the other pieces of modern life. Our safe passage since 1945 may reflect God's grace and patience as much as our ability to prevent nuclear war. There is no guarantee that our good fortune will continue.

Why now all of a sudden is there so much fuss and talk about nuclear war? What is shaking up the quiet waters of the past forty years? Why should Christians be facing up to nuclear war now if they haven't for the past forty years? Why is this issue so pressing now?

At least eight deadly changes make the threat of nuclear war especially urgent now. In the past most Christians were able to slide by without facing up to nuclear war—but that time is past. It may not be comfortable and we may not like it, but these eight deadly changes bring us face-to-face with the growing threat of nuclear war.

Multiplying Bombs

The term "warhead" is typically used to refer to nuclear weapons. I will generally use the somewhat impolite word "bomb" to remind us that we are talking about a destructive package of power. "Warhead" is a technical and less frightening term that emotionally insulates us from the devastation of nuclear weapons. We'll look more carefully at how such terms provide us with emotional insulation in a later chapter.

In the early days of the arms race, each missile carried one bomb. In 1966 the United States took the lead in developing a technique called "MIRVing" (Multiple Independently-Targetable Reentry Vehicle), and the Soviet Union quickly caught up. The MIRVing procedure makes it possible to place several bombs on each missile. Each bomb can be aimed at a different target. Between 1970 and 1975, 550 of the U.S. Minuteman missiles were "MIRVed," allowing them each to carry three bombs instead of one. In a short time the number of bombs on these missiles in underground silos tripled from 550 to 1,650. This deadly change means that without building or installing any new missiles, the number of potential targets like cities or military bases quickly jumped from 550 to 1,650. Missiles on submarines have also been "MIRVed" so that each one carries between 3 and 14 bombs. Each Trident II submarine missile will be able to carry 17 bombs. A single MX missile will carry 10 bombs. This first change has allowed both superpowers to multiply rapidly the number of nuclear bombs they can throw at each other.

Hitting the Bull's Eye

A second deadly change is the increased accuracy of modern bombs. It's hard to be sure a missile will hit the bull's eye after traveling 6,000 or 7,000 miles between two continents. The older missiles of the 1950s and 1960s weren't very accurate. You really couldn't count on them to hit a very specific target like a submarine port or a missile silo. Today it's a different story. In the early 1980s new guidance systems were installed in the U.S. Minuteman III missiles so that at least 50 percent of the time they will arrive within 600 feet of their target—not bad after traveling from another continent! Although the Soviet missiles have generally lagged behind the American ones in accuracy, some scientists estimate that now certain Soviet missiles might get within 1,200 feet of the bull's eye.

Future accuracy is even more striking! The second phase of the MX missile and the Trident II missile may be accurate enough to place at least half of the bombs within 300 feet of the targets. Recent jumps in technology mean that the superpowers can be sharpshooters who hit the bull's eye thousands of miles away. This change is deadly because it means that both sides are more easily tempted to strike first, since their chances of hitting the target are so good.

Striking First

The public military policy of the U.S. until recently was known as MAD, for Mutually Assured Destruction. Because the older missiles weren't very accurate, they were aimed at large population centers. Both sides knew that their bombs weren't accurate enough to hit each other's missile silos or bomber bases. They both knew that if one side struck first the other side would have many untouched bombers, missiles, or submarines that could still be used to strike back. So each side threatened to blow up the other's cities in revenge if it were attacked. It was this logic that gave us MAD, or Mutually Assured Destruction. We hoped to defend ourselves by convincing the Soviets that we would blow them to pieces if they tried anything, and vice versa. This is also called "deterrence," which simply means that you try to stop the other guy from hitting you by promising him terrible revenge.

Think of two feuding families, standing at opposite ends of a long room, pointing guns at each other. Both families know that they can't shoot straight enough to knock the guns out of the hands of their enemy. If one family starts shooting, the other family can return the fire and shoot straight enough to kill at least half of the family that fired first. So each family "defends" itself by scaring the other one so bad that neither will shoot in the first place.

This MAD policy slowly changed toward a "first-strike" or "counterforce" policy as the weapons became more plentiful and more accurate. A counterforce policy means that accurate missiles are aimed at enemy weapons instead of cities. Now each side tends to reason like this, "Since I have 10 bombs on each of my missiles, I have a good chance of destroying 8 or 9 of my enemy's missiles with just one of mine. By using 100 of my missiles I can wipe out 800 or 900 of his missiles. And if each of his missiles has 10 bombs, I will be destroying 8,000 to 9,000 of his bombs, which otherwise might hit my country. Since he can do the same thing to me, he'll probably try to hit me first. So I'd better strike him quickly before he attacks me. Hitting him first is the smartest thing to do."

The U.S. policy of a counterforce or first-strike option gradually emerged over several years and was confirmed by Presidential Directive 59 issued by President Carter in August 1980. The accuracy of the MX missile and the Trident submarine missile makes them good first-strike weapons. We can probably assume that the Soviet Union is also moving in the first-strike direction.

Why is the first-strike policy such a dangerous change? It's a deadly shift because whoever hits first gets a big advantage. The side that strikes first doesn't have to worry as much about being hit back since many of the enemy's weapons are already knocked out. In a time of international crisis when both sides think that the other side might strike first, the pressure rises on both sides to beat the other guy to the draw and get the big advantage of hitting first.

One protection against an enemy's first-strike is to launch your own missiles "on warning." If your satellites report that the enemy has fired his missiles, you quickly launch yours so that your silos are empty when his missiles arrive. This gives you only about thirty minutes to get your missiles out of the ground before the enemy missiles arrive. Such a "launch on warning" policy is extremely dangerous because accidental warnings—and there have been some— could easily trigger a major war. Inching toward a first-strike policy shakes up the stability of the past twenty years. Even more sobering is the fact that none of the nuclear nations have agreed *not to use nuclear weapons first.* The Soviets have indicated a willingness to endorse a "no first use" policy, but the U.S. has consistently rejected it.

Playing with Nuclear War

The idea of a "limited" or "controlled" nuclear war tags along with the first-strike policy. Under the MAD doctrine both sides threatened to blow each other up in an all-out nuclear war. War was the ultimate and unthinkable evil. With the technological refinements of the late 1970s and early 1980s, many military planners are now talking about fighting small or limited nuclear wars. Since nuclear war isn't out of the question, the strategists say we should be prepared to fight one and limit the damage as much as possible. Not only do they think that a small nuclear war could be limited; some argue it could even be won.

Vice-President George Bush has said that a nuclear war could be fought and won. U.S. Deputy Secretary of Defense Frank Carlucci said in 1981, "I think we need to have counterforce capability. Over and above that we need to have a war fighting capability." In mid-1982, U.S. Defense Secretary Weinberger issued a five-year plan which accepts nuclear war fighting as a necessity and calls for the U.S. to prepare to fight a "protracted" or drawn-out nuclear war.

President Reagan, in remarks to reporters, said, "I could see where you could have the exchange of tactical (nuclear) weapons against troops in the field without bringing either one of the major powers to pushing the button." This remark about limited nuclear war stirred up a flurry of protest in Europe, since it seemed to forecast precisely what many Europeans had feared—a limited nuclear war limited to Europe!

Such talk by government officials reveals a shift toward actual preparation for nuclear war. Admiral LaRocque, who heads the Center for Defense Information, describes the growing acceptance of limited nuclear war this way:

> The illusion that nuclear war could be controlled and limited and used to achieve some practical objectives is fed by intoxicating technological developments. Refinements of superaccurate missiles, computers and satellites lead many technicians and bureaucrats to think in terms of a controlled nuclear war. The illusion of "controlled nuclear war" has been spawned by war games and the persistent assumption that in every war there is a winner. There will be no winners in a nuclear war.[1]

A limited nuclear war might begin with the use of small nuclear weapons in Europe, the Middle East, or on some other battlefield in the world. Some believe it could start with a small nation experimenting with its new nuclear toy. U.S. Secretary of State Haig talked of firing a "demonstration" nuclear bomb to prove to the other side that NATO or the U.S. meant serious business. Such comments along with official U.S. policy confirm the American willingness to use nuclear weapons in a limited way.

Would a small nuclear war stay limited? Once the line between regular and nuclear weapons is crossed, is there any way to be sure that exploding a few nuclear weapons on a battlefield won't ignite an all-out nuclear exchange? This is a hotly debated issue. On the one hand, as U.S. military planners talk more and more about sitting on, or limiting, a nuclear war, many other defense analysts argue that *any* use of small nuclear weapons would almost certainly burst into a major nuclear war.[2] International security experts on the Palme Commission recently issued a report that says, "The idea of fighting a limited nuclear war is dangerous."

U.S. Civil Defense funds were dramatically increased by 89 percent between the 1982 and the 1983 fiscal budget to prepare for "crisis relocation" of citizens during a nuclear attack. This is another sign of the increasing preparation to fight a nuclear war. This growing talk of fighting, winning, limiting, and controlling nuclear war by many U.S. military planners is another deadly change. It's a shift that drags all of us closer to the brink of nuclear holocaust.

No Lids on the Arsenals

In 1972 the U.S. and the Soviet Union agreed to slow down some aspects of the arms race in a treaty known as SALT I (Strategic Arms Limitation Talks). The SALT I treaty has expired, and a new SALT II agreement, accepted by the Russians, was rejected by the U.S. Senate. Even though SALT II was not signed by the U.S., both parties are complying with the spirit of the agreement in most areas. *In spite of attempts to stop*, the arsenal of strategic bombs keeps right on growing. Between 1970 and 1980 the number of strategic or long-distance bombs on the U.S. pile jumped from nearly 4,000 to about 9,000. The Soviet pile grew from some 1,600 to about 7,000. And so the piles of bombs on both sides are growing daily. It's estimated that on the average, three to five new bombs are produced daily by the superpowers.

There are nearly 50,000 nuclear weapons in the world today with the explosive power of approximately one million Hiroshima bombs. Among these 50,000 weapons the U.S. and the Soviet Union have about 18,000 strategic bombs— large ones that travel a long distance. The rest are smaller tactical weapons made for short-range use on a battlefield. Many experts expect that the number of strategic bombs alone will jump to between 26,000 and 31,000 by the mid to late 1980s if no ceiling is placed on the nuclear buildup.[3]

Even as the nuclear freeze movement was growing in early 1982, the Reagan administration announced plans to build 17,000 *more* nuclear bombs over the next ten to fifteen years. Some of these will replace older ones, while many are for new weapon systems. In late March 1982, President Reagan asked for *a special increase* of 400 million dollars in the 1983 military budget to speed up nuclear bomb construction.

Even with the SALT I treaty in the early 1970s, the superpowers kept right on stacking up their bombs. While a treaty such as SALT I did stall some aspects of the arms race, it didn't slow down the growth of new weapons. Treaty limitations often ban outdated weapons which aren't very crucial anyway. The superpowers have simply not been able to put *effective* lids on their arsenals. They have *not* been willing to stop making nuclear weapons. This sad fact is a change from the optimism of the early 1970s when it looked as though treaties might be effective. And so the deadly race moves ahead. A nuclear freeze or a START (Strategic Arms Reduction Talks) agreement could slow things down, but they aren't likely to get rid of the 50,000 or so nuclear bombs that are *already* scattered around the world. And many people are skeptical about START talks since previous negotiations and treaties have not halted the arms race. The loopholes and ineffectiveness of past arms limitation treaties make a freeze quite attractive.

Super Weapons

It's not only a problem of growing piles of bombs. A more serious change is the whole new set of superweapons on the drawing boards. This new generation of weapons is frightening because of their technological sophistication and unbelievable firepower. They will certainly push the arms race ahead, and they clearly show that neither side is seriously interested in slowing down. History shows that every time the U.S. jumps ahead with a new and better weapon, the Soviets catch up three to five years later. See Appendix 1 for examples.

There is a whole array of new U.S. nuclear weapons scheduled to come out in the mid 1980s. The neutron bomb is already in production. Plans to begin producing 100 MX missiles each carrying 10 bombs are under way. The first of at least 15 Trident submarines started floating in 1981. About 4,000 cruise missiles are to be built by the end of the decade. These small, 25-foot-long missiles are easy to hide from enemy spy satellites. That fact scares the Soviets and increases tension all around. Approximately 100 new B-1 bombers are planned, with the first due in the air by 1986. Surely the Soviets will follow with their own versions of the weapons they don't already have.

These new U.S. weapons are already in the early stages

of production. There are many other conventional weapons being built: large naval carriers, fighter bombers, better tanks, and many more. The Pentagon is also experimenting with laser weapons and killer satellites. A major portion of the space shuttle program is devoted to military experimentation in space. In 1982, President Reagan announced plans to make nerve gas, breaking a thirteen-year moratorium in producing chemical weapons. It appears that the Soviets are already producing and possibly using these chemical weapons which kill by attacking the human nervous system. The list could go on and on. The Soviets are also doing a fairly good job of cranking out new weapons.

The important point is that *all* of these weapons are coming *on top* of what we already have. They will be stacked on top of the 1,052 land-based missiles, the 32 submarines, and the 376 intercontinental bombers that the U.S. already has in place. These deadly new instruments will greatly enlarge the present American pile of some 26,000 nuclear bombs. These superkillers will rock the stability of the last twenty years. They are the U.S. answer to new Soviet weapons. And in turn they will certainly push the Soviets to respond with bigger ones. This is the deadly change that lurks beneath the shiny glamour of these new toys of war.

Cranking Up

The early 1980s saw a seventh deadly change. The American government cranked up the largest military buildup in peacetime history. All government programs—health, transportation, education, research, social services, and environmental protection—were cut *except* the military. In 1981' and 1982 massive amounts of money were transferred from human services—child care, housing, health care, and programs for the elderly—to deadly services, the military. The government's proposed military spending amounts to 1.6 trillion dollars for the fiscal years 1983-87. Some Pentagon leaks suggest it will be much closer to 2.2 trillion. These figures account for all U.S. military spending. Nuclear weapon programs receive about 15 to 20 percent of the military budget. In October 1981, President Reagan called for 186 billion dollars for new nuclear weapons such as the B-1 bomber and the MX missile.

Now it's hard to imagine 1.6 trillion dollars. It sounds like a lot of dough. Using the lowest estimates, this amounts to about four dollars per day for every American man, woman, and child. This adds up to nearly $1,460 per person each year. Over the five year period of 1983-87, that is equivalent to $7,300 per person or nearly $30,000 for a household of four. This doesn't mean that each person will actually pay $7,300 in military taxes over the five-year period. Some will pay more and some will pay less.

Here's another way to imagine 1.6 trillion dollars. If you spent one million dollars each day since the birth of Christ, only half of it would be spent by now. Using the most conservative estimates, this means that the U.S. government alone will spend about 34 million dollars per hour or 820 million dollars per day for the military over this five-year period. That's right—34 million dollars an hour! These figures will vary slightly as the Congress or president shifts priorities each year. But such minor variations will not change the massive shift of money from human services to deadly services.

The embrace of gigantic military spending means that over 30 percent of the government's spending goes for military efforts. When the cost of past wars and benefits to veterans are included, the real military chunk of the U.S. budget is nearly 45 percent to 50 percent. The Reagan military budget request for 1983 is about 260 billion dollars. Even with inflation taken out, this is a real increase of 36 percent above pre-Reagan levels of military spending. The planned increases of 7 to 9 percent above inflation will bring the direct military budget in 1986 to 360 billion dollars.

It's hard to imagine! A single billion dollars would fill a string of 1,000 cars each with a million dollars. The 1983 military budget of 260 billion dollars is equivalent to a line of 260,000 cars each loaded with a million dollars. Bumper-to-bumper, these million dollar cars would stretch from Chicago to Washington, D.C., nearly 600 miles.

This enormous buildup involves more than just a larger

number of nuclear bombs and shiny new superweapons. It calls for 150 more ships for the navy, 4 new army divisions, five more air force wings, a Rapid Deployment Force, new tanks, missiles of all sorts, helicopters, and fighter planes. The list goes on and on. See Appendix 2 for a list of some of these weapons and what their cost could buy in human service programs.

The new superweapons come with a price tag that's not very cheap.

	Cost Per Single Weapon
100 B-1 Bombers	$400 Million
100 MX Missiles	$500 Million*
15+ Trident Submarines	$1.2 Billion
479 F-14 Fighters	$21 Million

*Some estimates are twice as high.

The point of all this is simply that the American government with the support of many people made a deliberate decision to shift *enormous* amounts of money from life-giving services to deadly services. It seems clear that we are getting ready for war. This massive change, when we are not even fighting a war, will burden the American people for years to come and makes war the government's major business. The deadly buildup brings all of us in the international community closer to the cliff of nuclear disaster.

The Contagious Bomb

Nuclear weapons are contagious. Nations who control nuclear weapons have power—power to threaten and bully other nations, power to get what they want. In the fifties and sixties the world was like a street corner where two of the teenagers had machine guns and all the other kids had sticks and stones. The two machine gunners ran the show. The kids with sticks and stones wanted machine guns in the worst way so that they too could act tough, run the show, and get what they wanted.

Today their wish is coming true. The bullies have lost control as the nuclear machine guns spread around the world. This is a serious change—the eighth one that pushes the world closer to the valley of death. We can't really blame the other kids for wanting to trade in their sticks and stones for nuclear weapons. Americans would certainly want to do the same thing if they had been sitting on the sidelines for thirty years. The contagious spread of nuclear weapons means that we are entering a completely new ball game in world politics.

It was one thing when two superpowers had a kind of gentleman's agreement that they wouldn't use these terrible weapons. But it's quite another ball game when ten countries have nuclear weapons in their closets. The nuclear club is growing. Six countries have nuclear weapons now. Ten more could build them within three or four years, and sixteen additional countries could construct bombs by the early 1990s. Some nations that could build nuclear weapons may choose not to. As many as 25 countries could have the bomb in the next ten years. The nuclear club is listed in Appendix 3.

In 1968 a nonproliferation treaty designed to stop the spread of nuclear weapons was signed by 114 nations, but 50 nations refused to sign. It's difficult to stop the spread of nuclear weapons for a number of reasons. They can be made from reprocessed nuclear by-products from nuclear power reactors such as TMI (Three Mile Island). There are already 55 countries which have nuclear power or research reactors. Twelve of these countries have refused to sign the nonproliferation treaty. In the treaty, the U.S. and the Soviet Union agreed to limit their stockpiles of nuclear bombs. Since the superpowers haven't stopped building bombs, many of the smaller countries see no reason why they should stay out of the race. The new director of the International Atomic Energy Agency believes several countries will soon acquire nuclear weapons, and he says there's little his agency can do to stop them. Many analysts believe that some nations which signed the treaty are secretly developing nuclear bombs.

The spread of nuclear weapons around the world is a

dangerous change from the calmer days when only two or three countries had the bomb. Now there's even a "how-to" book published in 1981 that describes how to build a nuclear bomb.[4] It's not that easy—it costs a lot of money for materials—but it's no longer a secret. Simple common sense suggests that as more countries and more people make more and more bombs, the chances grow that someday, somewhere, someone will use them. As nuclear weapons spread around the world, the chances grow that a small country with little to lose, or one bent on retaliation, or one eager to show off its adolescent muscles will explode a bomb. It's hard to keep such a nice shiny toy in the closet forever! This contagious spread of nuclear technology is another deadly change that makes the threat of nuclear war such an urgent issue today.

Perhaps the most frightening underlying theme in all of these changes is an eerie sense that we are being led toward the nuclear cliff by technology itself. Military policies tag along after our technical advances. The idea of a limited nuclear war is only possible because of engineering improvements. Is technology leading us by the hand to the nuclear abyss?

RUMORS OF NUCLEAR WAR

We have looked at eight changes, eight warning flags that signal the growing threat of nuclear war in some form. What are the chances, really, that nuclear weapons might be used or that a nuclear war might begin? Certainly no one knows for sure. We don't sit in God's chair. But even though such things can't be predicted accurately, we can get a reading on our direction. Listen to some trustworthy scientists and statesmen. These are not twenty-year-old left wing radicals; these are seasoned veterans who have watched the arms race closely for many years.

Four Minutes

The Bulletin of the Atomic Scientists is published by scientists concerned about the threat of nuclear war. The journal has a clock on its front cover. The scientists have used the clock since 1947 to show symbolically how close, by their estimates, we are to nuclear doomsday. Recently they moved the hand of the clock from seven minutes to four minutes before midnight because "the world seemed to be moving unevenly but inexorably closer to nuclear disaster."

Awesome Threat

Recently eleven eminent American physicists, including four Nobel prize winners, wrote a letter to President Reagan urging him to halt the nuclear arms race because it "poses the most awesome threat of all." Pope John Paul II recently sent a special delegation of four distinguished scientists to meet with President Reagan and President Brezhnev to convey his concerns about the urgent threat of nuclear war.

Very Likely

George Kistiakowsky, an eighty-year-old Harvard chemist, helped to build the first bomb, and later served as President Eisenhower's science advisor. He believes a nuclear war is very likely before the end of the century if the arms race isn't stopped. In a recent interview he said, "I am so old that I probably will not see it, but most of you will probably be involved in a nuclear war."[5]

A 50-50 Chance

Defense analyst Richard Garwin, one of the country's leading experts on nuclear weapons, told the American Association for the Advancement of Science that the probability of a nuclear war by the year 2000 was "at least 50-50 with a much higher probability for limited nuclear war." Helen Caldicott, leading spokesperson for Physicians for Social Responsibility, also believes the chances of some type of nuclear war are 50-50 over the next several years.

Closer Every Day

Herbert Scoville, Jr., president of the Arms Control Association and former senior official in the Central Intelligence Agency, said, "I am convinced that a nuclear war would be an unparalleled disaster for mankind. I am also convinced that each day is carrying us closer to the outbreak of a nuclear war."[6]

Destroy Ourselves
Admiral Hyman Rickover, the father of the U.S. nuclear navy, retired at the age of 82. In his farewell remarks to the U.S. Senate in 1982, he said, "I think we will probably destroy ourselves, so what difference will it make? Some new species will come up that might be wiser. . . . The lesson of history is: when a war starts, every nation will ultimately use whatever weapon it has available. That is the lesson learned time and again. Therefore, we must expect if another war—a serious war—breaks out, we will use nuclear energy in some form."

A Good Chance
Rear Admiral Gene R. LaRocque, director of the Center for Defense Information, described the threat this way:

> It is increasingly clear that nuclear war is an unrelenting and growing threat to hundreds of millions of people. World War III with nuclear weapons *can* happen and almost certainly *will* happen unless all governments confront this most uncomfortable reality. Each new weapon introduced, each new resort to military force, increases the likelihood of nuclear war. You and I and our children have a good chance of being destroyed by nuclear weapons before the year 2000 unless positive steps are taken to avoid this catastrophe.[7]

Flipping the Big Coin
No one of course knows the exact probability of nuclear war and no one knows if or when, but a broad spectrum of seasoned scientists, arms specialists, and statesmen are telling us that the chances are growing every day unless we break out of our present rut. It's described in many ways—as the ultimate threat, the greatest peril, the final epidemic, an unbelievable holocaust, and even as "the murder of God."[8]

These are all ways of saying that the situation is *very* serious. All other problems fade far, far into the distance in the face of nuclear war. Other threats facing humankind are merely tiny footnotes on the pages of history. It's a shattering experience to understand the horrors of nuclear war and then to hear reputable scientists say that the chances of it happening are like flipping a penny and hoping to get heads. Beyond that, it's depressing to see the superpowers blindly plodding on toward the nuclear cliff while some churches and many Christians silently—and some even loudly with Bible verses—support the race toward death.

TRIGGERS OF NUCLEAR WAR

How might a nuclear war begin? What are the triggers of nuclear war? Although there are many ways a nuclear war might start, we will only look at seven possible triggers.[9] A look at these triggers and some safety latches that could fail is convincing evidence that the security brought by nuclear weapons is a very fragile one at best.

Growing Crisis

How might a nuclear war begin? Although not the most likely way, one of the superpowers might start a nuclear war in a moment of international tension such as the Cuban missile crisis of 1962. A nuclear war probably won't just drop in out of the blue. It's more likely to come after days of rising international conflict when one of the superpowers is threatened or embarrassed by a smaller incident. The possibility of a war starting this way increases as new, highly accurate missiles make a first strike on the enemy's weapons quite attractive. If the crisis grows and each side *thinks* the other might try a first strike, it becomes more tempting for both sides to go for the big advantage of hitting first.

A Spreading War

A more likely ignition point might be a regular war on a small battlefield. A country might use a nuclear weapon as a last resort if it were backed into a corner in a coventional war. Or if one of the allies of the superpowers were embarrassed by a defeat, a nuclear weapon might turn things around and help save face. The superpowers themselves might be involved in a small brush-fire war involving the U.S. Rapid Deployment Force, and find it very tempting to use a nuclear bomb to turn the tide in an impossible situation. Or as Secretary of State Haig has said, "fire a demonstration shot" to convince the other side that the U.S. means serious business. Once the nuclear line is crossed, there is no way to guarantee that a tiny conflict won't flare up into a major nuclear shoot-out. A recent study says its "nonsense" to believe that any kind of nuclear war could be controlled.[10]

Accidents

With thousands of nuclear weapons being transported and placed throughout the world, it's entirely possible that a nuclear war could start through pure accident. In September 1980 a mechanic accidentally dropped a heavy wrench in a missile silo in Arkansas. The missile exploded and blew off the silo's 740-ton concrete lid. The bomb on the missile was thrown out of the silo about 600 feet, but fortunately it didn't explode. Such a bomb exploding on a large city could cause 2½ million deaths.

Between 1950 and 1980 the Department of Defense reported 32 major accidents involving nuclear weapons.[11] Columnist Jack Anderson believes the number of accidents in that thirty-year-period was closer to 120. He also thinks that Americans should fear their own nuclear weapons as much as Soviet bombs.[12] Planes carrying nuclear weapons have crashed, and trucks carrying nuclear bombs have jack-knifed. As more and more nuclear bombs spread around the world, the chances of accidents steadily grow. An accident could do terrible damage, and it might trigger a war, depending on how and where it happened.

Goofs

There is also the possibility that technical or human error could ignite a war. In 1975 one of the U.S. satellites that watch Soviet missile launchings detected unusual heat. It thought the heat came from a Soviet missile headed for the United States. Surprised that the missile never arrived, U.S. officials later learned that the satellite had detected the heat from a fire in a Soviet natural gas pipeline. In June 1980 a computer error showed that rockets launched from Soviet submarines were expected in the U.S. in fifteen minutes. U.S. bombers and missiles immediately prepared for launching. The error was discovered in three minutes, and in twenty minutes the alert was canceled. In another case, a 48-cent computer chip malfunctioned and caused an alert. There also was the technician who played a computer tape of a simulated Soviet attack by mistake, and it was taken as the real thing for several minutes.

In a twelve-month period in the early 1980s, three false warnings activated U.S. nuclear forces. There have been as many as 151 minor false alerts in an eighteen-month period in the North American Defense Command. The U.S. government itself has warned, "Despite the most elaborate precautions, it is conceivable that technical malfunction or human failure, a misinterpreted incident or unauthorized action, could trigger a nuclear disaster or nuclear war."[13] John L. Kirkley, editor of *Datamation* magazine, recently described the possibility of error in computers that control nuclear weapons:

1. The more complex the technology, the more prone to fail. And, ironically, the failure is likely to be in one of its smallest and simplest components.

2. Efforts to correct the complex system usually breed additional errors . . . like using gasoline to douse a fire.

3. We all seem to be slightly insane. The idea of pointing nuclear tipped missiles at each other is mad enough, but to rely on complex technological systems that may not work or that may even cause the disaster we seek to protect ourselves from, is even more lunatic."[14]

An increasing number of scientists are warning that our real national security is declining as we rely on more and more sophisticated electronic gadgets for our safety.[15] The accident at the TMI nuclear plant is a sober reminder of what can happen when several "fail-safe" backup systems fail on top of human error. There is a real sense in which the enemy of our survival is not the Soviets, but sophisticated nuclear weapons themselves. The danger to our future safety lies as much in the instruments of war as it does in the hands of human aggressors.

Mad Behavior

It's also possible that irrational behavior of some sort could plunge us into nuclear war. Such mad behavior might show up in two ways. Persons controlling the switches that fire nuclear weapons or national leaders might lose their cool under the pressures of an international crisis. Today about 100,000 persons are involved with nuclear weapons in the U.S. armed forces. In the late 1970s between 4,000 and 5,000 people were kicked out of U.S. nuclear weapons programs each year because of drug abuse, negligence, and misconduct. Such large numbers of disciplinary cases related to nuclear weapons is frightening.[16]

In the summer of 1981, CBS News in its five-night documentary "The Defense of the Nation" reported that U.S. submarine commanders have the authority to fire nuclear weapons if communications with headquarters break down. While all precautions are taken, it is possible that two missile silo commanders working together or a submarine commander for unknown reasons might lose his mind and shoot off some nuclear-tipped missiles. The president or secretary of defense in a moment of utter panic or in the crunch of an international dispute could lose his cool and do the unthinkable. Such sorry scenarios are not likely, but they could happen.

Teenage Countries

With the frightening spread of nuclear weapons, it's also thinkable that a smaller country, perhaps one with a tradition of terrorism and revolution, might use a newly acquired nuclear bomb to squash an internal squabble or to show off its "macho" power in the international community. A state with a long history of ethnic or religious wars with neighbors might relish using a nuclear bomb to punish a pesty aggressor. The spread of the bomb shakes up the quiet days of the past when only the superpowers taunted each other with the big stick.

Terrorists

And finally the seventh possibility, that a terrorist group will use the bomb, grows as more and more people learn how to make it. A terrorist group without much to lose might find a small nuclear bomb helpful to prove their point, to grab media attention, or to embarrass a hostile government. Even a small nuclear bomb like the one dropped on Hiroshima can do some nasty damage. A terrorist bombing might stop at that, or it might invite retaliation or even drag the superpowers into a big war with a nuclear exchange.

RUNNING SCARED

It's shocking and terrifying to face up to estimates that the chances of nuclear war are 50-50 over the next years. To look at our children, our friends, our pets, our homes, and our possessions, and to realize that they may have a 50 percent chance of being destroyed before the end of the century shatters our hope—our key to life itself. Our own life, our work and efforts could also be blown to bits with the flip of a nuclear coin. Such poor chances would be bad news from a surgeon at the operating table. And yet those are precisely the odds that some esteemed observers are giving us. Facing up to such a threat terrorizes us. And for many people, facing up to nuclear war means running scared.

The threat of nuclear war paralyzes our emotional circuits. Fear hangs heavy in the air. There's fear that the Russians might actually strike first and blow us up. We fear that a bold young dictator might explode a nuclear bomb to grab world attention. There's fear that a computer error might fire a missile by accident. We are afraid that our leaders, caught in a tight international jam, might lose their cool and let everything go. We fear that we might be survivors, dying a slow agonizing death from burns or radioactive fallout. And there's fear that even if we live, our children and grandchildren might carry the burden of genetic mutations. Perhaps the greatest fear—the one deep down inside —is that neither we nor anyone else can do anything to stop this drift toward death. Such fears are a heavy load, almost too heavy to carry.

Pretenders

In many ways we cope with the fear of nuclear holocaust like persons facing death—as though the threat were
a gigantic terminal cancer spreading throughout society. Re-
searchers have discovered several emotional stages that individuals go through when faced with a terminal illness.
Interestingly, the reactions of many people to the threat of
nuclear war parallel these same stages of coping with one's
personal death.

We are tempted to be *pretenders*, pretending that the
concern about nuclear war is a hoax, just something that the
media made up. And if we stop talking about it, it will disappear. It's an impulse to deny it all. We doubt whether these
surgeons, these prophets of nuclear war, really know what
they're talking about. After all, we say, no one really knows
what will happen. Or we may deny it by avoiding the subject.
We refuse to read or talk about it. Deep down inside we sense
that the predictions are probably on target, but we simply
can't face up to them and we cope by avoiding the topic. We
push the whole thing aside. It's just too much to handle emotionally, and we shift conversations into other directions.
The size of such a disaster boggles our minds and paralyzes
our emotional circuits. So we avoid any talk of nuclear war
and pretend that it's not a real possibility. But we can't
pretend it away. No matter how hard we shove it aside, no
matter how hard we pretend, it haunts us, it nags us, it
follows us, and sometime or other we know we must face up
to it.

Downers

Others are tempted to be *downers*. They fall into the
pits of despair. They are crushed under the weight of this
threat. They are depressed because they feel trapped and see
no way out. They are overwhelmed by the terror and sink into
depression. They don't run away from nuclear war. They
don't deny it. They face up to it, but it's too much to bear. The
thought of all their work and loved ones being foolishly
blown up in a few years cuts the thread of meaning that
holds their life together. Meaning evaporates from everyday

work; household chores, technical tasks, and professional duties suddenly seem irrelevant. The normal routines of life are suddenly empty, hollow exercises. They seem downright pointless if everything might be gone in a few years. Why work hard and try to make a difference if a nuclear holocaust is just around the corner? Activities which usually bring joy and satisfaction suddenly seem like a trivial waste in the face of nuclear destruction. Why go on? Why try if nothing matters? What can anyone do anyway? All of this leads to depression, to feelings of hopelessness, and to a massive resignation to fate.

Flailers

And finally there are *flailers*, those who jump on every passing bandwagon and ride on every fad. They swing at the nuclear monster with all their might, trying to knock him out with a mighty wallop of frenzied action. Panic is their response to fear. Instead of running away or falling into depression, some of us want to stand up and feverishly beat this dragon in the face. We abruptly change priorities, as in time of war, to devote all our energy to fighting the nuclear monster. We frantically flail at the wind with a sense of hopeless despair. Such outbursts of action will soon burn out and won't endure over the long haul. They reflect an inner chaos and anxiety rather than a mature spiritual commitment to the work of peace.

These are three normal reactions to the terrible possibility of nuclear war. Anyone can easily be caught up in one or more of them. We are all inclined to pretend, to flail, and to fall into depression. They are normal impulses that many of us feel, and they have an uncanny similarity to the reactions that come when we're faced with death. In a later chapter we will look at some ways Christians can respond with integrity.

FEAR GOD

Christian faith doesn't let us remain stuck in these valleys of despair. Jesus Christ leads us beyond the ruts of fear. We do some pretending. We are depressed sometimes and we do some flailing around, but the love of God gently prods us beyond these responses to fear. Fear is not God's gift. It's our reaction to a threatening situation. God doesn't give us a spirit of fear. He touches us with quietness, love, and self-control (2 Timothy 1:7). God's gift is love and his perfect love casts out fear (1 John 4:18). Jesus reminds us not to fear those who kill the body, only those who destroy both soul and body (Matthew 10:28).

The words of Isaiah nudge us out of the pits of paralyzing fear.

> Do not fear what they fear, nor be in dread. But the Lord of hosts, him you shall regard as holy; let him be your fear, and let him be your dread. And he will become a sanctuary.
>
> *Isaiah 8:12b-14a.*

As we fear God, he becomes our sanctuary, our place of refuge. God's presence nudges us away from fear, even the fear of bombs. His love gives us firm courage and hope to live joyously even in the face of nuclear war. His promise that death is not the final end helps us defeat depression. The arms race is built on fear and breeds fear. God's gift is hope; and hope is the only solid foundation which pries us from fatalism and resignation. God's Spirit gives our peacemaking efforts spiritual focus and persistence. He helps us endure over the long haul.

Isaiah reminds us that we really should fear God rather than the physical threats around us. Now the fear of God has two sides. On the one hand, it means a profound respect and reverence for God's demand for total allegiance. It means a holy appreciation for his vision of peace and justice echoed by the prophets and exemplified by Jesus. It means a joyous acceptance of his call to be peacemakers. The peace of God in our hearts must be translated into a peacemaking witness in our nuclear age.

The other side of the fear of God is terror for those who hear his message, but don't act. God's wrath will be unleashed on those who refuse his call to turn swords into plowshares and bombs into solar collectors. Those who know the way of peace and sleep on the dream should dread his wrath. We rightly fear his anger if we fail to confess our allegiance to him and join his peaceable kingdom. We ought to shake in the face of God's wrath as his judgment descends on our long silence on nuclear war. Christians who know the gospel of peace and yet silently condone nuclear weapons have good reason to fear God's judgment.

Disciples who walk and talk the way of peace discover God's presence with them. He becomes their sanctuary. His love provides a refuge and casts out fear. He brings a firm, calm grip on life, even when the world is at the nuclear brink. These disciples have cut their ties to the war machine and its logic. They have turned around and are walking away from the dangerous cliff. They are going back to God. They invite others to turn also and come home before it's too late. They are no longer enslaved by the forces of death; they now work diligently to affirm life and hope even in the face of impending doom.

And so our fear sometimes gets twisted around. We fear nuclear weapons that can kill the body. Our silent support for the bomb shows utter disrespect for God's kingdom of peace. When we truly fear God, when we respect his way of peace, we will join in his peacemaking and work under the canopy of his blessing.

THE NUCLEAR THREAT: A GIFT?
False Security

The threat of nuclear war is terrible and we have good reason to fear it, but the threat also brings along some gifts. The helpful thing about nuclear war is that it reminds us as nothing else can that true security can never be found in guns and bulletproof vests. We want to believe that we are secure, safe, and protected. We build walls, install burglar alarms, lock car doors, and put guns in our closets to defend ourselves and our possessions. In the name of national security, nations build bombers, target missiles, commission submarines, and develop neutron bombs.

We stubbornly cling to the illusion that more burglar alarms and more bombs will finally make us secure. We long to be in a place where no one can touch us, in a safe house where hoodlums can't enter, in a safe country protected from invasion. We do everything we possibly can to make sure that the worst will never happen.

But in spite of all our frantic efforts, there simply is *no* way to guarantee security. The young President Kennedy, who forced the Soviets to back off in the Cuban missile crisis, was cut down himself by a sniper's bullet. After the United States spent over 25 million dollars to protect Egyptian President Sadat, he was killed in a second. The prophet Hosea warned years ago of the false security provided by weapons. He suggested that trusting in the instruments of war may bring on the war itself.

> Because you have trusted in your chariots and in the multitude of your warriors, therefore the tumult of war shall arise among your people, and all your fortresses shall be destroyed.
>
> *Hosea 10:13b-14a.*

And so it is today:

> We pay for more security and are more insecure;
> We build stronger defenses and are defenseless;
> We trust in bombs and are scared;
> We protect life by threatening to destroy it.

There simply is no foolproof way to guarantee security. In fact, the words of Hosea point to the realities of nuclear war—the harder we try to be secure, the more insecure and threatened we become. Despite the prophet's warning and history's lessons, we desperately want to believe that we can once and for all make ourselves secure. The threat of nuclear war shreds that belief. It yanks off the mask of false security and leaves us standing defenseless—naked in the face of destruction.

There simply is no defense against nuclear weapons! Like lightning, nuclear bombs can not be stopped. Neither side has "defensive" missiles that can shoot down incoming ones. Once an enemy fires nuclear missiles, we cannot protect ourselves from them. No matter how hard we try, we simply cannot defend ourselves from a nuclear attack or the nasty radioactive fallout that spreads around after an explosion.

The U.S. civil defense plan calls for massive relocation of millions of people from high-risk areas to safer, rural areas. The success of the plan depends on *three to five days of warning time.* In other words, we need cooperative and friendly enemies who give ample warning time! Civil defense shelters near an explosion would be worthless, although in rural areas away from exploding bombs, shelters would reduce levels of radiation from fallout.

The most elaborate civil defense plans in the world won't save us from nuclear bombs. At best they are a shabby and false security blanket to soothe our fears, a blanket that will be shredded in a nuclear war. At worst, civil defense plans are a cruel trick to make us believe we are secure so we won't protest the nuclear arms buildup. Perhaps they're a cheap way of muffling our cries of fear.

This is the gift of the nuclear threat; it smashes our illusions of security and reminds us of the biblical truth that try as we like, we will never find safety in chariots or bombs. While that fact has always been true, we have desperately tried to make ourselves safe. Nuclear war *once and for all* shatters that false hope. As no other threat can, it peels off our shell of false security and reveals our utter dependence on God as our only place of refuge. His presence and the witness of his spirit provide a source of security, a firm anchor, and a quiet confidence. This spiritual security doesn't stop bullets or missiles. It doesn't provide a mysterious shelter against nuclear bombs. But it does provide a calm and quiet spirit that can not be crushed by bombs or bullets.

God's X-Ray

The gift of nuclear war is also found in its X-ray of the human heart. Modern humanity with all its sophistication and expertise is capable of producing unbelievable terror and destruction. We appear to be so civilized, so educated, so cultured, and so polite. We are people who have left our primitive ways far behind. But an inspection of our weapons of war shows we are capable of planning and executing the most primitive forms of brutality and violence. Nuclear war reminds us that we aren't as far away from the early, primitive days as we like to think. It reveals as nothing else can the boiling hatred that erupts when humankind rebels against God and his ways.

In the past, some wars appeared to produce more good than evil. A little evil, it was said, was necessary to achieve some good. In the name of defense, conventional wars are often justified. Such ethical fuzziness is gone in the face of nuclear war. The ugly face of a sinful humanity is unmasked by nuclear war. As nothing else can, nuclear war symbolizes the teamwork of the forces of hatred, greed, fear, dominance, and pride. Each nuclear-tipped missile is a symbol of the worst that the human community can produce. The gift of nuclear war is that it clarifies once and for all the rebellious nature of a people running away from God, trying to run their own show and doing a poor job of it.

The destructiveness of the feelings of anger, envy, revenge, and meanness that well up in all of our chests is multiplied millions of times over in the bomb. We too are connected to it. We are not innocent bystanders. The bomb represents the underside of our human spirit—the dark, nasty side. It symbolizes the arrogant impulses of rebellious humans, impulses that we share with the rest of humanity, and in that sense the bomb is also our thing. Certainly we don't threaten to use it, but it does represent the streak of unregenerate sin in all of us. And in that sense we are all involved with it.

Precious Life

Being shoved up against a monster like nuclear war and looking it straight in the eye is a lot like going to a funeral. It's not pleasant, but it does remind us that life is precious. As I leave a funeral, I always have a new appreciation for how quickly life can be snatched away. And then I resolve again and again to live more carefully, more tenderly, more joyfully, and more fully since life can be snuffed out so quickly. I guess this is a personal confession, but for me facing up to nuclear war has:

given me a new respect for life,
prompted me to care more tenderly,
taught me to hold life more gently, and
helped me to laugh and cry more freely.

For me this has been part of the gift. I know it's sad and tragic that it takes the ugly prospects of war to open the gift of life, but that's how life and death are. And that's how we are. And that's part of the gift.

Peace Makes Sense

The prospect of nuclear war also comes as a gift because it underscores the sensible nature of God's peace. From the days of the early church some Christians have said that faithful discipleship means living the way of peace, even when the nation demands military service. Taking Jesus' command to "love enemies" seriously often seemed too simplistic, like idealistic pie in the sky. The biblical vision of beating swords into plowshares just wasn't realistic; it sounded downright foolish. But now in the face of nuclear war, God's foolishness and Jesus' simplicity begin to make a lot of sense. In the midst of nuclear threats to destroy millions of people, God's logic sounds more reasonable and wiser than ever. And so in this sense the darkening cloud of possible nuclear destruction clarifies and confirms the truthfulness of God's mandate for a peaceable kingdom. And that clarification of God's will is also a gift of nuclear war.

Family Reunion

And finally, another gift is coming out of this threat. The prospect of nuclear war, like nothing else, is bringing God's children together. Billy Graham preaches the gospel of peace in Moscow, of all places. Unthinkable! Thousands of East German Christians walk in public demonstrations against nuclear weapons. Unbelievable! Over half of the active Roman Catholic bishops in the United States endorse a nuclear freeze! Amazing! We won't become one big happy family, but we are extending hands of fellowship across denominational lines. We are joining together to witness to the gospel of peace—Southern Baptists and Friends, Catholics and Presbyterians, Mennonites and Lutherans, and on and on. Not through rigid organizational structures, not by denominational decrees, but in spontaneous worship and witness a common voice is emerging. The movement *is* growing, and it's a beautiful witness to the prince of peace.

QUESTIONS

1. Are there other changes that make our situation today quite different from ten years ago?
2. What has enabled us to live safely with the bomb since Hiroshima?
3. Which of the triggers of nuclear war do you find most threatening?
4. What do you think about when you hear scientists estimate that the chances of nuclear war are 50-50 over the next years?
5. Which of the three reactions to nuclear war, such as "pretending," do you experience personally? Are there additional ones you feel or sense in others?
6. What are the similarities between facing up to nuclear war and coping with a terminal illness like cancer?
7. Are there other aspects to the gift of the nuclear threat?
8. Do you agree that "the bomb is also our thing" in the sense that it reflects impulses of hatred and rebellion common to all of us?
9. As Christians we often say that our security is in God. Do we really mean that? If so, what does it mean?

2
THE SECRETS

THE NAGGING QUESTION

A nagging question festers in the conscience of the Christian church. Why have we been so quiet about nuclear war? Why have Christians not spoken out against the construction and use of nuclear bombs? Why have we been so silent over the past decade as the arms race plunged ahead? That is the central question of our age that cries out for an answer. In recent months church leaders have started speaking out. Denominations have issued declarations and statements on peace. But for the most part average Christians have been silent. Where have we been? Why have we been so slow to face up to nuclear war? That nagging question haunts our conscience and will torment the historians who study the church's witness over the last twenty years. We have a lot to say about the little issues, but mostly silence on the big question of the day. Why?

Ignorant Bliss

I suspect there are many reasons, even some very good ones, for this uneasy silence. First of all, many of us are only beginning to discover what nuclear bombs do. For a long time that was a secret of American foreign policy. The official U.S. photos of the Hiroshima and Nagasaki destruction were classified information until the late 1970s. I was born a few days after the bomb was dropped, but until recently I really

didn't know what happened at Hiroshima. Of course I knew
that the U.S. dropped an atomic bomb on Japan, but so
what—a bomb is a bomb. What I didn't realize is that a nuclear bomb is not just another bomb. After going to school for
twenty years and teaching for ten years, I finally discovered
the horror of Hiroshima. I saw the pictures and that was
enough—they told the whole story. I recently learned for the
first time what a nuclear bomb would do to my own hometown.

The effects of nuclear weapons have been known for a
long time by the experts who make bombs and foreign policy,
but these facts have been hidden from us in the foggy jargon
of technical language. The people—average men and
women—have not known what these weapons do. We know
things would be bad if one exploded, but we know very little
about their specific effects. Few Christians know how much
damage a single bomb would do to their hometown.
Knowledge of the bomb's awesome power hasn't really
penetrated our minds. So one partly excusable reason we
haven't spoken up on this issue is ignorance. We haven't
known the facts. In this case ignorance certainly is bliss.

The Creaking Bridge
Second, we have assumed that the church's traditional
teachings about "just wars" also fit nuclear war. There have
been individual Christians and some traditional peace
churches who for a long time have said "no" to any participation in war. But the majority of Christians across the
theological landscape have felt it was their Christian duty, although not a pleasant one, to defend their country for
freedom. The Christian teaching that defensive wars were
just wars allowed us to do this with a free conscience.

Today we are beginning to realize that the idea of a just
war simply doesn't fit in the nuclear puzzle. In a major nuclear war even the defenders are killed. There are no winners.
Property and homes are blown into rubble on a massive
scale. Millions of innocent people are killed in an instant or
die from radioactive fallout drifting in on their homes
hundreds of miles from the attack. The just war bridge that

carried the church's doctrine of war across the ages is creaking, groaning, and crumbling under the burden of the nuclear age. We must turn anew to the Scriptures to discover a faithful Christian response to war. Nuclear war technology has raced far ahead of our theology. Now our theology is struggling to catch up.

Far Away

A third reason for our silence is the farawayness of nuclear war. Talk of nuclear war is often abstract, high in the sky of wordy concepts and theories. It seems so far away and irrelevant when it's wrapped up in the tissue of technical jargon. All of us, our homes, our children and our grandchildren, would be touched by a major nuclear war. A submarine launched missile is only fifteen minutes away from us. And ironically, while it may seem years away in the hazy distance, more than any other war, nuclear war is very close-by, and could be right at the doorstep of most of us in a few minutes. And that is part of the secret.

Our "Savior"

We have also been quiet about the bomb because of our fear of communism. Our government told us that the bomb would protect us and save us from a communist takeover. The bomb provided security and made religious freedom possible. This at least is what we were led to believe. And there was little reason to speak out against something that promised to save us from destruction. But now we are learning that the bomb also threatens to destroy us. Our savior might turn into our destroyer.

Close Up

It's not pleasant to get close to this demon. There's little comfort and delight in facing up to the gory details of nuclear war. But face up to them we must. For too long we have looked the other way. For too long we have pretended it's not possible. The horrors of nuclear war have been covered up with big words and abstract terms, making them sound acceptable and thinkable.

Before Christians can speak out about nuclear war we must at least know what we're talking about. Grim as it is, we must see the terrible human suffering that flows out of nuclear war. This is also one of the secrets. And it can no longer be hidden. We must get close enough to understand the agony and terror that real people like you and me would feel in a nuclear war—if we were among the survivors. We must imagine—as much as we dislike it—what would happen in our community to our neighbors and to our friends. We must see the destruction smashing down on our countryside, our historical sites, our streams, our homes, our parks.

And then we must realize that in an instant, American bombs would bring the same terror and destruction to other homelands across the world. The family names, street names, language, ethnic and racial tags would be different, but the memories, emotions, pain, and terror would be the same in these other homelands around the globe. Before we can speak, we must bring nuclear war down out of the sky of abstraction and see in vivid detail what it does to people and to places. Then, and only then, can we speak.

PEEWEE BOMBS

On August 6, 1945, a huge butcher knife hit the chopping block of history with a mighty wallop. It left a gigantic crack on the block of human history. The famous physicist Einstein said *everything* has changed since the nuclear bomb dropped on Hiroshima that day—everything, that is, *except* the way we think. Persons like me, born on this side of that crack in history, came into a different world than the folks who were born before the cleaver hit. What happened that day that makes things on this side of the crack so utterly different?

The Little Boy

A peewee bomb called "little boy" was dropped from an American bomber on the Japanese city of Hiroshima. Three days later, on August 9, 1945, another nuclear bomb exploded over Nagasaki.

Compared to the regular World War II bombs, this "little

boy" was a giant, but alongside today's bombs he was a mere peewee. The biggest bombs of World War II packed only ten tons of dynamite (TNT), but the "little boy" carried a destructive wallop of some 15,000 tons of dynamite—1,500 times more powerful than the bombs on the other side of the crack! This was a gigantic leap in the history of human destruction. For the first time a single airplane with a small crew could destroy a large city in seconds.

And now a few years later a few persons pushing buttons have the power to literally blow up much of the world. On this side of that historical crack collective suicide is possible, but it's more than that. There is also the power to obliterate buildings, hills, rivers, plants, and animals—the power to twist God's created order and to genetically disturb unborn generations. Those of us on this side of the crack live in a very different world, a very fragile one. We live in the shadow of the "little boy" with the awareness that a few people hold the triggers that could shatter our world bringing widespread death and devastation.

This book is about nuclear war. To understand nuclear war we must see what the "little boy" did. Hiroshima is our yardstick, our point of reference for understanding nuclear war. The destruction at Hiroshima was real. It wasn't an experiment in a laboratory, a computer prediction, or an abstract possibility; it did happen.

I am frustrated every time I try to describe nuclear war in words. They seem so empty and hollow. They do a poor job of communicating the terror and the pain. The realities of nuclear war are far beyond the fence of our daily experience. They are so utterly different, that they're impossible to imagine. It's hard to connect with such terrible destruction, hard to imagine it, and hard to feel it. Our words simply can't communicate all the ugly things that happen so fast in a nuclear explosion.

Photos and films tell the truth much better.[1] Truthful words about the effects of nuclear war sound like tearjerkers. Writers who correctly describe the effects of the bomb are accused of peddling fear. But to cover up the realities of nuclear war with pleasant words and impressive technical terms is downright dishonest. Governments have held the secret by not truthfully telling us what happens. I will try to describe it honestly, and it will sound emotional; but unfortunately that is the nature of the subject.

What Did the "Little Boy" Do?

What did the "little boy" do that day in Hiroshima?[2]

He killed at least 100,000 persons—fathers, grand-mothers, teenagers, children and babies.

He burned and injured at least 75,000 others—mothers, uncles, sisters and neighbors.

He created some 5,000 A-bomb orphans—children without parents.

He left about 179,000 survivors—people who were directly or indirectly touched by his destruction.

He killed or injured 90 percent of the medical personnel and destroyed 42 out of 45 hospitals.

He destroyed or severely damaged at least 60,000 homes and buildings.

He scorched the ground with temperatures of 7,200 degrees Fahrenheit and melted stone, steel and concrete.

He ignited a massive firestorm that devoured everything— men, pets, factories, cars and homes in a circle running 1.3 miles out from the explosion in all directions.

He smashed and burned to ashes a 5 square mile area in the city.

He seared the exposed skin of people standing 2.2 miles away from the explosion.

He wiped out an entire city in a few seconds.

The "little boy" whipped that city; he shook it; he battered it; he butchered it; and he slammed it into the ground. And when he was finished, it was dead. In a few seconds his nuclear butcher knife had slaughtered tens of thousands of people. In minutes the life of Hiroshima was blown out like the flame on a giant candle.

The American scientists were surprised at the "little boy's" power. They had only expected 20,000 deaths. Perhaps that's why President Truman remarked, "This is the greatest thing in history" when he got a note saying the bomb had been successfully dropped on Hiroshima. Things look quite differently however, depending on whether you drop the bomb or stand beneath it. It looked a bit different to the people in Hiroshima. Carved in stone in the Hiroshima Peace Memorial Park are these words to the dead: "Rest in peace, for the mistake shall not be repeated." What looked like a triumphant success to an American president, felt like a tragic mistake to those who were half alive, to the thousands of bleeding, burning bodies, to those who heard the moaning cries of pain.

Spots of Ash

Near the center of a nuclear blast the heat is so high that people and some objects don't even melt—they just turn into steam or vapor. Farther away the eyeballs melt, and the skin drips off the body. But in the center, nothing is left— there are no bodies to bury because they are completely burned to ashes. Morton Sontheimer, a member of the first team of Americans to enter Nagasaki, described how that city looked after the bomb:

> An open field. Occasional low humps of stone, bricks, mortar. No wood, no bodies. It was in a ghastly way, neat. Clean, even.... I looked down. My feet were in a circle of fine white ash, not thick enough to feel through my boot soles.... Had that spot been a man? A woman? A child? An oldster? Beautiful? Ugly? What color? No answer. All human ashes look alike.

> Nothing left to bury. I had seen many of those spots on my way to Point Zero.... Later I learned to distinguish the small irregular oblong spots, many fewer, that had been animals—dogs or cats, I guess. Altogether there were thousands of spots. It occurred to me that they marked the most instantaneous deaths in the history of the world.[3]

The Mushroom Club

The "little boy's" deadly poison lives on. It lives on in the bodies of the survivors who still live today. It lives on in the children of the survivors. And it will live on in the genes of

A portion of the Hiroshima downtown shopping area before the attack.
(National Archives Photo)

A partial view of the destruction in Hiroshima. *(National Archives Photo)*

An area of Hiroshima where parts of some sturdier buildings were not completely leveled. *(National Archives Photo)*

Nuclear ruins along the river in Hiroshima. *(U.S. Air Force Photo)*

their grandchildren. The naughty "little boy" commands respect for his enormous blast and sizzling heat, but those nasty results were soon over. The effects of his deadly radiation, however, live on today. They live on in the form of cancer in the lungs, breasts, and thyroid. They live on in leukemia, in eye cataracts, in mutations, and in mental retardation. In all of these the "little boy" is still with us today.

Some Japanese parents have formed a Mushroom Club. They are the parents of children who were in their mothers' wombs when the "little boy" came. Some of these children have smaller than normal heads and bodies, and some are retarded. One seventy-year old mother recently said, "My biggest fear is that I will die without anyone to take care of Kazuko [the child]. Kazuko always tells me that she will die first because her body is weak."[4] These, these are the little children that the "little boy" left. They are still with us today in the 1980s. His deathblow lives on.

Swimming in Death

His death blow also lives on in stunted minds. Robert Lifton, a psychiatrist, captured this fact in the title of his book *Death in Life*, in which he describes the psychological effects of the "little boy" in the lives of the Hiroshima survivors.[5]

Lifton calls the sudden immersion in death a "death imprint." The survivors found themselves swimming in a pool of death—it was on all sides of them. The death was so unnatural, so bizarre, so indecent, and so absurd that even death itself lost its meaning. A professor in Hiroshima said, "My body seemed all black, everything seemed dark, dark all over; then I thought the world is ending." A minister walking through the streets said, "The feeling I had was that everyone was dead. The whole city was destroyed. I thought that all my family must be dead. It doesn't matter if I die. I thought this was the end of Hiroshima, of Japan, of humankind."

Other survivors said they weren't sure they were alive. They felt like ghosts, like people walking in dreams. The line between the living and the dead had vanished. Even the living felt as though they were dying. There were no bodies to bury near the center of the explosion. There were no possessions to pass on. There were no people to pass on the memories. Funeral rituals, possessions, memories—the warm comforts that normally give meaning to death—even these were gone. Even the meaning of death itself was vaporized—gone like a mist.

Lifton also found people "closing off" their emotional feelings, "psychic numbing" he calls it. They were emotionally dazed and stunned. Their normal emotional reactions were cut off. They became emotional robots. It was a way of protecting themselves from nervous breakdown. If they felt nothing, then nothing was happening. It was the only way they could exist without falling apart.

Other survivors were nagged by guilt. Had they survived at the cost of someone else's death? Why were they singled out to live? And many felt they had not done enough to help others. They had neglected their public duties. They had refused to help close friends. They had literally run away from the terrible thing. And now days and months later they were tormented with shame and guilt. They hadn't done enough. Others had died because the survivors had turned and run away.

Black Rain

And there was fear:

> Fear that they had been touched by the "black rain," the rain that brought the radioactive fallout back to earth;

> Fear that they had been contaminated by the invisible nuclear radiation;

> Fear that they would get the "A-bomb disease."

There was immediate fear that within hours or days the disease would visit their families with severe diarrhea, high fever, loss of hair, and, yes, death itself. All around them the disease was at work. At any time the bomb in their body might strike again.

According to Lifton the fear created two rumors. Word

passed around that the entire city of Hiroshima would be desolate for 75 years, until the disease died out. The second story, told with great emotion, was that trees, grass, and flowers would never grow again in the city. It seemed as though life itself was being stamped out.

The fear lingered on after those early days. As leukemia and cancer of the breast, ovaries, lungs, and thyroid began popping up, the survivors had a keen sense that they were a link in a deadly chain that would stretch over several generations. And soon all the bad things—miscarriages, skin diseases, mental retardation, early death, and cancers of all sorts were rightly or wrongly blamed on the "little boy." There was fear that their children and their children's children would be sick or deformed. Since no one, including the experts, knew the long term effects of the "little boy's" work, fear sank deep into their beings, fear that someday, somehow, his deadly work might catch up with them. That fear still lives on today.

Other people feared the survivors and avoided them. It was said that they were contaminated by death. They carried the stigma of death and people didn't want to go near them. It was cruel treatment for those who had already suffered so much at the hands of the "little boy."

Vaporized Hope

Finally, hope itself was ruptured. Life's meaning was shattered. Purpose, pride, dignity, and humanity itself was in shambles. Have we really allowed this to happen? Has humankind really kicked itself like this? What kind of God allows these things to happen? What divine purpose can be found in the smoking rubble and searing pain left by the "little boy"? These urgent "why" questions hung heavy in the night air—unanswered—and the silence soon turned to bitterness and despair. The symbols of hope were gone. They were smashed to bits.

The War Game, a film simulation of a nuclear attack on Britain, captures this death of hope in a scene a few months after the attack. Young orphans in a refugee camp are asked what they want to be when they grow up. One after another

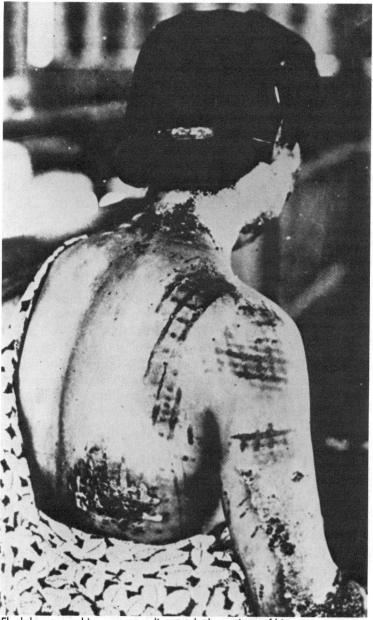

Flash burns on skin corresponding to dark portions of kimono worn at the time of explosion. *(U.S. Department of Defense Photo)*

the reply is the same, "I don't want to be nuthin." There is nothing more tragic, nothing more deadly to the human spirit than the evaporation of hope. Nuclear war in both its threat and its act vaporizes hope. And it is precisely at this point, more than at any other, that the bomb is a stranger to Christian faith—the faith that nurtures hope.

THE BIG BOYS

There's another part of the secret. The "little boy" grew up. At Hiroshima he packed 1,500 times more destructive power than the largest World War II bombs. But the "little boy" was heavy. He weighed four tons. In the 1950s technological progress made it possible to pack seventy times the "little boy's" power into a bomb that only weighed a ton. Since then scientists have learned to tuck more and more power into smaller and smaller bombs.

The power of a bomb is measured by tons of TNT. A ton of TNT is roughly the same as the destructive power in one ton of dynamite sticks. The largest World War II bombs had the power of 10 tons of TNT. The "little boy" dropped about 15,000 tons of TNT on Hiroshima. A kiloton is equal to 1,000 tons of TNT. So the "little boy" was a 15K (kiloton) bomb. One megaton, a common bomb size, is equivalent to a million tons. Thus, a one-megaton bomb packs a mighty wallop of a million tons of TNT. That is roughly seventy times more destructive power than the "little boy's"! It's hard to imagine a million tons of dynamite, but we must try to, because a megaton is a standard yardstick in the bomb business.

100,000 Dump Trucks

How can we visualize the power of a one-megaton bomb, equivalent to a million tons of TNT? Imagine filling the box-cars of a freight train with a million tons of dynamite.[6] It would take a lot of boxcars. The train would be 300 miles long, and it would take six hours to pass at full speed! Yes, 300 miles long. Now that's a lot of dynamite in a single bomb!

We can also visualize the power of a one-megaton bomb with dump trucks each loaded with 10 tons of dynamite. A one-megaton bomb would fill 100,000 of these trucks each with 10 tons of dynamite. This string of dump trucks would stretch bumper to bumper from Washington, D.C., to Columbus, Ohio, about 379 miles, if each one was twenty feet long. That's a lot of power packed into a small bomb weighing less than a ton! The older U.S. Titan missiles carry a 9-megaton bomb. The dump trucks (each with 10 tons of TNT) carrying the TNT equivalent for a single Titan missile would stretch bumper to bumper over 3,411 miles—from sea to shining sea. The Soviets have 20-megaton bombs on some of their missiles and are reported to have tested a 50-megaton one. All this boggles the mind and is quite impressive, or should we say depressive?

200 Hiroshimas

The trend today is toward smaller, more accurate bombs, and more of them. Big bombs aren't very efficient. They make a big bang, but the damage they make doesn't increase directly with their size. A two-megaton bomb, for example, doesn't double the damage of a one-megaton bomb. The U.S. Minuteman III missiles and the new MX missile in development carry several 335-kiloton bombs. Such a bomb is equal in power to 335,000 tons of TNT—one third of a megaton—or about 33,500 of our 10-ton dump trucks. But such a small bomb is over twenty times more powerful than Hiroshima's "little boy." A single Minuteman III missile carries 3 of these bombs for a total wallop of over 60 Hiroshimas. The new MX missile will carry 10 of these 335K bombs, packing a total power of over 200 Hiroshimas. Not bàd for a single missile! These "big boys" have taken us far beyond the days of the "little boy."

Another way of describing these "big boys" is to compare them with the firepower used in World War II and in Vietnam. The U.S. exploded a total of about five megatons of TNT in World War II and about six megatons over eight years in Vietnam.[7] A *single* submarine carries more than that today. Counting only strategic (long-distance) nuclear bombs, the U.S. has nearly 5,000 megatons of firepower and the Soviets have about 8,000 megatons! That's a lot of dump trucks loaded with dynamite! Figure 2.2 provides a summary of our

1 Kiloton (1,000 tons of TNT)

15 Kilotons (15,000 tons of TNT), size of the Hirsohima bomb.

1 megaton (1,000,000 tons of TNT), 70 times larger than the Hirsohima bomb.

Figure 2.1. Graphic Presentation of Bomb Growth

progress in firepower, from the days of the "little boy" to those of the "big boys."

UNIT	POWER EQUIVALENT
One Ton of Dynamite	1 Ton of TNT
Largest Regular Bombs	10 Tons of TNT
One-Kiloton Bomb (1K)	1,000 Tons of TNT
Hiroshima Bomb (15K)	15,000 Tons of TNT
One-Megaton Bomb (1M)	1 Million Tons of TNT
U.S. Bombs in World War II	5 Million Tons of TNT
U.S. Bombs in Vietnam	6 Million Tons of TNT
U.S. Strategic* Bombs	4,500 Million Tons of TNT
Soviet Strategic* Bombs	7,500 Million Tons of TNT
One MX Missile	3.3 Million Tons of TNT (223 Hiroshimas)
One Submarine with Trident II Missiles	19.2 Million Tons of TNT (Over 1,200 Hiroshimas)

*Long-Distance Nuclear Bombs

Figure 2.2. Nuclear Bomb Power

THE MURDER OF GOD

The "little boy's" secret is gradually being disclosed today. Usually his work is described by counting smashed houses and broken bodies. But there is a deeper layer to his secret—one that the Scripture helps us unravel. A clue to his work is found in the story of the judgment day in Matthew 25:31-46. The King says that every time we feed, clothe, and visit someone we are feeding and clothing him. Every time we turn someone away, we are rejecting Jesus himself. Even when we push aside a retarded or stigmatized child, we are pushing away the Lord himself. In the biblical language, "As you did it to one of the least of these my brethren, you did it to me." It is another way of saying that God himself is present in each of us. His Spirit is with us. We are created in his image. The touch of his Spirit is on us even when we stray. As he came in the flesh in Jesus, so he comes today in each of his little and big people.

Now this concept is especially moving as we face up to

nuclear war. For this means that behind every face is the face
of Jesus. Behind every Soviet and American body is the body
of Jesus. When we threaten to blow up a Soviet city, we are
doing it "as unto Jesus," who is represented in all those lives.
If we fry humans alive with the bomb, we have burned the
Lord himself. What the "little boy" did at Hiroshima he did to
Jesus. Behind every Japanese face—every soldier, every child,
every uncle—was the face of Jesus. As the "little boy" "did it
to one of the least of these," he did it to Jesus.

As we support the development, construction, and use
of nuclear weapons, we prepare to "do it unto him." And if
that day comes and we do it again, we will have "done it unto
him." It is in this sense, as Dale Aukerman has pointed out,
that Jesus becomes the central victim in nuclear war.[8] Put
another way, we are talking about the murder of God. When
his own creation—of which he is a part—rises up and exe-
cutes itself, God has been murdered. When "little boys" kill
even the littlest of children, they have killed God himself.
Jesus has been the victim before in the many wars down
through history. God has been murdered many times. But
never, never before has the planned execution been on such
a grand scale.

THE SECRET IN THE CLOSET

The bomb seems so contemporary, so far removed from
the biblical story. What could such an ancient record have to
say to such an utterly modern issue? The gap seems wide,
but a closer inspection shows some striking connections.
Surprisingly the old story has a lot to say about the bomb.

Savior or Destroyer

We must get right to the heart of the matter. The bomb
is the chief idol of our times. And as a good idol, it plays the
role of a god, demanding worship and respect. The trickiest
aspect of this idol is its hidden nature. This is the idol we
keep stored in the American closet. We proudly fly the flag
out in the front lawn as a symbol of freedom, but the real
idol—the bomb—we keep hidden in the closet. Most of us
have never seen it, but it is there. And it is worshiped. At a

recent commissioning of a new Trident submarine, a high-ranking military official said, "We all pray that because of her service at sea she will never fire a shot in anger." Note the religious language, "commissioning," "prayer," and "service."

At first it doesn't seem fair to say that we worship this idol. We don't work in the plants that produce nuclear weapons. We don't vote in the legislatures that order new weapons. We don't attend the commissioning services for new Trident submarines. In fact, most of us have never even seen a nuclear bomb or the missiles and submarines that carry them. So how can we worship something that we haven't seen? We don't fondle this idol and don't literally kneel down and worship it.

It is, nevertheless, our secret idol, a sacred object in our national closet. And even though we hardly ever see it, its presence touches all aspects of American foreign policy. Our policymakers know it's there, and other countries know it's there. And when the diplomatic going gets rough, there are vague references to "what we might have to do if worst comes to worst." Daniel Ellsberg reminds us that even though this nuclear idol hasn't been exploded since Hiroshima, it has been respectfully "used" in U.S. foreign policy at least twelve times in situations like the Berlin Crisis (1961), the Cuban missile crisis (1962), and to protect the Persian Gulf (1980):

> Again and again, generally in secret from the American public, U.S. nuclear weapons *have* been used, for quite different purposes: in the precise way that a gun is used when you point it at someone's head in a direct confrontation, whether or not the trigger is pulled.[9]

Many Christians are pleased to live in a country that wants to be "militarily strong." They are glad their country invests trillions of dollars in a "strong defense" to "protect and preserve their freedom." All of these beliefs, we must understand, betray that our faith rests squarely on the bomb. The bomb creates the impression of "military might," "strong defense," and "superior strength"; without the bomb all of these notions would crumble. Countries without nuclear weapons are not important military powers.

An idol promises to do something for you. It brings the rain or repells evil spirits. This idol, we say, protects our religious freedom and makes it possible for us to worship God. We have to have this idol, we contend, in order to worship God. What can be more idolatrous than to insist that we can only worship God if we have the bomb? Spiritual worship does not depend on external conditions. The idolatry of nuclear weapons is the ultimate idolatry, for the very idol that promises to save us may turn on us and literally destroy us. The false savior may return as a destroyer. The source of our salvation becomes the very weapon of our extermination.

We may never get a peek at the bomb. Christians never deliberately set out to worship it. The bomb, like most good idols, quietly nudged its way into our consciousness. Much of its seductive power lies in its ability to stay quietly and secretively enshrouded in the closet. For the most part we are not even aware of its prominence. But we do pay tribute to it every time we express pleasure in our nation's military might. That muscle is only possible because of the big stick which stands in our national closet.

The Idol's Grip

It's easy to measure the loyalty that the bomb commands. Share the World Peace Pledge with some friends or neighbors, and see how they respond.

> In light of my faith in Christ I am prepared to live without nuclear weapons in my country.

This simple statement gets to the heart of the matter rather quickly. The reaction of people to such a phrase reveals the strength of the bomb's devotion. Experiment with this statement and see what happens. You may discover that the bomb has a loyal following. Emotional reactions, more than ritual knee bending, are the best clue to our affection for the bomb. Tragically, many Christians may reject the statement. And this is the great scandal of our times, that Christian disciples kneel in front of the bomb along with the rest of the crowd.

Undressing the Bomb

The Bible reminds us that we often don't recognize idols at first glance. They are like wolves in sheep's clothing. This idol is no exception. It dresses up in very attractive clothing. It wears a pious mask. It speaks some impressive lines. But as we have already seen, it's not what it appears to be. It is described as the protector of freedom and the preserver of peace. It makes the world safe for democracy. It defends our vital interests and watches after our national security. It makes religious freedom possible and guards the safety of the free world. It slows the growth of godless communism. And if handled properly, it will never be used. These statements adorn the idol's mask in its professional wardrobe. With a biblical understanding of idolatry we shouldn't be surprised that a nuclear attack submarine was recently named the *Corpus Cristi*, meaning the body of Christ.

Good idols cleverly dress themselves up in religious phrases to cover up their true identity. But we are not deceived because we have already been to Hiroshima and we have seen what the "little boy" was really like. His name like those of most idols was cute, but when his mask was stripped off we saw his vicious and nasty ways. Those who see with their eyes and hear with their ears know that idols must be undressed, for only in their nakedness do we see their real nature.

Long-Distance Killing

This idol also wears a pleasant and comforting coat of "distance" as one of its clever disguises. Hiroshima seems so far away, yet it's so near. Nuclear war seems so far away, but it's close-by. The missiles, although far in the distance, are only 15 to 30 minutes away. The killers who push the buttons won't see their victims bleed, smell their burning flesh, or hear their cries of pain. The victims—average people—will be far away from the killers and from those who decide to wage war.

Long-distance killing removes the terror of nuclear war as well as our sense of moral responsibility. It's one thing to pull a trigger and see your victim writhe in pain at close range, but it's quite another thing to kill millions at a distance without needing even to glance at the bloody mess you make. Distance allows us to be all the more ugly. This all adds up to making nuclear war about the nicest ugly war one can have. This coat of distance must be ripped off our idol. Everything which seems so far, far away will be very, very near, very close, right at home.

The coat of technological distance hides the idol's work and provides emotional insulation between the killer and the victim. This allows nuclear killers to do things they ordinarily couldn't do. In a documentary on the "Defense of the Nation," CBS News interviewed an American missile commander in his underground silo. When asked whether he knew where his missiles were targeted, he said, "No." Then he added, "I don't want to know because I'd get too emotionally involved." In other words, if technological distance were gone and he knew exactly where his bombs were aimed, he probably couldn't handle the emotional and moral responsibility. Thanks to distance, he can "do his job" without feeling guilty or worrying about the damage and loss of life which will result when he pushes his button of lethal destruction.

Roger Fisher, a Harvard law professor, offers a modest suggestion for the prevention of nuclear war.[10] The secret code which the U.S. president uses to command the firing of nuclear weapons could be placed in a small capsule and implanted, much like a pacemaker, in the body of a presidential aide. The aide would be with the president at all times and would carry a butcher knife in his briefcase. If the president ever needed to fire nuclear weapons, he would first have to kill his own aide with his own hands. He would have to realize the terror of death and see the blood on his hands and on the White House carpet before he ordered the death of millions. Fisher reports that Pentagon officials frowned on his proposal because, in their words, "It would distort the President's judgment." I'm not sure whether Fisher is serious, but his modest proposal rips the coat of distance off our idol. Things do look and feel quite different when we're close up.

GOD'S COMPETITOR

Now idols have always gotten in the way of the people of God. He was aware of this in the early days when he asked his people to "have no other gods before them." In the Old Testament, God was a jealous God who wanted a monopoly on the worship and devotion of his people. But time and time again they ran after other gods, after all sorts of idols in the land. And we still do today.

So it shouldn't come as a surprise that once again we are running after other gods, even ones stored in closets. This idol is occasionally dusted off respectfully, with great awe at the christening of a new Trident submarine or in the dedication of a new missile system, but for the most part it's in the closet—deep in the water, deep in the underground silos, or high in the air. But it *is* there and it *is* worshiped.

In the biblical story the people didn't completely forsake God when they ran after other idols. They usually clamored after the heathen gods at the same time that they worshiped God. And so it is with us. We say we worship God, but we also quietly kneel before the door of the closet and worship the bomb. We print "In God We Trust" on our coins, but we truly trust in the bomb.

The Big Mystery

In the biblical sense an idol competes with God for the worship and adoration of his people. There are some uncanny parallels between the bomb and our images of God. Our words, language, and concepts are too limited for both of them. The bomb plays god in a very real sense. Mystery is at the center of the divine. His ways are higher than our ways. His peace goes beyond our understanding. His qualities and work supersede human comprehension. In a similar way the bomb is enshrouded in mystery. We don't completely understand how it works. We can't comprehend its destructive power. We can't predict half of its consequences. Like God, it cultivates mystery, makes us curious, and we worship.

The Big Power

God is portrayed as all-powerful, the mighty force that creates, moves, and sustains the universe. The power of the bomb is also awesome. As the scientist Oppenheimer watched the explosion of the first test bomb, words from a sacred Hindu text flashed into his mind:

> If the radiance of a thousand suns were to burst into the sky, that would be like the splendor of the Mighty One.... I am become death, the shatterer of worlds.[11]

The bomb also has the mysterious godlike power that can blow up thousands of acres with a few pounds of plutonium. Like God, the bomb too can move mountains and shake up the universe. The bomb's ability to destroy, parallels God's ability to create.

The bomb represents the highest, or should we say the lowest, achievement of scientific knowledge. The best scientific minds and brightest engineers of our day spend their careers perfecting the bomb. It is a symbol of our collective intelligence, and like the all-knowing mind of God it commands respect. God guides the course of history. He arranges the books of nations on the shelf of history. He is in control, nudging history forward. The bomb also signals control. The nations holding the bomb in their closet can control events. They dominate international politics. They get what they want. They keep others in line. The controlling influence of the bomb again has a striking resemblance to God's power.

The Nuclear Apple

Several biblical stories help us understand this nuclear idol. When God created the good garden, he planted a fruit tree which held the key to supreme knowledge. The urge to "be like God, knowing good and evil," was the promised reward for biting into the apple. Such an apple was very attractive. It was hard to toss it aside. The nuclear apple is no different. Countries scamper after the bomb so that they too can be like little gods, knowing good and evil. Biting the nuclear apple brings an artificial sense of ultimate power, the power to decide what is good and evil for other nations.

The nations who have bitten the nuclear apple know what's good for the rest of the world. They know which countries should have capitalism and which ones shouldn't. They know which nations should freely determine their own destiny and which ones should fall into line with the wishes of the superpowers. They know who deserves foreign aid and who doesn't. They know who deserves more guns and tanks and who doesn't. They know which is the "right" side in every civil war. They know who should be spanked with sanctions and who deserves praise. They know what causes instability and revolution, and they know what makes for peace. They know everything—or do they? Churchill noted that after President Truman knew the atomic bomb worked he got cocky, "He told the Russians where they got on and off and generally bossed the whole meeting."[12] The bomb breeds arrogance! Like the apple, it tricks its worshipers into thinking they're as smart as God.

The Nuclear Tower

The biblical drama soon moved outside the orchard. A bit later the people gathered to build a city and a tower (Genesis 11:1-9). They erected the Tower of Babel high into the heavens in order to "make a name for [themselves]." The tower was a sign of their importance and great achievement. They would be respected. They would have a name that meant something, a reputation that demanded respect.

And so it is with the bomb. Those nations which clutch it in their closets make a name for themselves. They are feared and respected. According to the biblical story, the Lord came down to see the tower. He was repulsed by their ambitious drive to make a name for themselves: "This is only the beginning of what they will do; and nothing that they propose to do will now be impossible for them." And so he confused their language and scattered them so that they couldn't worship their towering idol. Someday the intense electrical pulses emitted when a bomb explodes may shut down our communication systems and confuse us. We too may be scattered and unable to worship our idol.

The Nuclear Calf

Another biblical image fittingly describes the bomb. As Moses was up on the mountain chatting with God, the people invented their own idol. "Make us gods who will go before us," they begged Aaron. And he gave them what they asked for—a golden calf. They worshiped it saying, "These are the gods who brought us out of the land of Egypt." How stupid! How idolatrous to declare that the golden calf had delivered them out of Egypt. How foolish to think that the calf would "go before" them as a protector.

The idolatry of the bomb, while much more subtle, is astonishingly similar. The bomb, we say, has delivered us from the hands of aggressors. It has been our protection. It has kept us safe for 35 years. It's remarkable that we haven't had a major war with the Soviet Union over the past thirty years. But no one knows why we haven't. Those who worship at the bomb's altar say the bomb has saved us. Yet no one really knows.

And the bomb will go before us; we can count on it to guard us, we are told. A naval intelligence officer recently said, "Nuclear weapons are an umbrella under which we conduct our foreign policy." The bomb goes before us, and under its frightening shadow we flex our diplomatic muscles. Because it goes before us, we threaten to use all sorts of sanctions if things don't go our way. The days of idolatry are not past—we still desperately want an idol to "go before us."

The Nuclear Beast

The biblical saga closes with another glimpse of idolatry. The calf grows up and becomes a beast. The beast rises out of the sea and is given power and great authority (Revelation 13). This beast is usually understood as a symbol of the Roman Empire. The Scripture then describes the idolatry of nationalism:

> The whole earth followed the beast with wonder ... and they worshiped the beast, saying, "Who is like the beast, and who can fight against it?"

The bomb gives the superpowers the authority and power of the beast. The citizens of the superpowers and their camps of allies follow the beastly nationalism with wonder. The bomb lends mystery and ultimate power to these modern beasts. And when a country builds the bomb, the peoples of the world are impressed, and in their hearts they chant, "Who is like it, and who can fight against it?"

The Bloody Altar

Idols have sacrificial altars nearby. They not only demand reverent worship and respect, but also sacrifice. In primitive societies and in the Old Testament, people or animals were sacrificed. As the supreme sacrifice, Jesus made animal sacrifice obsolete. Today he invites us to follow him and leave all else behind—to sacrifice our allegiance to other commitments for his sake. When a god is worshiped, other things have to be given up.

Modern sacrifices usually don't involve killing a victim. War, however, is one exception. It is the highest sacrificial ritual of patriotic religion. In the name of patriotic faith, soldiers are slain and sacrificed on the altar of nationalism. Dale Aukerman points out that the original meaning of the word "victim" referred to something offered in sacrifice to a deity.[13]

The victims of nuclear war will *literally* be slain on the altar of nationalism. Modern as we try to be, we aren't as far away from ancient sacrifice as we think. In fact, a nuclear war would take us back to the most primitive form of sacrifice. With no respect for age, beauty, sex, or status, humans would be burned and vaporized on the altar of nationalism. This modern idol is quite primitive, for it demands absolute allegiance—even the willingness to be chopped and burned in the name of freedom, patriotism, and defense.

Aukerman makes the keen observation that this sacrifice would be a profane and upside-down Pentecost. Instead of mighty winds and tongues of fire rushing down from heaven as a sign of the unity of the body of Christ, the primitive sacrifice of nuclear war will send violent winds and raging fires rising upward toward heaven as they devour millions. The odors of these burning victims and the radioactive fallout rising in the atmosphere will be a sign of the broken and shredded relationships in the global community. An upside-down Pentecost indeed!

As we sort out our loyalties and choose whom we worship, we must be very careful to understand that the bomb is an idol that demands burning sacrifices in the old-fashioned way. The apostle Paul urges us to live so that our lives will be a holy sacrifice giving off a pleasant aroma. If multitudes of Christians would stop kneeling before the bomb, their lives could become an acceptable sacrifice in the eyes of God—one that might prevent the sacrificial burning of millions of victims on the bomb's altar. If we keep on worshiping the bomb, we will not only speed up the day of sacrifice, but we may also find ourselves burning on the altar.

And if that day comes when the blood drips off the altar, the closet door will open and we will finally see the true nature of this idol. The friendly mask of the bomb will be ripped off. Behind the altar we will see the ugly face of the god we have so carelessly worshiped.

Centuries ago David the psalmist gave a striking description of both our nuclear idol and of us:

> They have mouths, but do not speak;
> eyes, but do not see.
> They have ears, but do not hear;
> noses, but do not smell.
> They have hands, but do not feel;
> feet, but do not walk;
> and they do not make a sound in their throat.
> Those who make them are like them;
> so are all who trust in them.
>
> *Psalm 115:5-8.*

If that great sacrificial day should come to pass, there will be no compassion, feeling, humanity, or emotion from our technological idol. The bomb in its mechanical sophistication utterly increases the human suffering and pain in war. Yet at the same time, as no other instrument of war, its long-distance missiles separate the killer from the victim so that those who work for the idol truly would not see, smell, hear, or feel the suffering they cause.

QUESTIONS

1. What are the "secrets"?
2. Are there other reasons for the Christian silence on nuclear weapons?
3. Some have said that Hiroshima was necessary to save American lives and end World War II. Do you agree?
4. Is religious freedom dependent on the bomb?
5. What are your reactions to the World Peace Pledge? Does Christian faith mean we should be willing to live without nuclear weapons?
6. Is idolatry a useful biblical image for understanding the bomb?
7. Can you think of other parallels between the nature of God and the bomb?
8. Are there other types of "distance" that keep nuclear war away from us?
9. Is it fair to say that we worship the bomb when we haven't seen it or deliberately intended to worship it?
10. Does our reluctance to give up the bomb say anything about its strength?

3

WHY NUCLEAR WEAPONS AREN'T NICE

SHATTERING CREATION

All of this is still far away. Most of us haven't been to Hiroshima. It's hard to imagine what one million tons of dynamite would do. Such numbers don't easily plug into our everyday world. Recently a colleague and I brought seventy Hiroshima bombs to our hometown. We described what a one-megaton bomb would do in our community.[1] It's not that we enjoy horror; we don't. We simply wanted to learn firsthand what a nuclear explosion would mean for our friends and neighbors. It was a way of yanking the big numbers down out of the sky of abstraction, and translating them into local details of human destruction. Somehow these numbers look and feel a lot different when they hit your hometown than when they're high up in the theoretical sky.

In the process of our study we discovered that our community was one of some 400 high-risk areas in the U.S. Figure 3.1 shows the locations of the high-risk areas.

Dumping 100,000 Trucks

I will summarize some of the key effects that happen when a nuclear bomb explodes.[2] You can apply the same description to your own community. The number of casualties would vary with the size of the city. The same bomb would kill more people in a larger city. We could choose

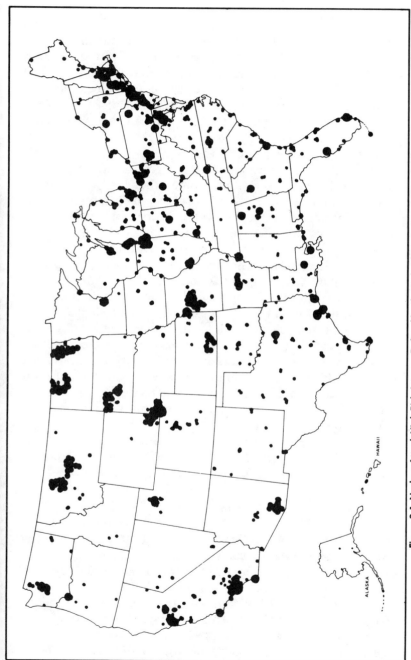

Figure 3.1. Nuclear Attack High Risk Areas as Defined by the Federal Emergency Management Agency.

any bomb size for our illustration, and the amount of damage of course would vary with the size of the bomb. A one-megaton bomb is the typical size that is used in many scenarios. Some of the bombs in today's stockpiles are smaller, and others are much larger. Remember that a one-megaton bomb could fill 100,000 dump trucks each with ten tons of dynamite.

A bomb can explode in the air above a target or on the ground. Usually it's exploded on the ground if the attacker wants to hit a missile silo or some other heavily protected target. A one-megaton ground burst would dig a huge hole in the ground nearly 1,200 feet wide and deep enough to bury a twenty story building. The damage from an air burst, on the other hand, fans out over a larger area and doesn't dig a crater in the ground. Another key difference is that an air burst makes little radioactive fallout. Like a giant vacuum cleaner, the ground burst sucks bits of dirt, buildings, and other junk high up into the air, makes them radioactive and then drops them slowly back to earth over the next days and months. A ground burst would be used on protected military targets, while an air burst is more likely over industrial centers. Military analysts often predict a "package" of both types of bombs over large military and industrial areas. I will describe the effects of a one-megaton bomb exploded about 6,000 feet in the air above its target.

A bomb releases its energy in five major ways as shown in Figure 3.2. Each of these produces different types of damage. We will look at the five effects separately.

Ground Zero

First, a brief overview may be helpful. As a bomb explodes, it forms a mile-wide fireball that flashes sizzling *heat* across the countryside. This is followed a few seconds later by a *blast* producing violent winds and rapid changes in air pressures, which smash buildings. At the same time, deadly rays of *radiation* bombard the ground under the explosion. The bomb also sends out a high-frequency radio wave called an *electromagnetic pulse*, which damages electrical and electronic systems in the same way that light-

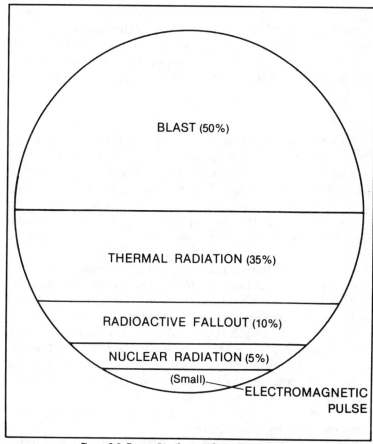

Figure 3.2. Energy Distribution of a Nuclear Explosion

ning does. Finally, the particles of radioacive *fallout* drop down on the earth for several hours and weeks after the explosion. All of this, except the fallout, happens very quickly—in a matter of seconds. In the wink of an eye, in a few seconds of time, God's good creation can be shattered and shredded to bits.

The point on the ground directly below the center of the explosion is called *ground zero*. This is the central point of reference for describing damage. The destruction diminishes as we move away from ground zero. In the following description, imagine that your own home or your hometown is at ground zero. In this way you can plug the description into your own setting and get an idea of what would happen around you. The calculations reported here apply to any geographical area under normal weather conditions in daylight.

Sizzling Heat

These bombs get *quite* hot. As a nuclear device explodes, it forms a fireball a mile wide. The temperatures are about 27 million degrees Fahrenheit, as hot as the sun itself! A sizzling flash of heat traveling 186,000 miles per second scorches the countryside in all directions. Thirty miles away, persons looking directly at the fireball receive retinal burns in their eyes. Fifty miles away from ground zero the fireball feels much hotter than the noonday sun.

Now back at ground zero things are *terribly* hot, so hot that they don't melt but turn into vapor. People, plastics, and plants are vaporized into hot mist in an instant. People have no idea what happened. They are burned alive, and if they're lucky their spots of ash remain. A mile and a half away from ground zero it's not so hot—here things melt. Steel, stone, and glass melt. Concrete explodes. Granite statues melt like butter. Skin melts and drips off the arms of people. Eyeballs melt and run down over the face. Here virtually everyone is fried alive. The sizzling heat penetrates everything like a giant torch cutting through jelly.

The blazing heat drops as we move away from ground zero. But things are still quite hot. About two miles away aluminum siding evaporates on the sides of houses. Even four miles away, wood, plastic, and fabrics near windows or lying outside houses start burning spontaneously. Five miles away the clothing worn by people standing outdoors ignites spontaneously. Even seven miles away from ground zero, newspapers and trash lying around outside houses burst into flames. At this distance people standing outside without protection suffer third-degree burns, the most severe kind. Ten miles away, persons without shelter receive first-degree burns similar to an instant sunburn.

After the heat flash, fires spring up all over the place. Wooden buildings, gas stations, cars, and natural gas lines explode and burst into flames. People are trapped in burning buildings and scorched by nearby explosions. In larger cities where some buildings are still standing, a massive firestorm would likely start as smaller fires grew together. The firestorm is like a gigantic fireplace. Cooler air rushes in at speeds of 100 miles per hour at the edges and forms a rising stream of hot air near the center. As the fire burns hotter and hotter, the chimney effect intensifies and sucks in more and more cold air, causing the fire to burn violently. A firestorm may burn for several hours, gobbling up several square miles, consuming everything in its reach, leaving only ashes.

Mighty Blast

About half of the bomb's energy is released in a powerful blast that does two things. It creates violent winds near the center that swirl around at 500 to 700 miles per hour. The blast rapidly changes the air pressure and creates a shock wave. This shock wave is like a wall of rock-hard air, similar to a tidal wave, that spreads out from ground zero at supersonic speeds. The sudden changes in air pressure create a giant shaking motion. Like a giant hand it suddenly shoves buildings in and then yanks them back again with tremendous force, like the mighty swat of a hand leveling houses in a child's play village.

Everything—houses, stores, libraries—crumbles like a cookie as the wall of hard air travels out from ground zero. Telephone poles and trees snap like plastic straws. Hospitals shatter like a broken drinking glass. Violent winds follow the shock waves and turn objects into deadly missiles flying at high speeds. Lawn mowers, tricycles, garbage cans, bricks, slivers of glass, all flying at hundreds of miles per hour, smash and slice whatever they hit.

In a few minutes it's all over. Everything is leveled in a circle that runs 2.5 miles out in all directions from ground zero. There are about 13,000 acres in this circle of total damage that is five miles wide from side to side. Everything, *everything*, has been smashed and flattened into the ground.

Wood-frame house before a nuclear explosion, Nevada test site. *(U.S. Department of Defense Photo)*

The same building after a nuclear explosion four miles from ground zero. *(U.S. Department of Defense Photo)*

80

Heat effects on a wood-frame house five miles from ground zero one second after nuclear explosion. *(U.S. Department of Defense Photo)*

Heat effects on the same wood-frame house about ¾ of a second later. *(U.S. Department of Defense Photo)*

Here and there a sturdy wall juts up through the heaps of rubble. Junk and debris are piled up like huge snowdrifts. Several feet of junk cover the streets. This is the inner circle of total damage.

Four miles away from ground zero, erect persons are blown 22 feet at 14 miles per hour. At this distance, lightly constructed commercial buildings are destroyed. Typical houses four miles out are smashed to bits. Even 5.5 miles away most houses are damaged beyond repair, and people standing outside are killed by the strong winds. At least 30 percent of the trees in this area break like popsicle sticks. Moving beyond six miles the damage declines, but it still reaches out some 15 miles in all directions, where it blows out doors, cracks plaster, and twists window frames. Glass might crack or break even as far as 30 miles away. When the mighty winds and changing air pressure quiet down, they leave the following levels of destruction behind:

Miles from Ground Zero	Acres	Damage
2.5	12,800	Total
4.0	19,200	Severe
6.5	51,200	Moderate
10.5	134,400	Light

Total Damage Area 217,600 Acres

Deadly Radiation

Nuclear radiation is the third thing that shoots out of the bomb. Like a giant X-ray machine, the bomb zaps the nearby area with its deadly rays. The invisible rays shoot through everything as they bombard the area near ground zero. A wall of concrete four feet thick is the only thing that stops them. The radiation kills anything that's still alive and contaminates rubble one mile out from ground zero. About two miles out, the radiation damage is quite small. Although the radiation is deadly at the center, the fire and blast effects are much worse and cause much more destruction. The circles of damage produced by the fire, blast, and radiation are summarized in Figure 3.3.

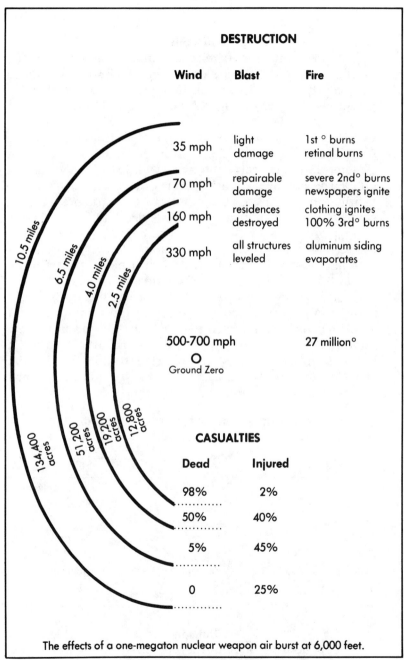

DESTRUCTION

Wind	Blast	Fire
35 mph	light damage	1st ° burns retinal burns
70 mph	repairable damage	severe 2nd° burns newspapers ignite
160 mph	residences destroyed	clothing ignites 100% 3rd° burns
330 mph	all structures leveled	aluminum siding evaporates
500-700 mph		27 million°

O
Ground Zero

10.5 miles
6.5 miles
4.0 miles
2.5 miles

134,400 acres
51,200 acres
19,200 acres
12,800 acres

CASUALTIES

Dead	Injured
98%	2%
50%	40%
5%	45%
0	25%

The effects of a one-megaton nuclear weapon air burst at 6,000 feet.

Figure 3.3. Heat and Blast Damage Zones

Super Shock

An electromagnetic pulse, commonly called EMP, is the fourth effect of the bomb's explosion. The EMP is similar to the electrical signal given off by lightning, except that it's hundreds of times stronger. And like lightning it burns out transistors and electronic circuits. As the EMP is picked up by power lines, it knocks out large electrical systems. The EMP damage would likely shut down communication systems and electrical services in a wide area. This would cut off power supplies, lights, phones, freezers, refrigerators, ventilation fans, pumps, computers, and elevators, making quite a mess on top of everything else. This could create serious problems for civilian nuclear power plants and other industries which can only be shut down by computer systems. How would we control nuclear power plants if the computing systems went dead? Would they melt down?

Survivors would have a hard time communicating and living in any normal sense. The power and communication systems could be repaired if they were not blown apart, but it might be months or years until a repairman arrived to fix them. Military officials are worried that a few bombs exploded many miles above the ground might shut down communication systems over much of the U.S.

ENERGY DISTRIBUTION AND EFFECTS OF A NUCLEAR BLAST

	Energy	Effects	Damage
Blast	50%	Explosive Shock High Winds	Buildings Collapse Flying Debris
Thermal	35%	Light and Heat	Burns and Fires
Radiation	5%	Gamma Rays, Neutrons	Deaths and Sickness
EMP	small	Magnetic Fields	Electrical Systems
Fallout	10%	Radioactive Particles	Contamination

SOURCE: Glasstone and Dolan, *The Effects of Nuclear Weapons*, pp. 6-8.

Hot Sand

Radioactive fallout is the bomb's fifth effect. When a

bomb explodes, it sucks dirt, junk, and other small particles up into the explosion and makes them radioactive. These bits and pieces go high into the atmosphere and then start falling back to the earth. The bigger, marble-size chunks fall back quickly near ground zero. The finer, sand like particles are carried by the wind and gently drift down to the ground over several days and weeks. Each little piece of fallout is like a tiny X-ray machine, that gives off its own deadly radiation as it lies on the ground.

An explosion in the air, like the one I described, makes little fallout. Ground bursts, however, really produce a lot of the nasty stuff. After a general nuclear attack involving both ground and air bursts, all areas of the U.S. would probably receive some fallout. Even places hundreds of miles away from an explosion would get "hot" dust hours and days later as the winds drifted across the country. The Federal Emergency Management Agency says that after a nuclear exchange "no area in the United States could be sure of not getting fallout, and it is probable that some fallout particles would be deposited on most of the country."[3] In other words, every area of the country can expect some.

Radiation is measured with a yardstick called a "rem." It's a standard way of estimating the extent of radiation damage to people. The deadly level is 450 rems, since about half the people receiving that much would die quickly. Exposures under 100 rems have no immediate effects, but they might produce long-term problems ten or fifteen years later in the form of cancer or early death. The U.S. Arms Control and Disarmament Agency estimates that a number of large areas in the middle and eastern United States will receive *at least* 1,000 rems of radio-active fallout radiation—over twice the deadly level. See Figure 3.4.[4] The fallout is blown around by the wind, and it piles up like snowdrifts, making "hot" spots all over the place. Without a Geiger counter the average person can't tell the "hot" spots from the "cold" spots.

A one-megaton bomb exploded on the ground makes a lot of fallout. If the winds are blowing from the northwest at 15 miles per hour, the fallout would form a cloud some 5 to 8 miles wide and 30 miles long toward the southeast. About

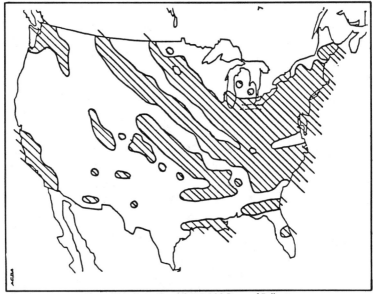

Figure 3.4. Areas Receiving 1,000 Rems of Fallout

3,000 rems of radiation would be falling from this plume as it drifted southeast several hours after the attack. The cloud eventually widens to 10-15 miles as it floats away from ground zero, and even 90 miles away the fallout levels are about 900 rems, or twice the deadly level. With many bombs exploding in different parts of the country and with unpredictable wind patterns, the "hot" sand would blow all over the place, and no one could be sure of being safe from it.

Three things happen as the fallout drifts back down to the ground in the hours and days after the attack. It decays at a fairly fast rate. For example, 1,000 rems of radiation would drop to 100 rems after 7 hours and to 10 rems in 49 hours. Although that sounds fast, it would still take 10 years for an area exposed to 3,000 rems to return to peacetime safety standards. Second, as the old fallout decays, new fallout arrives and increases the level of radiation. Third, persons are continually absorbing radiation. The seriousness of radiation sickness depends on the size of the dose and how fast you receive it.

All three of these processes are going on at the same time, so it's terribly hard for anyone to know how much radiation has been received. Placing any solid materials between you and the radiation gives some protection. Staying in a basement with sandbags around the windows would reduce outside radiation by a factor of 10, or from 4,500 rems to about 450 rems.

IN THE CELLAR

We've looked at how the five effects of a bomb spread out from ground zero. Now let's move five miles away from the explosion and consider how it might affect your family. Remember, you are five miles away, so anyone living closer to the blast is much worse off than you are. Imagine that it's an early spring evening.

You're a nurse and you've heard about an international crisis on the news, but it seemed far away. Local civil defense officials were urging people in your area to travel about thirty miles away in case of a nuclear attack. Traveling away seemed so foolish because you didn't know what you'd find there and, furthermore, an attack probably wouldn't happen. Besides, if worse came to worst, it seemed safer to take your chances at home in your own cellar since you at least knew where the food and water were located.

Your two children are playing outside, and your spouse is shopping two miles away. You are down in the cellar cleaning. A dazzling light flashes through the basement window. You run upstairs and the draperies around the windows are burning. You run outside looking for the children. Your son, who was playing out in the open, is in flames. His clothing has ignited spontaneously. His face and hands are scorched with third-degree burns. He's screaming. Newspapers and some trash sitting outside the house are also flaming. Wooden shingles on the roof of the kids' playhouse are smoldering. Your daughter, standing beside the garage, was protected from the blast's sizzling flash. She's safe. Horrified, she watches her brother burn, but she's afraid to go near him. She sees you at the back door, and you both run toward each other.

As you leave the house, you hear a rumbling noise. It's about fifteen seconds after the flash of heat, and now the shock wave is arriving. Violent, swirling winds pick up your daughter and slam her into a car, killing her on impact. Your burning son, who was running toward you, is crushed as a wall of your brick house tumbles down on him. Your house crumbles like a cookie. Two of the exterior walls are standing, but everything else caves in and blows away in the swirling windstorm.

Somehow the house misses you, but a flying bucket doesn't. It smashes into your back. You're also cut by flying glass and other junk. But you *can* walk. Suddenly the winds die down. The storm is over. Other houses in your neighborhood are smashed and burning. A nearby gas station is still standing. Its windows are blown out, and most of the shingles are blown off the roof, but miraculously the building shell is still upright. Here and there other sturdy building structures jut up through piles of rubble. In dazed shock you instinctively begin running toward the gas station for shelter, but a mighty explosion suddenly rips it apart before you get there. Again you are fortunate.

Now you see an old stone house that's still standing, and you run toward it in a daze. As you run you hear cries of pain and moans. You see people burning, but you're too stunned to stop. In the basement, seven other neighbors and some children are gathered. Some are trying to board up the windows. You fall on the floor exhausted. Suddenly you remember your spouse—where is he? And then it hits you—you'll never know; you'll never see him again.

The basement is dark. There's no electric. People are sobbing. Some are bleeding. Someone has a flashlight, and in the dim light they recognize you and come for help. They know you are a nurse and they beg, "Please help us." In the terror, even you had forgotten. Suddenly you remember the hospital; you should be at the hospital helping. There's no way to get there, no way to find out if it's even standing. So you tear up an old blanket in the basement and wrap some wounds. You do what you can to help, but it's not much.

You wonder whether your children are dead—maybe

one is still alive. You feel guilty hiding in a basement. You must go out and look. You must check for sure. As you move toward the basement door, another neighbor grabs you. "No, no," he says, "you can't go out. The radiation will kill you." You had forgotten about the radiation.

No one knows for sure. But some think they saw fallout coming down. Some are vomiting, no one knows from what. No one knows who was contaminated. Another neighbor tries to come in, but he is stopped. Your neighbors shove him outside so that he won't drag in the dreaded fallout and contaminate everyone else. And so you huddle together and try to survive. Everyone is afraid to go out for several days because of the dreaded fallout. No one knows for sure how much is there, nor how much was received. Life is bitter and morbid in the dark basement. You are alive, but it feels more like death than life. And many of those around you want to die.

PICKING UP THE PIECES
Nightmares

This imaginary episode gives us a personal glimpse of what nuclear war might be like five miles away from ground zero. The psychological torture would be just as bad as the physical pain and suffering. Fear would grip the survivors. It would terrorize every move.

Will another attack come?
Will I ever see my children again?
Will my children be sterile?
Will my grandchildren be deformed?
How much radiation did I get?
Was it a deadly dose?
Will the results show up five years later?
Is the radiation contagious?
Will my body be contaminated forever?
Can I drink water?
Is food contaminated?
How can I know things are safe?
When can I go outside again?

Will things always be contaminated?
Will the grass ever grow again?
Why should I go on living?
Why didn't I do more to help?
Why didn't I speak out before?
Has God given up on us?
Why keep on living?
Did God really let this happen?

Such questions flood the minds of survivors huddled in makeshift shelters. Fear, guilt, meaninglessness, and hopelessness paralyze them through and through. This is the psychological torture that flows from nuclear war. We have already seen the psychological reactions in Hiroshima—the immersion in death, the psychic numbing, the guilt for not doing enough, the hostile feelings, and the shattering of hope; these same emotional traumas will certainly follow the bomb's trail to other places. There is no reason to expect other people to act any differently. But there's more than just emotional pain. In a nuclear war there's also a body count.

The Mangled
There are all sorts of injuries and many ways of dying in nuclear war. There are direct injuries from the blast. The rapid change in air pressure ruptures internal organs, blood vessels, and eardrums. There are indirect injuries from the blast as buildings fall on people, and sharp objects jab into their bodies at high speeds. People are blown around and collide with all sorts of debris. All of this adds up to thousands of cuts, bruises, fractures, and punctured organs.[5]

The flash of heat and the vicious fires create thousands of burn injuries, many of them severe. Five miles away, everyone standing outside receives third-degree burns—the worst kind—that destroy the skin and leave permanent scars. Nerve endings are burned, eyeballs melt, hair is singed to the roots, the skin is charred black and peels off easily. A third degree burn over 25 percent of the body produces shock and requires complicated medical treatment. Flame burns from fires or burning stoves often sear the entire bodies of people who were protected from the fireball's initial scorching heat. There is flash blindness—temporary blindness—for a few minutes and retinal burns as far as thirty miles away for those who looked directly at the fireball.

Immediate radiation from the explosion as well as the later fallout produce radiation sickness and death. Over half the people exposed to 450 rems die quickly. Those soaking up smaller amounts experience loss of appetite, nausea, vomiting, headache, dizziness, internal bleeding, diarrhea, and loss of hair. Their weakened bodies are susceptible to the infection produced by burns and wounds. Those fortunate enough to live awhile can look forward to cancers of all sorts, early death, early aging, decreased fertility, cataracts, miscarriages, retarded children, and genetic mutations. The seriousness of any of these depends on the amount and rate of radiation exposure.

Two other types of injuries flow from a nuclear explosion. There are casualties from combined injuries. People die from burn infections because their bodies are so weakened by radiation that they can't fight the infection. Those who wouldn't normally die from just one type of injury, die from the stressful combination of several injuries.

And finally, injuries and death come from secondary effects. Pacemakers in hearts are stopped by the electromagnetic pulse. People dependent on insulin, cortisone, kidney treatments, special oxygen supplies, or visiting nurses can't receive them, and they also die.

The Body Count

A single bomb can mangle and kill an awful lot of people. The number of dead and injured left by one bomb staggers our imagination. The huge figures are hard to translate into dead and bleeding bodies. To get a feel for the size of the disaster let's look at what a single-megaton bomb would do to several cities. The number of dead would vary with how closely people live together and with the size of the city itself.[6]

These are the dead and injured that would be strewn about after a single-megaton explosion on each city. You can

City	Dead	Injured	Total
Atlanta	363,000	350,000	713,000
Boston	695,000	735,000	1,430,000
Detroit	783,000	954,000	1,737,000
New York	1,667,000	2,838,000	4,505,000
Los Angeles	816,000	1,194,000	2,010,000
Leningrad	890,000	1,260,000	2,150,000

see we've come a long way since Hiroshima. But it's unlikely that only one bomb would be used on a large industrial area. Two bombs, with the combined power of twenty megatons would really chop things up in New York City leaving the following casualties:

	Dead	Injured	Total
New York	9,583,000	3,654,000	13,237,000

That's right, 9.5 million dead in one city, snuffed out in seconds like the flame of a candle. I double-checked the source to make sure, and the figure is correct. That's an enormous pile of corpses from just two bombs. In our study of Lancaster County, Pennsylvania, with some 360,000 people, we estimated that if no one evacuated, a one-megaton air burst would leave the following casualties:

	Dead	Injured	Safe
Lancaster County	104,000	52,000	206,000

It's hard for me to grasp what it would be like to have 104,000 corpses lying around. How would we ever dispose of them and control disease? To understand what this would mean for our county, I reluctantly went back to my trucks for help. No, I'm not a truck driver, but trucks do help us comprehend the problem. Now with the 104,000 corpses, let's assume that one fourth of them were vaporized or permanently buried and that we only need to worry about getting rid of 75,000. I've never loaded bodies on trucks, but let's assume that on the average we get 100 bodies in each dump truck. We would need about 750 dump trucks just to haul the bodies out that weren't instantly cremated.

Now I know this sounds gross, and it's the kind of picture that repels all of us, but it's true! And we must understand that this is what we are talking about when we explode a nuclear bomb. Although it sounds crude, we must realize that the thousands of bodies left by a nuclear bombing would need to be hauled away by dump trucks or buried by bulldozers. There would be no time for funerals. Controlling rats, stench, and disease would be critical, so bulldozers and trucks would need to be used; *if* we could get anyone to drive them through the radiation and *if* we could find any equipment that would run. Now if it takes 750 dump trucks to haul out Lancaster's small number of corpses, think of the thousands of dump trucks it would take to clean up a Dallas or an Omaha, let alone a New York City.

We've looked at the number of dead and injured in specific cities. What would happen to the U.S. or the Soviet Union as a whole? Obviously, no one really knows. Military experts have all sorts of sophisticated computer programs to predict the number of deaths, but so many things could vary that we are left with a range of estimates from best to worst cases. A distinction is usually made between a "counterforce" attack aimed only at military targets and a general military-industrial attack on large manufacturing and population centers. The estimates look like this:[7]

ESTIMATES OF DEATHS IN MILLIONS

	World War II	Counterforce Nuclear Attack	General Nuclear Attack
USSR	20.0	4 to 28	42 to 100
U.S.	.4	2 to 20	20 to 165

Regardless of the final body count, it will take a lot of dump trucks to clean up after a nuclear war. And remember, these estimates don't include the injured. There may be as many injured as dead. As I've thought about these numbers and studied carefully what would happen in my own community, I'm struck by three conclusions:

Conditions after any nuclear war will be extremely bad. They will be terrible and filled with horror beyond our imagination.

A nuclear war will *not* be the immediate end of the world. Even the worst scenarios estimate that half of the people in most states and counties would survive the initial attack. It's possible that wild epidemics over several years could lead to the end of civilization, but no one really knows.

The survivors will live in a very different world. It will be an ugly, primitive, crude, brutal, and vicious world in every sense, a retreat to the jungle. The survivors are likely to envy the dead.

The Final Epidemic

In most disasters we turn to doctors for help. But could the doctors do anything to bail us out after a nuclear war? Frankly, they wouldn't be of much help. In fact, many doctors are saying that nuclear war would be the Final Epidemic. There are some good reasons to make such a prediction. The doctors and hospitals would be wiped out along with the rest of us. Most estimates of casualties predict a higher death rate for medical personnel because they generally live near urban centers, which are more likely targets than rural areas. Second, since hospitals are located in cities, many of them would also be gone.

In our local study we discovered that in a few seconds the number of hospital beds would drop from 1,334 to 226. If half the injured in our county needed hospital treatment, we would end up with at least 110 patients for each hospital bed. The 35 surviving surgeons would have to work in four operating rooms. Estimates of the number of injured victims seeking help from each surviving doctor range from 1,000 to 1,700 in large urban areas.[8] Physician H. Jack Geiger calculated that if 1,000 seriously wounded patients descend on one doctor who spends 10 minutes with each patient, the doctor would work 20 hours a day and it would take at least 8 days to see all his patients.

Such a clean, neat picture of medical care after an attack is a joke. Do you really think that the doctors would leave their own families stranded in makeshift basement shelters and walk or drive through deadly radiation to get to their offices? Think again! How would the patients get to the office? Without telephones no one would even know if the office was open, even if they could get there somehow. Think again! Would nurses, janitors, and X-ray technicians show up for work even if their hospital was standing? Probably not. In Hiroshima many of the emergency medical teams ran away. If a doctor made it to the office, how long would the medicine last without replacement? And how would the doctor work without light, electricity, and water?

Most victims will never find a doctor, even for a pain pill. And the few doctors who come out of hiding or who still have an office will be bombarded by thousands of injured crying out for help. In this situation physicians will need to use triage, the practice of dividing patients into three groups. They would refuse to help those who would die anyway, and refuse those who would eventually get better without assistance. They could help *only* those for whom medical care might make a difference.

The doctors who are courageous enough to work will be working without X-rays, lab tests, supplies, drugs, plasma, beds, and sanitary supplies. At best they will be putting on Band-Aids and wrapping strips of gauze around wounds. In a general nuclear attack, there will be no help from the outside. Medical care will be crude, primitive, and impossible after a nuclear exchange since many doctors and facilities will be gone. Medical treatment would be terrible even if the doctors and hospitals were still around.

A single airplane crash with 150 victims overloads the emergency system of even a large city like Washington, D.C., or Los Angeles. Such a crash is a speck of dust compared to a nuclear blast. Such isolated accidents can also receive help from outside the area. A single one-megaton bomb would produce some 10,000 severe burn cases in a single city. In the U.S. as a whole we have *at best* about 2,000 special burn beds. In Pennsylvania we have *only* 60 special burn beds. There are some 1.4 million hospital beds in the United States, but a *single* bomb over New York City would create that many injuries. In other words, we aren't prepared to

An aerial view of Nagasaki before the nuclear blast. *(National Archives Photo)*

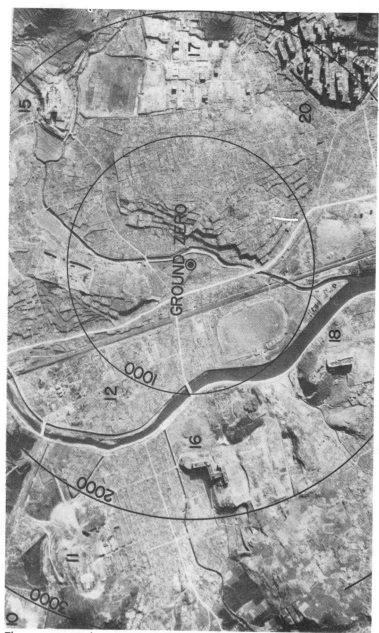

The same area photographed after the blast. *(National Archives Photo)*

cope with even one bomb, let alone hundreds! This is why physicians are telling us that there is *no* medical treatment for nuclear war. In their words, the only *sane* medical response is prevention.

Social Chaos

We have seen the ugliness left by a nuclear bomb. It's bad, but in some ways it's only the beginning of bad things to come. In the weeks that follow a nuclear explosion, communities will be thrown back into primitive times, with little or no electricity, lighting, refrigeration, telephone, water, or transportation. The survivors will be starting over again on a self-dependent basis in a very different and dark world.[9]

The social fabric of people, organizations and communication—all those things which normally support us—will be torn apart. The social props that routinely hold up our lives will be yanked out. We will be coping alone in a brutal and ugly jungle. Who will be in charge? Many of the elected leaders, along with police and firemen, will be killed. It will be impossible to have democratic elections. The strong, the loud, and the brutal will take charge.

We learned in World War II that in such conditions, civil order and polite behavior disappear. People become selfish, greedy, and violent, pushing and shoving to get to the head of lines. Everyone looks out for himself. Few care about the common good. Would Christians act any differently?

I live about 6.5 miles from the nuclear reactor at Three Mile Island. During the TMI accident in March 1979 I got a tiny glimpse of what happens in a moment of panic. Drivers butted into line at gas stations. People tended to look out for themselves. Some faculty ran off from their teaching jobs, leaving students behind. The phone lines were dead. It was difficult to get the "truth" about what was happening. Rumors were rampant. People acted irrationally and in surprising ways.

Social confusion and widespread fear jolted our quiet community into chaos. The aftermath of a nuclear explosion would be much, much worse. Whom could we trust? Whom could we believe? Friends, radio announcers, nurses, gas station attendants, and police might be gone, looking after their own families and themselves. Our social system that normally helps us cope with disaster—the doctors, psychiatrists, ambulances, prison guards, radios, and telephones—will be gone or badly shattered. New groups and helping relationships will emerge, but the general order of the day will be chaos, violence, stealing, looting, and anarchy.

With the social fabric unraveled, people will look out for themselves, trying to survive as best they can. The little things will make the difference between life and death. Now the search will be on for just *one* cup of clean, safe water. The cans of safe food will be carefully rationed. Blankets will be fought over and shared in the chilly basements. The law of the jungle is likely to become the law of society as individuals and families desperately try to make it with little food and poor shelter.

The Reign of Rats and Flies

The public health problems after a nuclear attack will be staggering.[10] The rotting bodies of people and animals will smell, and they will provide a rich breeding ground for insects and rodents. Survivors will be too afraid of radioactive fallout even to bury the corpses. A recent government study proposed that elderly folks should be recruited to clean up radioactive areas after a nuclear attack. The elderly would be drafted since they are already near death and would no longer bear children who might be genetically contaminated. This is a serious proposal! Surviving rats, mice, flies, mosquitoes, cats, skunks, and dogs will carry infectious disease. Human survivors—weakened by injuries, exposure, stress, malnutrition, poor sanitation, crowded shelter, and fatigue—will be especially likely to catch infections and spreading diseases. Poor sewage disposal, poor ventilation, little or no heating, and crowded conditions will provide a ripe breeding ground for contagious diseases.

Physicians are concerned that the carriers of epidemic disease may survive the radiation better than humans and give rise to outbreaks of infectious diseases such as hepatitis, encephalitis, plague, smallpox, and tuberculosis, just to name a few. Doctors will have few drugs to stop the spread of these diseases. It's also possible that radiation might produce new forms of diseases which would be difficult or impossible to control. Three summary points paint a very gloomy medical picture after an attack:

Diseases would spread easily and rapidly.

People would be weakened by all sorts of injuries and would be much more susceptible to contagious diseases.

The medical system of doctors, hospitals, ambulances, and drugs would be helplessly shut down.

Many physicians are trying to make it clear that we can't count on them to bail us out after a nuclear attack.[11] The doctors will be just as helpless as the rest of the survivors. There will be virtually *no* medical care. The best medical preparation before an attack will be worthless. In fact, some physicians believe it is immoral for them to assist in civil defense planning. Such planning, they say, is a cruel and immoral hoax, which dupes people into a false sense of security. There is absolutely *no* medical treatment for this disease! Our destructive capacities have far exceeded our caring capacities. Physicians say that when treatment of a disease is impossible, prevention is the only alternative. Do we hear them? Do we believe them? Are we willing to work for prevention?

Cockroaches Inherit the Earth

The most shocking and startling thing I've learned about nuclear war is *what we don't know about it.* In a careful study of the effects of nuclear war, the U.S. Office of Technological Assessment concluded that *the effects which can not be calculated in advance are just as serious as those which can be calculated.*[12] In other words, the scientists are saying that the ugly effects of the fire, blast, and radiation which we can predict *are only half of the story.* The other half of the story, those things we can't estimate in advance, will be just as bad as the things we can scientifically predict. Now that is a sobering and shocking conclusion! Put another way, it means that scientists really don't know half of what could happen. Yet in spite of not knowing half of what might happen, nations continue playing with nuclear matches and threaten to use them.

For example, cockroaches and some other insects can survive about a hundred times more radiation than humans. Some birds and other smaller animals die more quickly than humans from radiation. This means that the cockroaches will survive a nuclear blast much better than humans and many other animals. Insects are much less likely to be killed by fallout than humans. Now the critical point is simply this: different animals and insects dying at different rates will botch up the whole created order. It will disturb and twist the balance of nature which is crucial to life on our planet. How will insect populations be controlled if their natural predators, birds, die off at much faster rates? Will this increase crop damage by insects? No one knows. Will the cockroaches inherit the earth along with the meek? One can imagine genetic mutations producing huge cockroaches that take over. Now probably that won't happen, but the fact is that we really don't know what will happen when we shake up God's created order!

The Big Experiment

There are many other uncertain things. Scientists debate the extent to which many nuclear explosions would "thin out" the ozone layer in the upper atmosphere, which protects us from the sun's rays. If the ozone were depleted by 20 percent, the sun would blind unprotected eyes of humans and animals. Some scientists estimate that exploding only 10 percent of the superpowers' nuclear arsenals would destroy 40 to 70 percent of the ozone layer. Thinning the protective ozone layer would cause burning and blistering of plants, animals, and unprotected humans. It also might produce long-term changes in the climate, which in turn could affect a lot of other things. Humans can wear sunglasses and clothing as protection from the sun's scorching rays. But what about the animals that don't have sunglasses and special clothing? What would they do? How might this disturb the beautiful harmony in nature? If vegatation were scorched, how would this affect erosion, flooding, crop production, and forest fires? Again scientists don't really know how serious these changes might be.

Two scientists estimate that even a "limited" nuclear war using some 2,000 to 3,000 megatons on only military targets would irreversibly lower the earth's temperature; reduce rainfall in the mid-latitudes; destroy the wheat-producing areas of North and South America, Europe, Russia, and China; and advance the polar ice sheets until much of Canada and the northern U.S. and Europe were covered with glaciers thousands of feet thick.[13]

It's also clear that many nuclear explosions would increase genetic mutations. These might double among people exposed to a range of 20 to 200 rems of radiation. But again, scientists can't predict exactly how these deformities might emerge in later generations.

We also know that radiation exposure increases the chances of many kinds of cancer. It's certain that cancer rates outside the combatant countries would rise because of radioactive fallout drifting around the world.[14] Certainly not all the survivors would get cancer, but the rates would definitely climb. How much they would increase we don't know.

The results of an experiment are normally uncertain. And as you can see, the nuclear experiment is a rather large one, since the world is the laboratory and its outcome involves the fate of the earth.[15] It's the sort of experiment we may only be able to do once. Social scientists pay a great deal of attention to the ethical dimensions and the psychological impact of experiments when their subjects are human guinea pigs. There has been surprisingly little moral reflection over the ethical implications of the big experiment that involves all of us. And we may have only one chance to experiment with the fate of the earth.

PLAYING WITH NUCLEAR MATCHES

We are like children playing with matches when we threaten to use nuclear weapons in the face of such unknown horrors and uncertainties. The words of Jesus on the cross seem strangely appropriate in the face of such blindness: "Father, Father, forgive them for they know not what they do." And we must join in that prayer, "Father, forgive us, for in spite of all our science we really don't know what we're doing. Forgive us for playing with nuclear matches in your beautiful garden."

I have tried to show why these nuclear matches aren't nice. In summarizing their ugliness, two things stand out. On the one hand, nuclear war *is* war. The generals have often said that war is hell. The saturation bombings of cities in World War II killed more people than the Hiroshima and Nagasaki bombs. Any war is terrible and horrible. Nuclear war is a member of the family of violence. Whether people and property are destroyed by regular war or by nuclear war matters little. Biblically and spiritually it's hard to justify any type of war. The Word of God condemns violence in any form.

On the other hand, nuclear war *is not* war. John Sommerville contends that to use the word "war" for nuclear destruction is deceptive and misleading. Simply putting the adjective "nuclear" before war gives the misleading impression that nuclear war is just another kind of war. When we think that way, we assume that all our previous ideas about war also apply to nuclear war. They don't! Sommerville argues that since we have a special term for killing one's self, suicide, and for killing an ethnic group, genocide, we need a special term for nuclear devastation to remind us that it's not just another type of war. He suggests "omnicide" since we're talking about obliterating several nations as well as the natural creation. I think he's on target because it's one thing to say we're preparing to fight a nuclear war, but it sounds a bit different to say we're preparing for omnicide.[16]

What are the ways in which nuclear war is *not* war? It is fundamentally different from conventional war in several ways:

The large number of people killed by a single bomb;

The enormous amount of physical destruction over wide areas;

The control of so much destruction by so few people;

The speed of destruction, which allows no time for escape, sur-
render, or negotiation;

The disruption of the created order of nature;

The genetic contamination of future generations;

The destruction of innocent civilians hundreds of miles away;

The total shattering of economic, medical, and political
systems;

The severe psychological damage caused by fear before and
after an explosion.

For all these reasons nuclear war is not war. It represents a
gigantic leap backward in human ugliness. It's in a league all
by itself. We must understand that we have left the peewee
league of the "little boy" far behind.

THE CROSS AND THE BOMB

I suggested in the previous chapter that the biblical
symbol of the idol helps us see the demonic power of the
bomb in our time. The chief idol of an era competes for allegiance on an even par with God. Wealth, or mammon, was
the chief rival in Jesus' day. Like God, it captured the total affection of the people. Mammon still reigns today, but men
rarely die for it. Mammon still commands respect, but
mothers won't sacrifice their sons and daughters on its altar.
But people will die for their country. Nationalism, with the
bomb as its emblem, does reign supreme. It's an idol that demands a burning sacrifice, a willingness to die for the sake of
the country.

The Choice

Jesus said we are faced with choices. We can't give ultimate devotion to two masters. We can try to serve two
masters, but in the end we will serve one and hate the other.
And so Jesus urges us to decide, to choose our lords carefully
and to understand their demands for complete loyalty.

The cross is a symbol in the biblical story which reveals
the nature of both God and the bomb.[17] The cross unveils
God's will and demonstrates how he deals with violence. At
first glance the cross and the bomb look quite similar. Both

are hideous instruments of torture. The cross was the Roman bomb. It was the god that "went before them." The apparent peace of the golden age of the Roman Empire was only possible because the cross lurked in the shadows. And so it is today. Peace built on nuclear threats, freedom dependent on atomic bombs, and international cooperation based on sanctions are not real. Peace and freedom imposed by the bomb's shadow are artificial and shaky.

While the cross in one sense was the Roman bomb, the crucifixion transformed it into our central symbol of Christian faith. The death of Jesus disclosed the very nature of God's love and clarified once and for all how he copes with evil. Today we see the cross from the perspective of the resurrection, and from that vantage point the cross and the bomb stand in stark contrast. Symbols always point us toward something else. On this side of the crucifixion the cross emerges as the key sign of God's kingdom, while the bomb pulls us toward nationalist worship.

The bomb and the cross are the dominant symbols of our time. They represent two utterly different kingdoms. They stand far apart. They both invite us to worship. They both expect ultimate allegiance. In a real sense the bomb stands against *everything* that Jesus represents. We must make a choice. It is difficult to worship at two altars at the same time when they are so far apart. Let's examine their differences before we choose.

Grace and Sin

The cross stands as a sign of God's grace, a sign of his willingness to suffer and become the sacrifice for the sins of the world. God himself in Jesus becomes the innocent victim and takes the place of those who deserved to die. In his death, sins are forgiven. His willingness to be the innocent victim is a sign of enormous grace. The bomb stands far apart as the ultimate sign of sin. It represents the collective efforts of unforgiven hearts and lives that are severed from God and from each other. The bomb is the corporate banner hanging over a community that has turned its back on God. It is the chief manifestation of sin in our times.

Love and Hate

The cross is a sign of God's love and caring. For God so loved the world that he gave his only son. Greater love than this has no man. Here we have love at its best—true compassion and caring for the human predicament. The bomb on the other hand is a bundle of vicious hate. Like no other symbol in history, it stands for the worst kind of revenge. And so we have, side by side, love at its best and hate at its worst.

Forgiveness and Revenge

The cross communicates God's forgiveness. He's willing to erase the past and start over again. He's willing to forget, to talk, to make up, and to move forward together. The bomb is the modern weapon of retaliation. In the strategic policy known as MAD in the 1970s, the bomb could only be used for massive revenge. It couldn't protect or defend a country. It could only threaten devastating retaliation. The bomb became a defensive weapon only in the sense that its ugly threat of retaliation might make an aggressor think twice before hitting. And so it stands today as the central symbol of revenge in our modern culture—not based on an eye for an eye, but on the principle of 100 bodies for an eye. You scratch my eye and I'll blast your body to bits—that's the threat of the bomb. And it's quite a contrast to God's way of turning the other cheek.

Reconciliation and Separation

The cross bears a message of reconciliation. It brings hostile enemies back together. Jesus broke down the dividing wall of hostility. Adversaries are brought together in Christ. Through the cross, God fellowships with sinful humans. At the foot of the cross, bitter feelings mellow and hatred melts. The cross brings people together. It gathers them in, offers them peace, and unites them. The cross is the Great Gatherer. Those who kneel before it become God's agents of reconciliation in this world and cannot kneel outside the idol's closet at the same time.

In contrast to the cross, the bomb scatters and chases

people away. Instead of reconciling, it threatens. It intimidates, snarls, and sneers. It pushes nations farther and farther apart. It upsets and undoes the work of reconciliation. It increases the gaps, broadens the gulfs, and heightens the misunderstanding.

In the biblical sense, sin is separation from God. The bomb is truly the Final Separator. In the days and weeks after the bomb's burst, people are separated from each other. Communication lines are cut. Transportation is impossible. Families are torn apart forever. People are permanently separated from their homes and history. In the ugly aftermath of the bomb, there may also be separation from God. Survivors may unfairly blame the bomb on God's will and hold him responsible. They will say he shouldn't have allowed it. And that warped understanding of God's will may push them farther from him. It will be hard to believe and hard to have faith in God in the face of the Great Separator.

Salvation and Destruction

The cross is the sign of salvation for all. In the cross all are welcomed—black, white, American, Soviet, male, female, capitalist, and socialist. There is salvation for all who turn from their foolish ways and ask forgiveness. The cross does not discriminate. Everyone is welcome regardless of rank, race, position, or nation. Indiscriminate salvation flows freely from the foot of the cross.

The bomb cannot be accused of discrimination either. It offers destruction for all regardless of race, age, sex, or status. The bomb destroys indiscriminately. Just like the cross, it is no respecter of persons. It has no favorites. Destruction flows freely at ground zero. Titles, positions, and political status make no difference in the bomb's nasty swath of destruction. On the one hand, we have indiscriminate salvation; on the other hand, indiscriminate annihilation.

Service and Demand

The cross is the emblem of servanthood. Jesus, the man of the towel and basin, freely serves. He heals, he feeds, he teaches, and he freely pours out his life on the cross as the chief servant of all times. He was among us, he said, not as a dominating leader but as a servant, and his compassionate service cost him his life. But he was worshiping at the right altar.

In sharp contrast, the bomb is a sign of demanding domination. Nations who hold the bomb in their national closets control others. They influence events. They make things turn out in their favor. They break treaties and get away with it. They intervene in the lives of other nations, and they hold other countries under their economic thumb. The arrogant bomb stands in sharp contrast to the gentle posture of the chief servant, who willingly walked to the cross.

Humility and Pride

The cross is also the sign of humility. It was a humble Son of God who hung on the cross. He agreed to submit to the Father's will. In selfless form he voluntarily laid down his life. He quietly and truthfully answered the questions at his trial, knowing that his answers would lead to his death.

The bomb on the other hand is the ultimate symbol of collective greed, pride, and rebellion. It's the haughty sign of international superiority, the symbol of being number one. Piles of bombs measure the hungry greed of huge corporations which gobble up fat military contracts. They also reveal the greed of scientists who make a killing hustling lucrative research grants to develop bigger and better bombs. The bomb is the corporate expression of a rebellious, proud, and greedy people.

One and Many

There is also the theme of the "one and many" in these symbols. In the cross there is *one* death so that *all* may live. In the bomb there is *one* decision so that *all* may die. At the cross a single death brings life to many. In the bomb the futile attempt to protect life brings death to millions. The death of many is held in the hands of a very small number of people. One decision, one code, one command, one button brings death to many.

Coping with Evil

And finally, we have here two different ways of dealing with evil. The cross demonstrates God's method of nonviolent resistance. At first glance it appears feeble and flimsy like the response of a scared weakling. But in the end, God is triumphant. His apparent weakness strips the pleasant mask off the Roman Empire and shows it for what it was—brutal and ugly. The empty tomb, the witnessing apostles, the growing church, in the long run were all an embarrassment to the Roman and Jewish rulers. These signs showed how powerless the rulers were to stop the truth. They foolishly thought they could wipe out the truth by killing one man. But they couldn't. The truth lived on. Paul says that on the cross Jesus "disarmed the principalities and powers and made a public example of them" (Colossians 2:15). He embarrassed them publicly by showing how weak and powerless they were to stamp out the truth. The truth doesn't need to be protected or defended. And every attempt to squash it will fail and embarrass those who try, because in the long run the truth will overcome. It will be victorious because it *is* the truth. God simply fights evil with good.

The bomb deals with evil quite differently. It fights evil with evil. As we have already seen, it fights a little evil with *a lot* of evil! The bomb tries to stamp out a little evil with a bigger dose of the same stuff. But in the long run the bomb simply breeds more evil, and it takes bigger and bigger doses of evil to wipe out the new evil. And the vicious cycle goes on and on. That in a nutshell is the history of the bomb. A country makes a small bomb to scare off its enemies. And then an enemy country makes a bigger bomb to protect itself. And back and forth it goes as each side tries to build a bigger and better bomb to crush the enemy's threat. It never works. And yet people and nations are too foolish to realize it. We must understand that the cross and the bomb represent two utterly different ways of coping with evil.

We Must Choose

It should be clear by now that these are two very different symbols. They are the chief banners of our time. The crowds that follow them are marching in utterly different directions. And we must decide under which banner we will march. The tragic situation of our time is that many Christians can't distinguish the two. They live and talk and worship as though the cross and the bomb are stitched onto the same banner. They even use the cross, of all things, to justify the bomb. They do not understand the fundamental spiritual breach between these two signs. They see, but do not see. They hear, but do not hear. They worship, but do not know what they worship. Jim Wallis is correct when he says that the great evangelistic task before the church is to convert our own people from the bomb to the cross.[18] Which sign will we choose? Under which banner will the church live? In which direction will we march? At which altar will we worship? On which altar will we burn? There is a difference. And we must choose.

QUESTIONS

1. What mental images or pictures of life after a nuclear war fill your mind?
2. Is there any value in describing the effects of a nuclear bomb on our own community? It's not nice to scare people, is it?
3. Should Christians waste their time describing the dangers of nuclear war? Isn't this condemning the darkness rather than lighting a candle?
4. Do you agree with the physicians who think it's immoral to participate in civil defense activities?
5. Is there a moral difference between conventional war and nuclear war? Is nuclear war merely war?
6. Why has there been so little moral reflection about such a big experiment?
7. What might the scenarios of nuclear destruction look like from God's standpoint?
8. Are there other distinctions between the cross and the bomb?
9. How might survivors respond to God after a nuclear attack? How might such an experience change our Christian faith and our understanding of God?
10. Do you agree that the "evangelistic task" of the church is to convert our own people from the bomb to the cross?

4

CAN WE TRUST THE GIANTS?

THE LAND OF THE GIANTS

We live in a world where two giants stretch their arms all over the globe.[1] They are afraid of each other. Smaller countries fear the U.S. and the USSR. The giants woo the little countries over to their respective sides by baiting them with guns, tanks, fighter jets, and all types of foreign aid goodies. The giants fight and scrap over the little countries. And the little nations play the two giants off against each other. They pout, they whimper, and they threaten to buy guns from the other giant if they don't get what they want from the first one.

The Security Jam

The giants compete. They have different ideas about how the world should run. They twist the arms of other countries. The giants look out for their "vital interests," "security interests," and "national concerns" all over the globe. Scarce natural resources—oil, copper, uranium, and other precious metals—must be protected, they say. The giants guard shipping routes, making sure no one stops the flow of raw products and trade necessary for their industrial growth. And they protect friendly multinational corporations stretching around the globe.

All of this creates a security jam—the feeling of being caught in the corner of an extremely shaky world. "We live in a very dangerous world," President Reagan said when he ordered draft registration in a reversal of his campaign promises. Russian President Brezhnev recently described tensions in Europe by saying, "Not since World War II has the situation been so serious." We find ourselves in an unpredictable world, where revolutions can flare up almost anywhere at any time.

There aren't simple solutions. If the giants start giving in too much, they might get trampled. If they act too tough, they might touch off a war and blow things up. It's a real security jam. Acting like nice guys may bring terrible results. And acting bad may stall off the war. So what's to be done? On and on the competition goes—nip and tuck, back and forth, here a few gains and there a few losses. The giants deceive and they infiltrate, they bribe and they intervene, all in the name of "national security." This genuine concern to protect and look after their own interests as well as their friends' lies at the heart of the arms race. It's the basic source of the locomotive's steam. There's no easy way to get out of the security jam. If there were, we'd be out of it!

Bickering Giants

The giants see each other as the chief threat to world peace—and they really believe it. Each giant believes it must move in quickly to control brewing trouble spots before the other giant takes advantage of them. Like two fighting children they always have something to say about each other's business. And like arguing spouses they blame each other for stirring up unnecessary trouble. And so fear lurks in every corner. Each giant prepares for the worst. Both struggle to protect their people and their interests. If one sits back and does nothing, the other giant may gain a foothold and soon threaten its opponent's national interests. Neither can trust the other. And yet the more they threaten and snarl at each other, the more they scare each other and perpetuate a cycle of fear.

The Global Play

The struggle of the giants plays on an international

stage. The world community sits in the auditorium cheering and booing the performance. This complicates the drama and makes it hard to separate the real actions from the "showy" ones. No one knows when the giants really mean it or when they are just showing off. Since the whole world is watching, they have to be somewhat polite and pleasant so that they aren't seen as rude bullies. But they also have to look and talk tough so that they aren't taken as yellow weaklings. It's always hard to know what's really going on, when to take them seriously and when not to.

Following the giants' moves can be a fascinating hobby, but it's also quite scary because we all know they keep the big bomb in their backstage closet. And we never know when they might open the door and use it.

WHO'S AHEAD?

To win a race you have to stay ahead, and this race is no exception in the minds of most folks. The Soviets are sure the U.S. is ahead. Americans are afraid the Soviets are ahead. Are the Russians catching up? Are we still ahead? Are we falling behind? These simple questions, so important in a foot race, also shape our thinking on this complicated arms race. Several basic issues determine who's ahead in the nuclear arms race. What percent of your forces are ready at any moment? How many bombs do you have? How do you get them to your targets? Will they hit the targets?

The U.S. and the USSR each have three different vehicles to "deliver" bombs to their targets: missiles, submarines, and bombers. Missiles, sitting in underground silos, can carry their loads of bombs some 6,000 miles. A special re-entry system guides the bomb down to the target. Submarines each carry 16 to 24 missiles which shoot up out of the water and deliver their bombs. The third type of delivery vehicle, bomber airplanes, can fly over their targets and drop bombs by gravity. Cruise missiles, presently being installed on American B-52 bombers, can be launched several hundred miles away from their targets. This way the bombers don't have to fly over enemy territory or worry about enemy radar or antiaircraft fire. These three delivery systems are often called the "triad" since they form a kind of three-pronged nuclear fork.

THE THREE PRONGED FORK
Missiles
Each delivery system has its good and bad points. Land-based missiles are the most accurate and easiest to control because of their excellent communication and guidance systems. Land-based missiles, however, make very inviting targets. Enemy satellites can detect them, and they're sitting ducks for accurate enemy missiles. The U.S. worry about a "window of vulnerability" comes from fear that Soviet missiles might hit U.S. missiles in their silos. A missile is also hard to call home after it's been fired!

Subs
Submarines are on the move and hard to detect. They can jam each other's communications, making it hard to track and destroy them. If an enemy knocked out U.S. land-based missiles, American submarines could fire their missiles in retaliation. Submarine missiles in the past have not been as accurate as those sitting in silos. The submarines also have difficulty communicating with the outside when they're in deep water. This might create serious problems if an enemy strike crippled communications. What would a submarine commander do if he knew a war was in progress and his outside communications were cut off? Would he fire his missiles?

Bombers
The bombers can get up in the air fairly fast. During a time of crisis many bombers would be in the air continuously. If satellites give 20 to 30 minutes of warning time, other bombers could be off the ground and safe from an enemy attack aimed at their base. Unlike missiles, bombers can be called back before dropping their bombs if the war changes or the enemy surrenders. On the other hand, bombers are slow. In the past, pilots worried about enemy radar and fighter jets, but these are less troublesome since

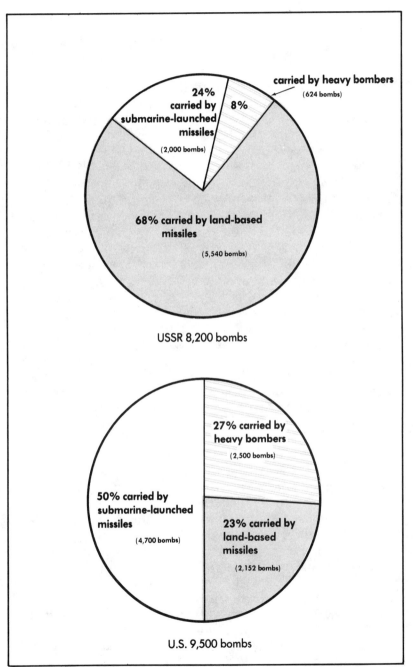

Figure 4.1. Distribution of U.S. and USSR Strategic Long-Distance Nuclear Bombs.   115

the new cruise missiles can be launched by bombers from outside enemy territory.

Three Baskets

The U.S. keeps its nuclear eggs in these three baskets— land-based missiles (ICBMs), submarine launched missiles (SLBMs), and long-distance bombers (B-52s). If an enemy wiped out one of the three baskets, the other two could still retaliate.

Both of the giants carry their bombs in these three baskets, but the number in each basket is quite different. About half of the U.S. bombs are on submarines, while about one fourth are on land-based missiles and one fourth are on bombers. The Soviets have almost 70 percent of their bombs on land-based missiles, about 24 percent on submarines, and less than 10 percent on long-range bombers. Figure 4.1 illustrates the differences.

ADDING IT ALL UP

So who's ahead? That depends on what you look at and whom you ask. It's clear that the U.S. has led the arms race historically. With one or two exceptions, the U.S. has always been several years ahead of the Soviets. But the Soviets have doggedly hung on. In fact, in recent years they have really closed the gap. An estimate of the present balance appears in Figure 4.2.[2]

Figure 4.2 includes *only* long-distance nuclear weapons designed to travel between continents. The numbers are rough approximations for several reasons. First, since new bombs are made by both sides each day, the actual number of bombs is hard to pinpoint. Second, different "watchdog" organizations give slightly different estimates. Third, the public never knows exactly how many bombs are around since some information is held secret by both sides. Some experts estimate that the number of bombs is probably higher than the estimates in Figure 4.2, but who knows? Fourth, exact numbers aren't terribly critical because there are plenty of bombs to go around.

So who's ahead? It all depends. If you look at the

	U.S.	USSR
LAND MISSILES	1,052	1,398
Bombs on Land Missiles	2,152	5,540
BOMBERS[1]	376	156
Bombs Carried by Bombers	2,500	624
SUBMARINES[2]	32	62
Bombs Carried by Submarines	4,700	2,000
Missiles Carried by Submarines	520	950
Total Delivery Vehicles[3]	1,460	1,616
Total Bombs[4]	9,500	8,200
Total Megatons[4]	4,500	7,500

1. U.S. bombers include 316 B-52 and 60 FB-111; USSR figures include Bears and Bisons.
2. Includes 1 Trident and 31 Poseidon submarines and only modern USSR subs.
3. Includes missiles carried by subs, rather than subs themselves.
4. These estimates may vary plus or minus 500 depending on the source.

* Includes only long-distance (strategic nuclear) weapons.

SOURCE: Center for Defense Information, Washington, D.C. (1982).

Figure 4.2. Estimates of U.S. and USSR Strategic* Nuclear Forces

number of land-based missiles, the Soviets are ahead. If you look at the accuracy of those same missiles, the U.S. leads. The Soviets have bigger bombs to compensate for their poorer accuracy. So if you count total firepower or megatons, the Soviets win. If you count the total number of bombs, the U.S. is ahead. Count submarines, and the USSR is ahead. Count bombs on submarines, and the U.S. moves ahead. If you look at the "readiness" of the submarines, it's the U.S. again. For example, it's usually estimated that only 15 to 20 percent of the Soviet submarines are on patrol at any moment, compared to 60 or 70 percent readiness of U.S. submarines. Consider the ability of submarines to hide undetected, and the U.S. has the edge. The Soviets have more nuclear missiles aimed at European targets. Soviet civil defense is better, but it's doubtful if that means much.

If you count the number of bombers, the U.S. is ahead. Many of the Soviet bombers are old propeller types, so they lose on that one. Count tanks in Europe, and the Soviets are ahead. Count land-based missiles in Europe, and the Soviets are far ahead. Count *all* types of nuclear bombs on submarines, bombers, and missiles in Europe, and they are approximately equally divided between Soviet and anti-Soviet forces.

Consider how evenly the bombs are divided among the three delivery systems, and the U.S. is ahead. In weapon quality, reliability, and accuracy, the U.S. is ahead. In fact, many experts feel that the U.S. is ahead in the most critical areas of comparison. And so it goes. Most independent experts agree that a rough balance exists between the two sides in the early 1980s. The 1982 report of U.S. Secretary of Defense Weinberger contends that at present there is parity, or equivalence, between the nuclear forces of the U.S. and the USSR. That simply means that when you take *everything* into account, both sides are about equal. This is one reason a nuclear freeze is so attractive.

When President Reagan said in a 1982 news conference that the Soviets "have definite nuclear superiority," numerous military experts, both inside and outside his administration, quickly rejected his contention.[3] He may have been refering only to land-based missiles in Europe; and if that's the case he was correct. Or he may have been trying to prod us into supporting his defense buildup. Perhaps he feared eroding American support for his massive military buildup more than he feared the Soviets! Even Americans who talk of Soviet superiority wouldn't think for one minute of trading in the U.S. arsenal for the Soviet arsenal!

Regardless of how you count and which weapons you look at, one simple fact is clear. Both sides have more than enough to blow each other up many times! The strategic (long-distance) bombs *alone* add up to nearly 12,000 megatons, which amount to some 840,000 Hiroshimas. And remember, these numbers *don't* include short-range (tactical) nuclear weapons, the smallest of which are twice the size of the Hiroshima bomb.

The total number of *both* strategic and nuclear bombs is shown in Figure 4.3. These are conservative figures because many experts estimate the total at 50,000 or more.

	U.S.	USSR
Strategic*	9,500	8,200
Tactical	16,000	8,000
Total (Approx.)	26,000	17,000

Grand Total 42,000

*These estimates may vary by plus or minus 500.

SOURCE: Center for Defense Information, Washington, D.C. (1982).

Figure 4.3. Estimated Number of All Nuclear Bombs

I've tried to show three things in all of this:

1. "Who's ahead?" is a complicated question, and the answer depends on which weapons and which characteristics you consider.

2. Both sides have more than enough firepower to blow each other up many times. When everything is considered, the giants are about equal.

3. "Who's ahead?" is the wrong question. We really should be asking, "How much is enough?"

In his remarks to the U.S. Senate in 1982, retiring Admiral Rickover, father of the U.S. nuclear navy, pointed out the foolishness of the "who's ahead?" question:[4]

I see no reason why we have to have just as many [subs] as the Russians do.... What's the difference whether we have 100 submarines or 200? I don't see what difference it makes. You can sink everything on the oceans several times over with the number we have and so can they. That's the point I'm making.

HOW MUCH IS ENOUGH?
Looking Tough

Cars and many other consumer products have a *use* value and a *prestige* value. A car provides us with transportation, but it's also a symbol of our social status. Both Cadillacs and Chevettes transport us, but they say quite different things about our social status. Things are much the same with bombs. They can be used both to destroy and to impress others. In fact, many military analysts think the most important reason for having bombs is not to explode them, but to cultivate an image of power. Nuclear nations assume that their security depends on their ability to project a powerful image based on their numbers of nuclear weapons.

It requires only a small number of bombs to do the actual destruction. But you can *never* have enough when you use them to impress others! Prestige is gained by piling up bombs endlessly. The superpowers want to impress their own people, their enemies, and the world community with their enormous collection of nuclear marbles. And it is quite an impressive collection—frightening at first and then almost funny! The giants want to look "impressive" and "tough." It's what the other countries think of you that counts. In other words, the prestige value of bombs is more important than their actual destructive power. The giants worry that if they don't keep expanding their arsenals they will *appear* weak and lose political leverage on global issues.

Bare Bones

How many nuclear bombs are necessary for a bare-bones, no-frills national defense? That question has often been asked and answered. In the beginning of the Cold War, President Truman was told that 400 atomic bombs would "keep the Soviets in line." In 1958 the National Planning Association concluded that 200 warheads would be enough to devastate a large country. President Kennedy's aides privately argued that 100 missiles carrying one bomb apiece would be enough to stop a Soviet attack. Secretary of Defense MacNamara said that 400 one-megaton bombs could easily destroy 76 percent of the Soviet industrial strength and 74 million of its people.

George Kennan, former ambassador to Moscow, contends that both sides could cut their nuclear arsenals by 50 percent and still have a strong defense. Numerous military analysts have argued that the U.S. could remove all its land-based missiles without weakening its defense. Removing these sitting ducks would also lower the possibility of a Soviet first strike on U.S. soil.[5] Recent secretaries of defense have been quite mum about how many bombs we need, for a good reason—the number we have far outstrips the number we need. Soviet society could be wiped out with just 5 percent, or about 450 megatons, of the U.S. strategic arsenal alone. What do we do with the other 95 percent, or "leftover" bombs? It's a problem of not having enough targets for all the bombs!

Leftover Bombs

Military analysts argue that the extra bombs are needed in case some are destroyed in a first strike, don't work, or miss their targets. And extra bombs are needed to impress and scare our adversaries.

The following numbers profile the prestige value or "overhate" power that's stacked up in our nuclear arsenals. Sometimes called "overkill figures," these rough estimates give us comic pictures of the problem. The numbers are crude, and it's not always clear whether strategic, tactical, and regular bombs are added together or separated. The figures will vary a bit depending on how they are calculated. But regardless of slight variations, the facts are quite plain. Both sides have enormous piles of bombs, far in excess of what is needed to prevent an attack. The numbers show how far we've come in the race, and they demonstrate that the name of the nuclear game is impressing ourselves and others; and in that game we can *never* have enough! I must confess that the figures are quite impressive, or should we say depressive?

Impressive Power

The U.S. has about 4,500 megatons of strategic firepower, far more than the 400 that former Secretary of Defense MacNamara considered adequate.

In 1978 the giants' TNT power in strategic weapons *alone* would have filled a freight train 3.5 million miles long, providing one Hiroshima-sized bomb for every 6,000 people on the planet.

The TNT firepower of 100 MX missiles would fill a freight train 100,000 miles long—long enough to circle the earth four times at the equator.

The U.S. has some 26,000 nuclear bombs, capable of destroying every Soviet city forty times over.

The USSR has about 17,000 nuclear bombs, capable of bouncing the rubble in every major U.S. city 25 times after the first hit.

Each of the 31 U.S. Poseidon submarines carries 160 bombs that can be aimed at 160 different targets. Each bomb is three times the size of Hiroshima's "little boy." One of these subs carries more explosive power than all the munitions used in World War II.

The Soviets' new Typhoon sub carries 168 warheads, each about fourteen times larger than the Hiroshima bomb. In other words, *one* of these Soviet subs packs about 2,350 Hiroshimas.

Each new U.S. Trident sub equipped with the Trident II missile in the mid-1980s can carry 408 bombs able to destroy 408 different cities. Unbelievable! Each bomb, carrying a blast five times greater than Hiroshima's, could easily flatten a city of 100,000 people.

The world nuclear arsenals contain the potential firepower of at least a million Hiroshimas. In dump-truck terms that's 100,000 dump trucks, each carrying ten Hiroshimas. Quite a keg of powder to welcome newborn babies!

The Age of Supervenge

We've come a long way from the days of the "little boy." Are we safer today? Do we feel more secure as overkill grows? We have moved beyond revenge. This is the age of supervenge—far removed from the old days of an eye for an eye and a bomb for a bomb. These are the days of massive revenge with tons of dynamite ready for each person, and hundreds of bombs for each city. In this age of supervenge, the promise of modern governments is that such awful and unbelievable threats will prevent war. More bombs will bring us peace, they tell us. Will they?

MORE ON ORDER

Now on top of all this, both sides have some exciting new weapons on order. It's hard to get accurate information about the USSR's plans. The American public usually has a better idea of what's on tap. We'll look briefly at some of the U.S. plans for new weapons; it's probably safe to assume that the Soviets are up to similar antics. As you read over this shopping list, remember that *these weapons come on top of what we already have.*

The Reagan administration calls a freeze dangerous since it would halt all these new weapons which are considered necessary for U.S. security.

Neutron Bomb

President Reagan announced in 1981 that the United States would build the neutron bomb. This nuclear weapon gives off about a third of its energy as deadly radiation. In contrast, only about 5 percent of a regular nuclear bomb's energy is released as nuclear radiation. Contrary to rumor, the neutron bomb does more than just kill people. Its radiation penetrates walls and steel much better than other nuclear bombs, but it also leaves a lot of fire and blast damage.

MX Missile

The United States plans to build 100 MX missiles in two versions. Each missile will carry 10 bombs, and each bomb in the second version will be about 30 times more destructive than the Hiroshima bomb. Each bomb can be aimed at a different target. The final version of the MX is expected to carry a bomb within 300 feet of its target. In other words, each missile can carry the destructive wallop of 300 Hiroshima bombs, and the 100 MX missiles together pack the power of 30,000 Hiroshimas.

Cruise Missile

The U.S. Pentagon is requesting about 4,000 cruise missiles by the end of the 1980s. In 1981 twelve cruise missiles were installed on each of 168 B-52 bombers. The cruise missiles, only about twenty feet long, can be shot from land, air, or water, giving them great flexibility. They can carry either regular or nuclear bombs. Skimming the earth's surface only 100 to 200 feet above the ground, they can travel 1,500 miles after being fired. This makes them quite nasty since they can sneak in under enemy radar. The small cruise missiles can easily be hidden from satellites in trucks or railroad freight cars. This development injects more fear into the arms race since neither side will know exactly where the cruise missiles are hidden. That kind of fear makes the whole situation shaky. Because they are so small and easily hidden, they will be hard to *ever* control in any arms agreement. The Soviets will likely follow the U.S. lead in making this provocative weapon.

Trident Submarine

In 1981 the first U.S. Trident submarine was commissioned. These boats are about 560 feet long, almost the size of two football fields end to end. At least 15 and perhaps as many as 30 of these subs are planned. The Trident I missile can travel 4,500 miles, giving the new subs about ten times more ocean area in which to hide than the older U.S. subs. Presently the sub carries 24 missiles with 8 bombs per missile, for a total of 192 bombs per sub. The Trident II missiles coming in the mid-1980s can carry 17 bombs, making a total of 408 individually targeted bombs per sub.

Bombers

The U.S. plans to produce 100 B-1 bombers with 14 scheduled to be in the air by 1986. The B-1 can travel 8,000 miles, drop nuclear bombs, or launch cruise missiles from outside the enemy's territory. It carries up to 30 cruise missiles. The U.S. is also developing a stealth bomber designed to avoid detection by enemy radar. These are due off the production line in 1989, only three years after the B-1 starts flying.

THE SOVIET THREAT

Can we trust the Russians? What about the Soviets? Most discussions of the nuclear arms race boil down to these simple questions. The *only* justification for the massive American arms buildup is the Soviet threat. Alan Wolfe has shown that the fear of the Soviet threat rises and falls more with American domestic politics than with objective changes in Soviet behavior.[5] American leaders repeat time and time again that the Soviet Union is a serious threat to American interests and to international security. U.S. Secretary of

State Haig put it this way, "Let us be plain about it; Soviet promotion of violence as the instrument of change constitutes the greatest danger of the world."[6] Again and again arguments about the arms race bog down on how we view the Russians.

Talk about the Soviet threat usually has several prongs in the minds of most Americans:[7]

Fear that the Soviets will move ahead of the U.S. in the nuclear arms race,

Fear that the Soviets will invade American shores,

Fear that the Soviets will gradually conquer the world through military violence, and

Fear that a Soviet nuclear advantage would impress other countries and give the Soviets more diplomatic clout as well as make it easier for them to use conventional military force.

Can we trust them or can't we? We can ask whether the Soviets have kept international treaties in the past. We can try to understand why they do what they do. And we can ask what the risks are if we trust them or if we don't. We already trust them in the sense that they could shoot missiles at us this very minute and the only thing we could do is retaliate *after* we've been hit.

Guns

There are three parts to the Soviet threat: arms, intervention, and ideas. The Soviets have engaged in a concentrated military buildup over the past ten years.[8] They were far behind the U.S. in the early 1970s, and in many ways now they have caught up. They have the largest conventional army and tank force in the world. They have rapidly expanded the number of nuclear missile launchers (both short and long-distance). Their modernized and enlarged navy includes several new types of nuclear submarines. A large percentage (12-14 percent) of their gross national product is devoted to defense spending. They may be developing a new intercontinental bomber as well as laser weapons for use in space. This is a real and formidable military buildup that can't be brushed aside as a joke. Whether it's a real threat to American security, however, is another question.

Butting In

A second aspect of the Soviet threat is their military intervention in other countries. The Soviets have used military force to regain control in Hungary (1956) and in Czechoslovakia (1968). They invaded Afghanistan in 1979 in order to strengthen their political control. Soviet influence undoubtedly led to the military crackdown in Poland in 1981.

The Soviets have also actively aided rebel movements and set up military bases in other countries around the globe. Their public policy supports wars of "national liberation." Revolutions are often ignited by economic injustice or domestic repression, and then the Soviets start aiding the rebels. Typically, then, the U.S. begins helping the ruling government to prevent a communist takeover.

The irony is that Americans who are proud of their own war of independence from the British often end up supporting dictators who are trying to stamp out freedom and independence movements. And the Soviets, known for their authoritarian government, end up assisting the freedom fighters. El Salvador exemplifies this pattern. The Soviets either directly or through their proxies have been active in countries such as Cuba, Nicaragua, Angola, Libya, Ethiopia, South Yemen, Syria, and Cambodia. The Soviets have supported revolutionary groups such as the Palestine Liberation Organization (PLO). The Soviet intelligence agency (KGB), according to news reports, is active in the U.S. And no doubt the American CIA is alive and well in the Soviet Union.

Squashing Freedom

The third prong of the Soviet threat is fear that they are out to conquer and control the world through military might. Khrushchev's words "We will bury you" suggest to many Americans that the Soviets are out to get us and crush freedom by military force.

Khrushchev's statement, translated properly, really meant that in the world of open competition, Soviet socialism will "leave capitalism in the dust." The Soviets see capitalists as imperialistic aggressors out to control other countries as they gobble up natural resources and protect new markets for their products. Naturally, Soviets think socialism is superior to capitalism, and in the long run they expect capitalism to collapse because of its own internal problems.

The Soviet willingness to suppress free speech, build walls, torture prisoners, and haul dissenters off to Siberia to maintain their system *is* a real threat to freedom and the rights of people. Deep in the American soul is a genuine fear that the long-term Soviet goal is to stamp out freedom in the world and put everyone behind bars and walls. Whether or not this is true, the Soviets do want to protect and expand their interests throughout the world, as do many other countries. The Soviets will use any opportunity to demonstrate the superiority of socialism, and they'll use violence when necessary. The Soviet threat of arms and ideas isn't a paper tiger—it's a real force in our world.

There are understandable reasons for some of the Soviet activity which make it appear more than just violence for the sake of meanness:

1. The Russian people historically have been plundered many times by foriegn invaders. In this century alone their borders have been invaded three times.

2. In World War II they lost 20 million people on their own soil and some 73,000 villages and cities.

3. They feel threatened by adversaries along all their borders—China to the east and NATO to the west.

4. They want to erase the international image that they are a second-rate, backward nation.

5. They see U.S. military influence around the world since World War II as a serious threat to their existence.

6. They want international recognition that they are a first-rate giant, in both ideas and arms.

You Must Remember

These factors don't excuse Soviet aggression, but they do help us understand why the Soviets flex their muscles. These psychological scars and factors have also been used by Soviet leaders to justify to their own people their enormous arms buildup.

A Soviet arms-control specialist, in a seminar I recently attended, said with deep feeling:

> You must remember that our country was invaded many, many times and we have determined that *it will never happen again.*

> You must remember that we have hostile enemies sitting on thousands of miles of our border and *we will not be invaded again.*

> You must remember that your country [U.S.] embarrassed us in front of the world in the Cuban missile crisis of 1962 and we have determined *it will never happen again.*[9]

The persistence and size of the Soviet threat reminds us of two things that are hard for Americans to accept:

> The USSR *is* an international giant and, like the U.S., it doesn't enjoy being a "number two" giant.

> The U.S. will not be able to race ahead in military might. The Soviets can and will catch up, as they have demonstrated in the past ten years.

So is the Soviet threat real? Yes and no. They are a real military force on par with the U.S., and they are actively peddling their ideas and helping revolutionary groups throughout the world. But the threat of their launching a surprise attack on the U.S. or invading American shores or trying to conquer the whole world by force is often exaggerated by the Pentagon as a scare tactic to get public support for massive military dollars. The Soviets have also had numerous political losses around the world as exemplified by setbacks in Egypt, Sudan, and Somalia.[10]

THE AMERICAN THREAT

Love your enemies. How do Christians follow such a radical command? To love an enemy means that first of all we try to stand in his shoes and see the world through his eyes. We look at things from his point of view and try to imagine how we'd feel if we were on his side of the fence. It's very important for Americans and especially for Christians to stand in Soviet shoes because things do look a lot different from their side of the fence. If Americans were Soviets, we'd probably act much the way they do.

In Soviet Shoes

The Soviets see imperialist aggression by capitalist countries as a *real* threat to world stability. They are frightened by American military power. The Soviets worry about the American threat. Through their eyes Americans have intervened time and time again in the affairs of other nations. When the Soviets look around the world, they remember and see many evidences of the American threat:[11]

1. They remember that the U.S. along with other Western nations invaded the USSR in 1920 in a futile attempt to crush their new revolution.

2. They know the U.S. is the only nation with hundreds of thousands (540,000) of troops stationed in over 200 military bases around the world. The U.S. supplies military aid, training, and advisors to at least 61 countries. For example, in 1982 one out of ten El Salvadoran troops was trained *in* the U.S.

3. The Russians are aware that between 1948 and 1980 the U.S. intervened by sending military troops or advisors on the average of once every eighteen months to countries such as Iran (1953), Guatemala (1954), Lebanon (1956), the Congo (1960), Vietnam (1960), Laos (1960), the Dominican Republic (1965), Cambodia (1970), and El Salvador (1982). All of these military interventions were "justified" to stop communism.

4. The Soviets see 350,000 American troops stationed just across their border in Europe. How would Americans feel if the Soviets had 350,000 troops across their border in Canada?

5. The Soviets know U.S. "electronic listening" posts sit near their borders in China and Turkey and formerly sat in

Iran. How would Americans feel if the Soviets had "listening posts" across their borders in Mexico and Canada in addition to what is probably already in Cuba?

6. When the Soviets look across their borders, they count *all* the anti-Soviet tanks and nuclear missiles. This includes NATO, French, and Chinese, as well as American, equipment. The total number of *anti-*Soviet weapons is always higher than their own.

7. When the Soviets look around the world, they see 168 billion dollars in U.S. foreign investments, and they know that American military power is primarily designed to protect U.S. economic interests overseas rather than to defend American shores.[12] The bulk of the U.S. military budget, about 80 percent, is used to "project power" in distant places to impress American friends and enemies. Only about 20 percent goes for the actual defense of the U.S. mainland.

8. The Soviets watched President Reagan create a Rapid Deployment Force in 1981. In three to five years it will be able to move 200,000 American troops and equipment anywhere in the world on 48-hour notice! In 1981, 6,000 American troops "played" war games in the Middle East for four weeks at a cost of 69 million dollars. In this "Bright Star" practice by the Rapid Deployment Force, B-52 bombers flying directly from the U.S. dropped live bombs on the Egyptian deserts. How would Americans feel if the Soviets were preparing a 200,000-troop Rapid Deployment Force designed for quick intervention anywhere in the world on 24-hour notice and they began "practicing" by dropping live bombs in Cuban hills? Is it any wonder that the Soviets might think the Americans are out to control the world?

9. The Soviets have also witnessed the U.S. using the threat of military force 215 times to gain political or economic ends, according to a Brookings Institute study. This included U.S. threats to use nuclear weapons.[13]

10. The Soviet Union saw the U.S. establishing *new* toeholds, or military bases, in 1981 and 1982 in Somalia, Kenya, Egypt, Oman, Honduras, and Colombia. The 1983 U.S. defense budget request includes 21 million dollars to construct

new U.S. airfields in the western Caribbean area.

11. The Soviet Union knows the U.S. was the largest arms merchant to the world community until 1981 when the Soviets themselves pulled slightly ahead. They saw U.S. arms sales jump from 1.8 billion dollars in 1970 to 17 billion dollars in 1980. They saw President Reagan offer 15 billion dollars in military sales to other countries in the first three months he was in office. They have seen the U.S. twisting the arms of its European allies and Japan to increase their military budgets. They know that the U.S. supplied over 45 percent of all the major weapons sold to the Third World in the past decade.[14]

12. The Soviets know that the U.S. provided over 70 percent of the ground, sea, and air forces in the Pacific and Indian Ocean regions at a cost of over 2 billion dollars in 1982.[15]

Two Naughty Giants

We must understand that when you look at the world through Soviet eyes it looks very different than when you look at it through American eyes. I'm *not* suggesting that the Soviets are the good guys and the Americans are the bad guys. *Both* of them want to flex their muscles and control international events. Americans must understand, however, that U.S. military arms stretching around the globe and our tough talk are two of the many reasons for the recent Soviet military buildup.

How would Americans feel if we switched historical roles with the Soviets? If the Soviets had been far ahead of the U.S. for the past thirty years in the nuclear arms race and if the Soviet Union had 540,000 troops stationed around the world, many not far from our border, I'm sure most Americans would be crying for an enormous military buildup. Can we understand how American military power truly scares the Soviets and only pushes them to build up their forces even more? Can we understand that the Soviet buildup seems like good common sense from their standpoint rather than an attempt to conquer the world? Can we understand why the Soviets might think it's actually the U.S. that's trying to conquer the world? If as Christians we want to take the first small step in loving our enemies, we must try to see how this thing looks from the other side.

The words of the Soviet arms-control specialist help us stand in their shoes once again. "You must remember," he said, "that from *our* perspective

your country first built the bomb,

your country first used the bomb,

your country refused to negotiate when you were far ahead in the nuclear arms race, and

your country refuses to declare that it will not use nuclear weapons first."

It's hard to take off our American glasses and see this deadly race from the Soviet point of view. But we must try hard to imagine what it looks like from their side. After we've looked at both sides, perhaps we'll be able to understand how the race looks from God's seat. So when Americans ask, "What about the Russians?" perhaps we should ask, "What about the Americans?" Can we trust the Americans? Can we trust either of the giants? Perhaps we can trust the Soviets about as much as we can trust the Americans. Each giant wants us to believe that he's the good guy and the other giant is the bad guy. So we probably need to be careful about both of them—because both are somewhat tricky.

THE CHRISTIAN THREAT

The real question that Christians should be asking isn't "Can we trust the Russians?" or "Can we trust the Americans?" but "Can we trust the Christians?" Can we trust the Christians to be faithful to the gospel of peace in times like these? Can we trust the Christian churh to be a good steward of the gospel of peace in an age of nuclear war?

Can We Trust the Christians?

This is a harder question because it's one that we *can* answer and it might require an unpopular witness. It's easier and safer to sit in our armchairs and speculate about whether or not we can trust the Russians because in the final analysis no one knows anyway. It's easier to debate that unanswerable question than to deal with the important question, "Can God's children be trusted with the gospel of peace?" Can I be trusted to be a faithful witness to the non-violent way of Jesus Christ today in the midst of these mountains of nuclear weapons?

The real question for God's people is, "What about us?" What has happened to us when the disciples of love quietly support the use of nuclear weapons designed to kill millions and fracture mother nature herself? What about us when the children of God even use Bible verses and Christian slogans to justify the making and use of nuclear weapons in American foreign policy? What has happened to us when even in a democracy we don't speak out about such murderous intent? That is the real question, and it's one we can answer if we're willing to face up to it.[16]

If Christians begin witnessing to the peaceable way of Jesus Christ, they will become a threat—a real political threat. Even in a democracy, Christians who stand up and testify that they are willing to live without nuclear weapons will be seen as political traitors. Christians who declare publicly that on the basis of their faith in Jesus Christ they do not support the production, holding, or use of nuclear weapons will be seen as political subversives even in "Christian America." But if millions of Christians throughout North America stood up and said "no" to nuclear weapons, public opinion propping up the arms buildup would crumble. The eyes of Christians throughout the world are watching the North American Christians to see whether or not they can be trusted to use their freedom of speech to speak a word of peace for humankind.

The Threat of Jesus

The Christian community will be a threat when it witnesses to the power of God. A witness to the love of God undercuts the authority of the state to demand ultimate allegiance, and strikes at the root of the state's power. Jesus' life and ministry was a threat to the political power of both the

Jewish leaders and the Romans.[17] His words of love, his acts of judgment, his caring deeds on the Sabbath, and his stinging parables shook the foundations of the Jewish and Roman power structures. He was a greater threat than Barabbas, who led a political revolt. Jesus was crucified as "King of the Jews." His loving ministry of the towel and the basin looked like a political threat even though he had no political ambitions. He didn't stop witnessing to the truth just because he was seen as a threat. He didn't take the advice of friendly Pharisees and run back to Galilee to hide. He quietly and persistently told the truth in the middle of Jerusalem's political stage, knowing full well that it would cost him his life. And it did.

The Threat of Standing Up

An old-time Bible story whose radical message is dulled by its familiarity also fits here. Remember Shadrach, Meshach, and Abednego? The Babylonian king set up an idol and told everyone to bow down and worship it. But the three Hebrew boys knew that they couldn't worship God and the king's idol at the same time. They knew where to draw the line. They knew some things were not Caesar's. They knew that when they were caught in a jam between allegiance to God and to Caesar, they had to obey God. They told the king they wouldn't kneel at his idol, even if their God didn't miraculously deliver them from the fiery furnace. And so while thousands of people kneeled down, they boldly stood up and told the king publicly,

> Be it known to you, O king, that we will not serve your gods or worship the golden image which you have set up.
> *Daniel 3:18.*

The kings once again are calling us to worship their golden nuclear idols. And those who don't fall down and worship will be a threat. They will be ridiculed. They will be unpopular. They will be called all sorts of names. If the Christians don't stand up today, millions may be tossed into a fiery nuclear furnace, and this time there may be no miraculous deliverance. We desperately need some Shadrachs, Meshachs, and Abednegos today. If millions of them stood up and refused to worship the nuclear idol, they would give a mighty witness to the gospel of Jesus Christ, and they might help to cool off the nuclear furnace that the kings of the earth have fired up. But in that witness they will be a threat.

GOD'S SIDE

The giants want us to take sides. They want God to take sides. The lesson of history is that both sides say God is on their side as they rush into war. No one enjoys fighting a war. It's a bloody mess. That's why God's name, his blessing, Bible verses, chaplains—the whole works—are used to justify fighting. Sprinkling religious words over a dirty task turns it into a cause and makes it worth dying for and easier to do.

This puts the Soviets at a disadvantage because as avowed atheists they can't cover their activities with God's blessing. And that fuels the American impulse to spread the icing of "God's blessing" thick on the American military cake—even on nuclear weapons. The fact that Soviets do not permit religious freedom turns the arms race into a religious crusade, convincing many American Christians that God's smile of approval shines on U.S. military efforts. God does smile when governments allow democratic processes, freedom of speech, and freedom of religion, because in those conditions his church is free to be the church. But to believe that he smiles when brutal military force is used to "protect" such freedoms is quite another matter. To think that he smiles when a so-called Christian nation uses nuclear weapons to "project power" around the world is far from the truth. To say that God blesses the threat to annihilate millions of people in the name of maintaining peace is profanity of the highest order. In the cross, God demonstrated how he deals with evil. He doesn't fight it with force. He fights evil with love—even if it means dying.

God doesn't take sides. He calls his followers to a third way that winds through the valley of the shadow of death. The superpowers face each other with their nuclear bombs piled high on their political mountains. The shadow of death hangs heavy over the valley between them. But God walks in the valley as it winds its way between the mountains of nuclear bombs. He calls us to walk with him in the valley between the two sides:

> Even though I walk through the valley of the shadow of death, I fear no evil; for thou art with me; thy rod and thy staff, they comfort me.
>
> *Psalm 23:4.*

Many Christians are climbing up the American mountain. They imagine God smiling over their shoulders. They have forgotten that God walks in the valley. And as in the story of Shadrach, Meshach, and Abednego, he calls them off the mountain and invites them to walk with him down in the valley—even the valley of the shadow of death. And so the question is not, "Is God on our side?" but "Are we on God's side?"

GAMBLING ON GOODWILL

Can we trust the giants? Can we trust the Christians? Hardly anyone or any nation is completely trustworthy. We live in a risky world. The arms race is a risky business. The stakes are very high. Arms control is risky. A nuclear arms freeze is risky. The Russians or the Americans might cheat. The process of disarmament is risky. If one giant weakens too quickly, the other might take advantage of it and move in for a killing.

Either way we turn, there are many risks. We can't avoid them. We simply will need to decide which risks we are most willing to live with. Do we want to accept the dangers of a nuclear arms race and take a 50-50 chance that a major nuclear war might break out in the next ten years? Or do we want to live with the risks that go along with a nuclear freeze and a gradual disarmament process?

We have gambled on threat for the past thirty years. Isn't it about time that we start gambling on goodwill? Now I'm not a gambler, but the Scripture suggests to me that if God gambled, he'd gamble on goodwill instead of threat. Isn't that what he did at the cross when he gave his son for undeserving sinners? Doesn't the Scripture call us to gamble on goodwill—to heap coals of love on our enemies? Shouldn't Christians plead with their governments to gamble on goodwill? As for me, I'd rather live in a world filled with the risks that come with a slow disarmament process than in one filled with the risks of a maddening arms race.

Goodwill has worked in the past! The U.S. and the Soviets have made 14 constructive and lasting agreements over the past 21 years that the Soviets haven't violated. The U.S. Department of Defense and the joint chiefs of staff reported in 1980 that Soviet "compliance performance under 14 arms control agreements has been good."[18] Maybe we can trust the giants after all? When the risks are so high—when the future of mother nature is at stake—gambling on goodwill makes a lot more sense than gambling on threat.

In 1982, Soviet President Brezhnev in a public letter to an Australian disarmament organization *repeated* his offer to halt the production and stockpiling of nuclear weapons:

> The Soviet Union is ready to reach agreement not only on the complete termination of all nuclear weapons tests, but also on ending their further production, and on the reduction and subsequent *complete* [italics mine] elimination of their stockpiles.[19]

Is he serious? Does he have a trick up his sleeve? We don't know. The Soviets have proposed a nuclear freeze several times before. As START talks were beginning, President Brezhnev again called for an immediate freeze. Why not gamble on goodwill and take the Soviets at their word? And why hasn't the president of "Christian America" made a freeze offer? President Reagan and Secretary Haig have repeatedly rejected the American grass roots freeze proposal as "too dangerous." Can we trust the Christians?

The issue will not be solved by simply trusting the Russians. There may be some good reasons not to trust them. But if Americans want the arms race to slow down, we will need to work with them and make some goodwill initiatives. We may need to cooperate with the Soviets even if we can't completely trust them. Any serious reductions of nuclear arms will need to involve *mutual* steps by both countries. We must understand that what is good for the Russians is also good for the Americans. It is in the best interests of *both* countries to slow down this deadly race. Who has the responsibility to take the first step?

LAUGHING WITH GOD

What shall we make of all this clamoring to be ahead? What shall we do with this huge pile of superhate? At first glance it terrorizes us. It's very scary, so scary that it's almost funny. The line between sanity and insanity is thin. The difference between terror and humor is fuzzy. The nuclear arms buildup is a serious issue—the ultimate threat, the final epidemic. What could be worse? Yet at the same time, when you step back and look at it from a distance, the foolishness of it all turns into humor.

Now I don't mean to be irreverent and I'm not trying to be cute. I simply think that from God's viewpoint this whole thing must look silly at times. As serious and as tough as the superpowers try to be, they must look like fools from God's seat. And believe it or not, there's even a Bible verse describing God's laughter. The psalmist must have seen this thing coming. More likely, modern nations act as foolishly as old-fashioned ones. Recall the supervenge figures as you read the words of the psalmist:

> Why are the nations in turmoil?
> Why do the peoples hatch their futile plots?
> The kings of the earth stand ready,
> and the rulers conspire together
> against the Lord and his annointed king.
> 'Let us break their fetters,' they cry,
> 'let us throw off their chains!'
> The Lord who sits enthroned in heaven *laughs them to scorn*
> [italics mine].
>
> > *Psalm 2:1-4 (NEB).*

Things haven't changed much! God's laughter echoes down through the valleys of time. Holy "ho, ho, ho's" reverberate through history as he sees the nations plot to do each other in. To suggest that this is a laughing matter for God doesn't mean he takes it lightly. His heart is heavy as he sees the weapons of violence piling up. He agonizes over the terror that already stalks the land. He suffers already for the terrible anguish and pain that could come. He despises the callous hearts and the open rebellion to his ways even among the churches.

So why does he laugh? Doesn't he have compassion? Doesn't he care? He laughs because the nations get caught in their own traps. They trip over the wires they set for each other. They blindly go on refusing to learn from history. The giants refuse his advice and foolishly stumble and fall into their own plots. Again, the psalmist describes our times:

> The nations have plunged into a pit of their own making;
> their own feet are entangled in the net which they hid.
> Now the Lord makes himself known.
> Justice is done:
> the wicked man is trapped in his own devices.
> *Psalm 9:15-16 (NEB).*

In the apostle Paul's words,

> God has made the wisdom of this world look foolish.
> *1 Corinthians 1:21 (NEB).*

The giants are foolishly caught in their own traps. Their computers design bigger and better weapons, and they hope military superiority is just around the corner. They think brutal military power will guarantee security. From God's seat this is utter nonsense, pure foolishness that's only worth a chuckle.

We must learn to laugh with God. In fact, if we can't laugh with God, it means that we are also caught in the trap. The giants want us to believe that they can make us secure. They want us to believe that more military might will do the trick. They want us to take them very seriously, to accept their assumptions, to support their policies, and often we do. And that's why we need to laugh with God.

Laughing at something helps us realize its futility. Poking fun reminds us that things aren't all that they're cracked up to be. Giggling teaches us not to take ourselves too seriously. Chuckling with God reminds us that all this talk of getting ahead is really silly. It really doesn't matter. It won't save us. It won't give us more security. Laughing with God is a way of pulling the mask off the giants. It's another way of undressing our idols. It helps us see the wisdom of God's ways.

We do need to laugh about this matter because many Christians, of all people, get caught in the snares of the superpowers. They begin to believe what the giants say. They begin to trust in the giants, and when that happens, God laughs at us as well. We must learn to laugh with God because in that chuckle we see the foolishness of our ways and begin to see things the way he sees them. But how long will he laugh? When will his laughter turn to holy rage at our foolish disobedience?

The more you think about it, the more hilarious the arms race must seem from God's vantage point.

The citizens of the most "secure" nations are most gripped by fear.

The nations with huge military budgets are threatened by economic competition from low military spenders.

The "one nation under God" leads the world in destructive power.

The toughest military nations are decaying spiritually and economically.

The giants risk destroying themselves in order to save themselves.

The most modern nations threaten the most primitive type of war.

The race for security brings insecurity.

With each new threat, the giants scare each other into new rounds of threats, and on and on it goes.

And so we must join in God's laughter. But how long will he laugh?

QUESTIONS

1. Can we trust the giants? Can we really gamble on goodwill in a violent world?
2. How might U.S. threats provoke Soviet military buildup? Is our security increased as we threaten our enemies?
3. How do things look different when we look at the world through "Soviet glasses"?
4. How important is it to you that the U.S. stays "ahead" in the nuclear arms race?
5. Are there signs that we can trust the Christians?
6. In what ways might a Christian peace witness be a political threat in a democracy?
7. Would you rather live with the risks associated with a nuclear arms race or with the risks involved in disarmament?
8. Is this really a laughing matter? How does laughing help us think about the giants?
9. How long will God laugh about all of this?

5
WHY THE ARMS RACE DOESN'T STOP

REACHING FOR THE BOTTLE

If the bombs are so ugly, the risks so high, the consequences so terrible, why don't we stop this race? We can call the bomb an idol, condemn the superhate, and laugh with God, but that doesn't stop the race. Why in the world does the race keep merrily rolling along? Elected officials, scientists, and generals in the Kremlin and Pentagon are hardly vicious folks out to blow up the world. They have homes and families too, and they want to preserve them as much as we do. Why can't we stop? We are like alcoholics who can't put down the bottle. We are like overweights reaching for more potato chips. George Kennan, a former U.S. ambassador to Moscow, recently described our foolish race;

> We have gone on piling weapon upon weapon, missile upon missile, new levels of destructiveness upon old ones. We have done this helplessly, almost involuntarily: like the victims of some sort of hypnotism, like men in a dream, like lemmings heading for the sea.[1]

Underwater Currents

What are the forces that push this race forward? What are the winds that blow us along? What are the hidden currents that nudge us ever closer to the brink of nuclear disaster? Many forces join together, forming a mighty ocean wave that sweeps us forward. Some of these currents are not easy to detect because they are hidden beneath the surface. A kind of social radiation, they are powerful but not visible.

These forces are what the Scripture calls the "principalities and powers." Paul mentions them several times in his letters (Colossians 1:16, Ephesians 1:20-21 and 6:11-12). He makes several points about them. They are visible and invisible. They were created by God. The authority of Jesus is above theirs. Sometimes they are manifest as spiritual forces of wickedness. Paul reminds us to be alert to these forces since they often work against God's wishes.

God created us with a need for order and with the ability to create orderly patterns. We couldn't survive as a loose assortment of individuals. To live and survive we create patterns or ruts of social behaviors, rules, norms, relationships, traditions, transactions, organizations, and established ways of doing things. Social pressures, fads, and winds of public opinion also blow us along. These forces are woven together like a giant social spider web.

Such social and spiritual forces are bigger than any one individual. They emerge over a long period of time as thousands of people interact. And they develop a force, a weight of their own, that propels them forward. They push people. They shape our behavior. They influence our ideas. We want our wardrobes and homes to conform to proper taste. The rate of inflation changes our spending habits. Such forces do shape our lives, in quiet but yet in real ways. This doesn't mean we are robots. We do make decisions, but these social forces funnel our decisions in certain directions. Interest rates, wages, intelligence, and the color of our skin lock us in or fix our place in life to a certain extent. Other "softer" forces like fads and public opinion also whisper in our ears and urge us to come along with them.

The apostle Paul makes it clear that God created us with the need and desire for structures. But he also says that these invisible principalities and powers can work for *or* against God's purposes. They can provide beautiful order and harmony in a family, church, or nation. Or they can bring chaos, fear, confusion, and destruction. Just like the people who nurture them, these forces can serve *or* they can master. They can help *or* they can hinder. They can build *or* they can destroy.

We give direction and shape to these forces. We set them in motion. We fertilize them, but we are also their products. These social waves reflect the spirit of our hearts. But they also shape our ideas and opinions. A strong surge of militaristic feeling in the country influences us. A growing tide of nationalism molds our attitude toward government. Bitter inflation and high interest rates bring out our meanest economic spirit. When these forces are fertilized with seeds of greed, they become vicious and breed more hatred in us. When they reflect sinful hearts, they stir up even more ugliness in others. They push us away from God and foster a false sense of order—an order that works against God's vision of wholeness and peace.

The Game Plays Us

There's a seesaw, back-and-forth rhythm here between these massive social forces and ourselves. On the one hand we create them, and yet they influence us. We control them, and yet they control us. We guide them, and they also guide us. We play the game, but the game also plays us. We run the arms race, and the arms race runs us. We are in charge of this dreadful race, but it also directs us. It's in our hands, and we're in its hands—at its mercy. The arms race is *not* beyond human control; but our perceptions, commitments, and beliefs must change before we will have the courage to stop it.

We must recognize this paradox, this strange situation, because if we don't appreciate the enormous social muscles that propel the arms race and understand how they twist our thinking, we will never break loose from them. It's only when we truly recognize their mighty power to control us that we will have the freedom and courage to break out of their grasp. If we think we're in charge when in fact we aren't, we'll always be the slaves of these social forces. If we let them roll us blindly along, we will never take charge and never escape their captivity. Tricky aspects of these social forces conceal their power:

Their hidden nature tempts us to think they don't exist.

They dupe us into believing we're in charge when in fact they often are.

And finally, when we realize their power they tempt us to believe there's nothing we can do.

There are two funny things about organizations. They quickly grow up and outgrow their clothing. They expand their turf and start doing things they were never set up to do. Second, they take charge of things. They start calling the shots and running the show. They switch to automatic pilot. Instead of serving people, they begin to dominate, to control, and to master people. They develop a life and history of their own that gains force and speed, and you have to be careful not to get in their way. They become self-propelled and it's hard to keep them in check. That's just how social groups and organizations are. Even good ones like churches and schools act that way. They can get out of hand too!

The arms race is no different. Like a huge locomotive that we pushed up the historical hill, it's charging down the other side now on its own steam. We are frantically grabbing the brakes, but they don't seem to work. It's running on its own steam now with a life and thrust of its own which is hard to stall.

The eerie thing about organizations is how they keep themselves in business. When huge military forces and weapons have been built up, we have to invent more and more enemies and dangers to justify their existence. And that's the irony; the very thing—the enemy—that we set out to stop has to be continually reinvented so we can justify our huge military machines.

George Kennan asks what keeps the arms race running if it's not our will and the wickedness of our opponents. He says,

> The answer, I think, is clear. It is primarily the inner momentum, the independent momentum, of the weapons race itself—the compulsions that arise and take charge of great powers when they enter upon a competition with each other in the building up of major armaments of any sort.... I see this

competitive buildup of armaments conceived initially as a
means to an end but soon becoming the end itself. I see it taking possession of men's imagination and behavior, becoming a
force in its own right, detaching itself from the political differences that initially inspired it, and then leading both parties,
invariably and inexorably, to the war they no longer know how
to avoid.[2]

Even powerful presidents seem powerless to pull the
brake. Most U.S. presidents since World War II have called for
the control of nuclear weapons, but they haven't been able to
control them. In his inaugural address President Carter said
one of his goals was to abolish nuclear weapons. And in his
farewell address Carter said again that nuclear disarmament
was one of the three most urgent issues facing the world.
And yet during his administration hundreds of nuclear
bombs were built! The race goes on in spite of what the
presidents say or do. In the last chapter we saw how fear and
genuine security interests were the basic force pushing the
race forward. But there are secondary pressures that also
generate the locomotive's steam. What fuels its fires? What
keeps it going?

NUMBER ONE

When Jesus was tempted on the high mountain, he was
given a chance to be number one. The tempter offered him
control over all the kingdoms of the world that he could see if
he would merely bow down and worship. The temptation to
be the big man on the block gets through to most of us. We'd
all like to be number one. Jesus' disciples also squabbled
over their pecking order. "A dispute also arose among them,
which of them was to be regarded as the greatest" (Luke
22:24). Jesus said this "number one" urge was typical among
the kings of the earth, but was out of place among his
followers.

The "number one" urge drives the arms race. Both of
the giants want to be number one. Each wants to be big man
on the block. Neither wants to play second fiddle. Each side
wants to make sure it has the most and best weapons. Each
is afraid it will slip behind and be dubbed a second-rate

power. It's unthinkable to most Americans that another giant might be our equal. There are many layers to this number one urge. The diplomats and politicians want to project a number one image. The Pentagon bureaucrats and corporate officers want to keep us on top of the global pecking order. And the masses of people, most of us, like the warm, proud, and satisfying feeling that comes from thinking we're number one. The most important question, however, is "Number one in what?" The giants are at the top militarily, but further down on some other ladders.[3]

NUMBER ONE IN WHAT?

	U.S.	USSR
Socioeconomic Standing	7th	23rd
Infant Mortality	15th	39th
Doctor/Patient Ratio	18th	1st
Life Expectancy	9th	35th

Figure 5.1. U.S. and USSR—Relative Ranking Among 141 Nations

YOU CAN DO IT, GIANT!

The builders of the Tower of Babel wanted to "make a name" for themselves. It must have been quite a challenge to build the first and highest tower in the world. We are still building towers today. There's a technological push in the arms race, a kind of engineering challenge that calls us. It's exciting and satisfying to see what fancy war toy we can come up with next. If we keep trying, if we do our best, maybe, just maybe, we'll be able to build the ultimate superweapon— that weapon of all weapons that no one will dare challenge. A killer satellite that could zap the enemy's communications satellites would prevent him from even firing a missile. Or maybe a laser beam could strike missiles or tanks without blowing up the whole environment. It might be just around the corner. We can do it if we try. It would be terribly embarrassing if the Russians built one first. The challenge of such tower building is hard to shake off. New toys are exciting.

This technological challenge captures the spirit of the scientists and engineers, and they work feverishly to build bigger towers. But do we really want to live in a world where killer satellites pollute the evening sky? This technological hope that the superweapon is just around the corner pushes the race ahead. But the belief that technology will save us also carries within it the seeds of our destruction.

TIT FOR TAT

In many ways the arms race is like two children squabbling, tit for tat, back and forth in a never ending action-reaction syndrome. Both sides want a "margin of safety," a polite way of saying that they both want to be ahead. As each side tries to get its "margin of safety," it scares the other side even more. A "margin of safety" looks good to us, but to the Soviets it looks like a threatening advantage for the enemy. And so back and forth it goes. One of the striking lessons of the history of the arms race is simply this: with few exceptions—such as Sputnik—the U.S. has always led in the development of new weapons. And the Soviets have always caught up a few years later. That in a nutshell is the history of the arms race. Appendix 1 shows the history of this titting and tatting.

In 1970 the U.S. developed the MIRVing technique, which places several bombs on each missile. In 1975 the USSR had it too. In 1981, President Reagan announced that the U.S. would start making the neutron bomb, and a few days later President Brezhnev said the USSR would follow with a similar "countermeasure." In early 1982 when President Reagan announced plans for making chemical and biological weapons again, breaking a thirteen-year freeze, he said the reason for doing it was because we *think* the Soviets are doing it. And so it goes, back and forth, tit for tat, each side responding to the moves the other side makes.

Each side tries to think of the worst thing the other side *might* try to do. What's the ugliest weapon they might come up with? What's the sneakiest attack they might try to pull off? Both sides prepare for the worst. Such fear and preparation for the worst pushes both sides further and further into the race.

The tricky thing about all of this is that each new weapon on either side is a new threat which does two things: (1) it turns the older weapons into antiques, and (2) it makes the enemy scamper around for another, similar weapon. So new weapons turn existing ones into old-fashioned junk and force the enemy to come up with another set of new ones. This makes for a great deal of economic waste and increases the threat of nuclear war as each generation of weapons becomes more dangerous. This tit-for-tat motion is not like the action of a mechanical ratchet, nor does it mean that the Soviets simply mimic and imitate American behavior. The history of the arms race however does show a general tit-for-tat motion between the giants, and it reveals that the U.S. does most of the "tatting." This rhythm, this swinging back and forth, pushes the race along.

BIG BUCKS

One of the things that fires the locomotive is money. Very bluntly, *the nuclear arms race pays off.* There's profit in this race for a small group of influential people. There's money to be made, and as we all know that's a hard lure to shuck off even in a business as deadly and as risky as nuclear war. Most military contractors would protest that they aren't after the almighty dollar. They don't sign military contracts just to make some fast and easy bucks. Rather, they say, they are performing a critical national service by contributing to "the nation's preparedness." They are helping to "make the world safe for democracy." They are building a strong national defense. Now that may be partly true, but it's also partly true that these are sweet apple pie and motherhood slogans that smoothly cover up some very fat and profitable weapon contracts.

As the Reagan administration's military buildup surged forward in the early 1980s, the stocks of military contractors led the Wall Street rallies. In a time of recession, when almost everything else was sluggish or dropping, the stocks of military contractors were rising. The financial carrot was very attractive. Many of America's well-known companies are deeply involved in the war business.

Cute slogans advertising products for friendly kitchens are sickening in the light of corporate involvement in the bomb business. General Electric says, "We bring good things to life." Monsanto reminds us, "Without chemicals, life itself would be impossible." Union Carbide, producer of nuclear bombs, advertises, "Today, something we do will touch your life."[4] These and other major corporations demand huge military contracts as their bread and butter. The companies need them to survive. They fight and lobby for them so that their corporate shops won't be shut down. Their corporate lobbyists twist arms and wine and dine both congressmen and Pentagon bureaucrats to get more and more lucrative contracts.

Over 42,000 workers are employed directly in the design and manufacture of nuclear weapons. That is only a small fraction of all military jobs. No one likes to lose his job. Corporations want to make jobs. These powerful incentives keep the arms locomotive rolling along. These huge corporations propose new weapons and accessories. The corporate lobbyists work closely with the air force, the navy, the army, and the U.S. lawmakers on Capitol Hill to aggressively promote and sell their dream weapons. They don't always sell them, but the corporate lobbyists are a powerful force that shoves the arms race forward.

Take Rockwell International for example.[5] The cheers rang out, and the champagne flowed on the day President Reagan announced his new military buildup. There were good reasons for all the noise. About half of Rockwell's revenue comes from government business. They make the new B-1 bomber. Plans call for 100 of these bombers at 400 million dollars each. That will mean at least 10 billion dollars in sales over the next several years, assuming there are no cost overruns or changes in the plane's price. Rockwell is also the largest MX missile contractor. The company will get a big chunk of the 10 billion dollars initially marked for MX production. And Rockwell is a major subcontractor for the Trident submarine now in production. The same company is also the prime contractor for the space shuttle program designed to monitor Soviet military activities in space. In

1982, Rockwell spent a record 400 million dollars to modernize and expand its plants for all this work, and that did not even include new expansion for the B-1 bomber. In 1980 its profits were nearly 280 million, and Rockwell's president Robert Anderson, is confident they'll keep rising.

It's often estimated that about one third of all scientists and engineers in the U.S. are engaged in military-related research. *Chemistry and Engineering News* reports that 25 billion federal dollars were slated for research and development (R & D) in fiscal 1982.[6] About 6.3 billion of that was for nuclear weapons. At least 100 billion dollars in federal R & D funds is projected for military research over the next four years. Think tanks, research groups, consultants, and special laboratories sprout up all over the place when such funds come spilling out. Many of the leading universities such as Massachusetts Institute of Technology, Harvard, and the University of California are hooked into the Pentagon's R & D pipeline. It's a hard habit to kick. The large corporations and the research scientists have an enormous appetite for military contracts. They are full of ideas for new weapons. And that economic appetite is one of the factors pushing this race forward.

Jesus was clear about the seductive power of money. It was the one thing, he said, that could capture the lives of people like a god. His reminder that we can't worship God *and* mammon, says a lot about financial greed. We are tempted to worship profit. We become enslaved to wealth. We bow at its altar and give up our lives, families, and other interests for pure, old-fashioned greed. Now greed has been around for a long time, and it never looked nice. But when the forces of ugly greed team up with the makers of deadly weapons, we really have a mean monster. Together, these forces thrust the locomotive forward. They are hard to stop because they often cover up their greed with sweet phrases, but they are the powers of death greedily at work in our midst.

THE IRON TRIANGLE

The forces propelling the arms race often team up. In a

sense they are different layers of the same system, or we can
think of them as different underwater currents flowing together with a common force. A study entitled *The Iron
Triangle* illustrates how these forces link up with each
other.[7] Gordon Adams studied eight corporations that hold
large military contracts. He shows how the military contractors, the Department of Defense, and the Congress work
hand in hand, as three corners of a triangle. He calls it an
iron triangle because information about its activity is
usually sealed off from the public. The three points of the
triangle work together in several ways:

1. Each of the military contractors keeps an office in Washington to lobby for its interests in Congress and to coordinate
its weapons manufacturing with the Pentagon and Congress.
Rockwell International, the company we looked at before, has
about forty people lobbying for military contracts from its
Washington office. Adams reports that five of the companies he
studied, spent 16.8 million dollars in "government relations
activities" over a two-year period. And 15.8 million of that was
charged off against their military contracts. This means that
taxpayers' money is used to convince congressional leaders to
vote for more money for more weapons, benefitting the companies and of course taking even more taxpayer money.

2. The corporations each have a Political Action Committee
which gives millions of dollars in contributions to the political
campaigns of senators and representatives on the
congressional committees which make decisions about
military spending. Through these Political Action Committees
the corporations also make contributions to the representatives whose local districts will benefit from the military
contracts.

3. A lot of people move back and forth between the points on the
triangle. Retired military officers and Defense Department employees get jobs with the corporations that make the weapons.
The Defense Department hires executives from the corporations. Aides to congressmen get jobs with the companies.
Between 1970 and 1979, 1,942 people moved back and forth
between jobs in different points of the triangle. Secretary of
State Alexander Haig is a good example of this shifting around.
He was the NATO military commander in Europe. Then he
worked in the White House as a chief assistant to President

Nixon. After that he became president of United Technologies, a major military contractor. From there he moved to secretary of state.

4. These close and cozy ties between the three points of the triangle are especially important for Research and Development. The contractors design new weapons and then try to sell them to the Congress and the Pentagon. The process goes smoothly because the corporate executives who previously worked in the Defense Department or in a congressional office have an "inside scoop" as to what will "fly."

Now all of this shouldn't come as a big surprise. It's the typical way people and organizations work together when they have similar interests. Lobbying, buddy systems, buying and paying off people, helping old friends, and working for a competitor—these things are not terribly new. But such cozy cuddling among the members of the triangle generates a lot of steam for the arms race. And it usually happens without public knowledge and may not be in our best interests.

THOSE DIRTY GUYS
The arms race is encouraged when we strip off the enemy's human face. Instead of seeing Russians as persons we think of them as communists. We hang nasty name tags on our opponents—villains, rebels, fascists, enemies, guerillas, aggressors. These labels keep us from seeing our adversaries as persons. Abstract labels make them sound like agents of the devil. They are treacherous and aggressive. You can't trust them. They are crafty and they'll trick you whenever they get a chance. They don't share the joy, compassion, delight, and emotions that other humans feel. They are beastly, not quite human. They torture. They are vicious and they don't respect human rights. They are just plain old "Japs," "gooks," "Commies," "pinkos," or "subversives."

Sticking labels on opponents serves a lot of purposes. Both Americans and Soviets do it. It simplifies life. People and nations are neatly sorted into "friendly" and "enemy" bins. These stereotypes become filters that sort out the news that we hear. We look for bad things that "prove" that the enemy is aggressive, and we tend to focus on things that make our country look good. If we hear something that doesn't fit the label, we toss it aside and doubt whether it comes from a truthful source.

Jerome Frank reports a study of American fifth and sixth graders who studied photos of tree-lined roads.[8] The children were asked why Russians plant trees along their roads, and they responded, "So people won't see what's going on beyond the road" and "To make work for prisoners." But when asked why Americans plant trees along roads the children said, "To keep the dust down" and "For shade."

Labels allow us to have a double standard. We see the same thing but interpret it differently. The communists are barbaric because they use chemical weapons. We manufacture chemical weapons to protect the world for democracy. The *same* thing on the one hand is terrible and cruel, and on the other hand it's an act of kindness and concern. These distorted images prevent us from trusting any sincere peace initiatives the enemy might make.

Dehumanizing the enemy helps us kill without feeling bad. How can kind American fathers who hug their kids, also go to work in the Pentagon each day and play war games designed to kill millions of people? If the enemy is a hated abstraction, we can plan torture without feeling guilty. Abstractions don't cry. Statistics don't bleed. Stereotypes don't feel pain. Emotional labels don't moan.

It sounds terribly cruel and uncivilized to plan the murder of millions of people, and most of us couldn't do it, not even the Pentagon planners. But when we put the labels of "enemy," "aggressor," and "troublemaker" on these people, we can plan to kill them in barbaric ways without feeling guilty because that's what such ugly creatures deserve. Inventing and constructing a terrible enemy also justifies a huge military machine.

Having mean enemies around is very important. It gives us an excuse for having a double standard of interpretaton. It takes the blame of our cruelty off us and puts it onto them since they "deserve it." Ugly labels make it emotionally easier for us to prepare for war, and they're another good excuse for a military buildup. It's always hard to tell which came first, the enemy or the military establishment, because enemies create military buildups and military machines also invent enemies.

Jesus was speaking exactly about this when he talked of "loving our enemies." It's hard to love a statistic. It's hard to love a barbaric aggressor. It's tough to be kind to a trouble-maker. To love our enemies means that we strip off all labels and begin seeing the people as God sees them. Soviet fathers love their children. Soviet grandparents want their children to live in a safe world. Soviet reactions to international events seem reasonable and sensible from their point of view. Loving our enemies cuts through the labels and tags we put on them. When that happens, we discover that some of their behavior makes sense from their side of the fence, and we discover that they are an awfully lot like us—and that makes it hard to kill them. Seeing enemies as people won't make them nice—they'll still do some vicious things—but it might slow down our reactionary impulses and remind us that we are hating and killing people, not animals.

GAPOSIS

"Gaposis" is a form of propaganda. It happens when one of the giants compares itself with just one military characteristic of the other giant and discovers a gap. It's be-hind. Both giants create and use gaps. Tom Wicker calls this disease gaposis.[9] Because public support of military spend-ing is necessary in the United States, gaposis is an especially contagious disease among Americans. One of the quickest ways to get public support for new military spending is to frighten people with a new gap. The ploy goes like this: "We are behind the Soviets in area X. There's a gap and they're moving ahead of us."

Gaposis has been a common disease in our history, and it has hit again. A gap frightens people into approving more military spending. The tragedy is that most of the American gaps have been artificially concocted to scare people. In other words, governments sometimes deliberately construct fear and threat. When President Kennedy took office, he talked about the "missile gap" based on CIA estimates that the Soviets would soon have a missile lead of three to one over the United States. Later we learned that the Soviets only had about 50 missiles instead of the 200 to 1,000 that the "gappers" had estimated.

Several gaps were recently manufactured. The "spending gap" refers to the Soviet Union's increased military spending. It's true that Soviet arms spending is increasing. Some U.S. officials contend there is a gap in military spending since the Soviets spend about 12 to 14 percent of their gross national product (GNP) on their military, while the U.S. spends only about 5 to 6 percent of its GNP on guns. So according to the gappers the USSR spends twice as much as the U.S.   False. This simply is not true because the U.S. GNP is about twice as large as the Soviet GNP. While the percentages make it look as though a gap exists, the actual dollar amount is nearly the same. In addition, the U.S. analysts calculated Soviet army pay by estimating what it would cost the U.S. to maintain an army as big as the Soviets' at U.S. wages and benefits. This makes Soviet military spending appear much higher than it really is.

In a recent article on the imaginary defense gap, Richard Stubbing says,

> Recognizing the impact of NATO, Warsaw Pact, Asian Allies and Soviet spending directed toward China and other factors, transforms an alleged 50 percent Soviet spending advantage into a 15 to 37 percent advantage for the United States. No cause for fright there.[10]

Beyond this, U.S. estimates often don't take into account the efficiency of Soviet factories. Many observers think Soviet military research and production is not nearly as efficient as in the United States. So the Soviets may be getting much less for their money than the Americans.

The "window of vulnerability" is a fancy slogan for another gap. Since the Soviets have more land-based missiles than the U.S. and since theirs are becoming more accurate, the gappers say the Soviets might be able to sneak through the U.S. "window" and blow up our missiles in a first-strike attack. This is a new version of the "missile gap."

It's true that in the future with accurate missiles the Soviets might be able to blow up many of the U.S. missiles in their silos. However, only 25 percent of the U.S. bombs sit on land-based missiles. About 75 percent are safe on bombers and submarines. The Soviets are the ones who *really* have the gap or window of vulnerability because 70 percent of their bombs are on land-based missiles and U.S. bombs are *already* accurate enough to strike Soviet missile silos. If the U.S. has a window of vulnerability, then three sides of the Soviet house are wide open! The Soviets really have something to be jumpy about. The American government fabricated the gap to help justify the new MX missile. Scaring the American people with a new gap is the easiest way to get public support for a new weapon like the MX missile.

The Pentagon recently printed a booklet, *Soviet Military Power*, which says the Soviets have over twice as many troops as the United States.[11] According to the Pentagon the Soviets have 4.8 million troops, and the U.S. has only about 2 million, so we have a real gap here. Or do we? It's not quite that simple. To get the high figure of 4.8 million the Pentagon included some Soviet internal security personnel involved in construction and railroad maintenance. The London Institute for Strategic Studies says the size of the Soviet forces is closer to 3.7 million.

But is it fair to compare U.S. and Soviet troop size and claim that there is a gap? The Soviets are worried about the Chinese on their western borders, and at least 25 percent of their ground troops are assigned to the Chinese border. Americans don't have to worry about the Chinese or the Canadians. U.S. troops plus NATO troops plus Chinese troops add up to about 9 million. The total number of troops in the Soviet army and among their allies totals about 5 million. So where is the gap? The Soviets are probably telling their people that they have the gap. And from the Soviet point of view, when they add up all the enemy troops, they end up 4 million troops short.

There are all sorts of gaps—tank gaps, chemical weapon gaps, spending gaps, missile gaps, bomb gaps, troop gaps. By playing with figures you can make a gap out of almost anything. We must understand that gaps are artificially created by governments to pump more money and support out of their people. Gaps are usually not fair and honest comparisons. They are scare tactics. Looking at a gap in just one area is usually unfair.

Furthermore, what's so important about being equal with your enemies on all counts? Rather than asking who's ahead, it's more important to ask, "Are our military resources big enough for our needs?" If they are—and they certainly are for both giants—why foolishly try to match the opponent on every single thing? An accurate comparison looks at the *total* defense needs and military resources of a country. The gaps fabricated by the superpowers play a role in pushing the arms race along.

WHITE LIES

Both giants accuse each other of using propaganda and they use it themselves. We all tend to make ourselves look good and our competitors look bad. The giants aim their propaganda at two audiences, their own people and the world community. Propaganda is often partly true. It's like a white lie; only half of the truth is told, or the truth is twisted out of context. It also suggests connections between issues that aren't really linked. Propaganda is tricky because you never quite know when you're being taken across. It's hard to pick up a newspaper and know what is fact and what is government whitewash.

As the peace movement grew in Europe to protest the deployment of U.S. and NATO nuclear missiles, both the U.S. and the USSR tried very hard to do two things. Both offered "peace" proposals in an attempt to give the impression that they were truly the peacemakers.

The Soviets proposed a freeze on European land-based missiles if the U.S. would drop plans to install 464 cruise and 108 Pershing II missiles in Europe in 1983-84. This Soviet "peace" proposal was a joke to Americans since the U.S. had no land-based missiles in Europe and because it would have frozen a clearcut Soviet advantage in such land-based missiles. President Reagan then proposed a "zero option," in which the U.S. would not install new missiles on European soil in 1983-84 if the Soviets would dismantle their 300 newly installed land-based missiles. The American proposal sounded ridiculous to the Soviets since it did not take into account hundreds of NATO and U.S. nuclear bombs on submarines and bombers, French and British warheads targeted at the Soviets, nor some 7,000 smaller, "tactical" nuclear weapons which the U.S. controls in Europe.

The giants also tried to paint each other as the bad guy. The U.S. Pentagon released a slick 99-page book, *Soviet Military Power*, which described Soviet military might sometimes accurately and other times falsely. It was lopsided because it didn't show or compare U.S. military might. Reading it alone would give any sensible American a sleepless night. It paints a frightening picture of the Soviets. A few months later the Soviets returned the favor. They printed *Whence the Threat to Peace*, a booklet which describes the serious threat of American forces. Both giants were trying to convince the western Europeans that the other giant was the bad guy.

The U.S. State Department has frequently charged the Soviets with using "yellow rain," a chemical weapon, in Southeast Asia and Afghanistan. This charge made headlines several times in U.S. newspapers and gives the impression that the Soviets are really playing dirty. There's growing evidence that chemical weapons are being used, but there's also some scientific doubt about the evidence. Some scientists evaluating the State Department's "facts" are not convinced of the proof. Regardless of the facts, this accusation made excellent propaganda for the U.S. because it confirms the worst American suspicions that the Soviets are indeed bad guys. It gave the U.S. an excuse to start making chemical weapons, and it rallied public opinion behind the massive U.S. military buildup. Such shaky information could have been held until there was definite proof; instead, it was cleverly used by the U.S. State Department *before* it could be disproved.

As the revolution in El Salvador began boiling, the U.S. State Department released a white paper blaming the situation on outside, communist aggression. It provided "evidence" that weapons were being shipped to the rebels in El Salvador from other communist countries. When the "evidence" of the white paper was carefully examined, it became clear that much of it was shaky or misinterpreted. But the truth didn't matter. The U.S. government had captured many headlines which gave the American people the *impression* that the revolution in El Salvador was inspired by communist outsiders. The State Department wanted to give precisely that impression because they wanted to send huge amounts of military aid and American advisors into El Salvador to influence the outcome of the war. Certainly the American people couldn't say "no" to sending American money and advisors into the country if the communists were taking over. Undoubtedly some guns did come into El Salvador from socialist countries. The root of the problem in El Salvador, however, arises from internal economic injustice. U.S. propaganda in the white paper gave the *impression* that outside communists were the major cause of the whole thing.

Another example of how propaganda works can be seen in the United States' different views of Poland and El Salvador. In 1982 the U.S. made a film called "Let Poland Be Poland," which condemned the violence in Poland during the military crackdown. The film was a message to the USSR to keep out of Poland, and it played up all the violence. At the *same* time the film was shown on television stations around the world, the U.S. made a decision to send millions of dollars in new military aid to El Salvador to support a government that had killed thousands of its own citizens the previous year. The United States was telling the USSR to let Poland be Poland and at the same time it refused to let El Salvador be El Salvador. Violence in Poland was terrible and condemned, but violence in El Salvador was quietly swept under the carpet.

Both giants should have been keeping their hands off both Poland and El Salvador. Which is worse, wholesale imprisonment or wholesale assassination? The violence in both countries was terrible. But the government propaganda in the U.S. gave the American people the impression that the Soviets were the bad guys and the Americans were once again the good guys.

Now let me be very clear. Both sides whitewash the truth like this. The Soviets are just as good at it as the Americans. It's not a one-sided thing. However, Americans find it hard to believe that their government would deceive them. We want to believe that our government's story is the only story. Someone has said, "Both the Soviet people and the American people are brainwashed, but the Soviets know they are." Who knows? We must open our eyes and ears and realize that both of the giants whitewash their stories, and all the whitewashing propels the arms race along.

SANITIZED HATE

Pleasant words also spur this race. As we have already seen, nuclear war is pretty nasty. Its effects are ugly, bloody, and violent beyond our imagination. Now it's uncomfortable to face up to such terror all the time. So gradually over time, polite technical terms begin to cover up the vicious truth. These words are like emotional shock absorbers that help us withstand the jolting idea of nuclear war. They make it sound reasonable. They place some distance between us and the terror. They blur the suffering so we really don't have to face up to the destruction we're planning.

The technological jargon makes things sound complicated to average people. The impressive words and pleasant technical terms relieve us of guilt. We don't feel so guilty and bad when we can describe terror in pleasant terms. This is the process of whitewashing or sanitizing hate. It happens gradually over time. For the most part it's not a deliberate deception. It's just the natural human inclination to describe very bad things with pleasant and polite words. This verbal veneer allows us to go about our business without getting all upset about what our country is doing.

Pleasant verbal masks must be stripped off our idol. We must dig underneath the words to see what they really mean. Consider a few examples. A "surgical first strike" doesn't sound all that bad. Doctors do surgery to correct problems and to help people. Well in this case, it means "helping" your enemy by taking his missiles out of their silos. But it really means blowing up the enemy's missiles and killing 2 to 20 million people, depending on which computer prediction you use. Not so nice after all!

The new MX missile has a "bus" in its nose cone. Buses are useful; they transport passengers and drop them off at stops along the way. It turns out that the MX bus has some violent passengers on board—ten nuclear bombs, each the size of thirty Hiroshima Bombs. And like a good bus, this bus drops off its passengers along the way at ten different targets—cities or military installations.

"Collateral damage" is another term in the vocabulary of nuclear war. It's sort of vague. What it really refers to is the civilian death toll. It just sounds better to say we did a lot of collateral damage than to say we killed a lot of people. "Countervalue strategy" is another bit of jargon, which means aiming missiles at cities rather than at military targets. So when someone says, "Our countervalue strategy will result in higher collateral damage," what they really mean is, "By targeting missiles on cities we will kill a lot more people." Not very complicated after all, is it?

We could go on and on with examples, but the point is simply that all these technical, nice-sounding terms are deceptive labels on ugly hate. They are ways of sanitizing hate, of making it sound pleasant, comfortable, and sophisticated.

We saw how the survivors of Hiroshima underwent "psychic numbing" after the attack as a defense against insanity. The technical jargon of nuclear warfare is a preattack version of psychic numbing. It's our way of numbing our senses to the terror of nuclear war even before the attack. But that false sense of reality pushes us even closer to the danger itself. It's a way of planning for terror without terrorizing ourselves in the process.

This sanitizing process dulls our senses to what we really are doing. It gives the brutal business of death and killing an image of modern civility. This verbal padding absorbs the emotional jolts and allows us to push the arms locomotive along without much anxiety or guilt.

BARGAINING CHIPS

Another source of the locomotive's steam is bluffing. Ironically, getting ready for arms control treaties is one of the things that actually speeds up the race. Now that sounds funny at first. If the point of arms control talks is to put a stop to the race, why does it work the opposite way? Superpower agreements such as SALT and START grow out of hard bargaining sessions.

Any good bargaining requires some bluffing. It's like a giant poker game. You never know what the other guy is up to. Everyone wants to come away from the bargaining table looking good. You give a little here and a little there, and you get some here and you get some there. It's not a very black and white situation, but in the end you want to convince yourself and your friends that you got a "good deal."

Now when bargaining with nuclear bombs, you want to go to the table with your pockets loaded so that you can give up a few weapons without really hurting yourself. You take along some obsolete weapons and three or four new ones. And remember, the other guy is doing the same thing. So when you get to the table, you offer to give up some of your outdated weapons, forcing your opponent to give up something too—probably an old weapon he didn't really want either. Then to make yourself look good you even offer to give up one of your new weapons. You act as though you really wanted it—even though you built it for the purpose of giving it up. You say, "Aw shucks, we'll be good guys and give up our chemical weapons." That of course forces the other guy to give up a big weapon too—one which perhaps he also built to give away.

In the end you want to walk away from the bargaining table looking good to everyone. To the doves you say, "We really gave up a lot and have set new limits on arms," but you don't tell them that you only gave up junk. To the hawks you say, "We really didn't give up anything, but we sure forced the other guy to give up weapons right and left," but you don't tell them he gave up his junk.

Unfortunately that is how arms talks often go. It's called "bargaining from a position of strength," looking and sounding tough so that you can force the other guy to give up a lot. When President Reagan announced plans to make chemical weapons in 1982, he said, "This step will provide strong leverage towards negotiating a verifiable agreement banning chemical weapons." In other words, these new chemical weapons were deliberately made to use as bargaining chips. President Reagan was slow to negotiate with the Soviets in order to buy time to build bigger and better weapons. He wanted plenty of chips at the bargaining table. The president initiated START talks only after the nuclear freeze movement created intense grass roots political pressure to begin talking with the Soviets.

New weapons are also used as bargaining chips back home. President Carter reluctantly agreed to support the MX missile in order to "buy" U.S. Senate votes for the Salt II treaty.[12] Carter lost on both counts. He got an MX missile that he really didn't want, and the Senate didn't approve the SALT II treaty. So the public lost an arms control treaty and on top of that got stuck with a new weapon.

Another irony of arms control is that when a nation is "ahead" it doesn't want to negotiate because it has an advantage which negotiations might hurt. And a nation that's "behind" doesn't want to negotiate because it won't have a chance to catch up. It's a rare moment when both parties really want to negotiate.

This doesn't mean that negotiations are always useless. Some new weapons systems such as the ABM (anti-ballistic missile) have been stopped through negotiations. However, the point of all this is that the process of arms control itself actually produces *more* weapons. That sounds crazy but that's the way it works, and that's another factor that pushes the race ahead. This doesn't mean we shouldn't support arms control treaties. We should support them, but we must realize that in the process they are likely to produce more weapons, and we should scrutinize them carefully to see whether only obsolete weapons are given up.

ANTIQUE THINKING

Einstein's famous quote needs repeating. *Everything*

has changed since the first atomic bomb except the way we think. In other words, there's a lag between our thinking and our technology. We hear a lot about the gap between the USSR and the U.S., but the real gap is between our weapons and our thinking. Our traditional ideas of war such as winning and losing, offense and defense, advantage and disadvantage grew out of a world of bows and arrows. Those concepts make sense on the battlefield if you're fighting with rifles and tanks, but they're antique concepts in the face of nuclear war. Our technology has raced far ahead of our thinking.

In the past, war produced some benefits. The victorious country expanded its territory, enlarged its empire, acquired new seaports, controlled new diamond mines, or took some slaves. These payoffs made the suffering and horror of war seem worthwhile. There won't be many goodies left to plunder after a nuclear war—in fact, I can hardly think of any. If one nation managed to blow up another nation, it would be years before the smashed country was decontaminated. Who would go and clean up the debris with contagious disease and radioactive hot spots all over the place. If the Russians blew the Americans to bits, do we really think they would want to come over and clean up the radioactive mess afterward? What would be in it for them? And would we really want to go over to the USSR and clean up afterward?

Concepts like winning and losing are old fashioned in the face of nuclear war. It seems pretty clear that both sides in a nuclear exchange will look more like losers. There won't be any winners. I've already shown how the concept of being ahead is somewhat archaic. The truth of the matter is that both sides are slipping behind in their own security.

Even a term like defense is slippery. It's an idea that almost sounds sacred. Certainly, we say, everyone—individual and nation—has the right to self-defense. It certainly is all right to build and threaten to use nuclear weapons in national self-defense. But remember, *there is no defense against nuclear weapons.* That's a hard fact to accept, but it's true. If the U.S. shoots some nuclear missiles at the Soviets, there's not one thing they can do about it except take them on the chin. They can fire some of theirs back in revenge, but they can't protect or defend themselves against the ones we send over.

In the past most weapons could be used both for offense and defense. But nuclear weapons *can not* be used for defense in the traditional sense. They can be used three ways. They can be used to hit the enemy first, they can be used in revenge to hit back at an enemy after he has hit you, and they can be used to threaten revenge—to scare your enemy so bad that he'll never do anything to you in the first place. In this third sense, nuclear weapons are used in a type of "defense" which is actually a threat of ugly retaliation to encourage your enemy to "cool it." Modern defense is not defense in the traditional sense; rather it's a threat of terrible revenge *after* you've been hit with nuclear weapons. It's like killing a burglar's family in revenge after he has broken into your house. There's simply no way of keeping the nuclear burglars out of the house if they decide to come in. All we can do is unload revenge on their families.

However, we still have a Defense Department and a secretary of defense. We are urged to support defense spending for a strong defense. All such talk gives us a cozy sense of security when in fact there simply is *no* defense against nuclear weapons. Perhaps defense departments built on nuclear arsenals should more accurately be called Offense and Revenge departments. But that wouldn't work because who would support increased spending for offense and revenge? Or perhaps the Defense Department should be called the War Department as was the case in World War II.

One of the basic realities of war in the past was the connection between the number and size of weapons and a country's ability to win. Traditionally, more and bigger weapons meant greater strength and better chances of winning. Today the link between military strength and winning has been snapped by nuclear weapons. Just adding more weapons doesn't increase security or the chances of winning. In fact, many argue that at some point we cross a line with nuclear weapons where the old formula reverses itself and more weapons mean less security. Have we crossed that threshold? The old-fashioned tie between number of weapons and winning is a hard idea to break in our minds.

Terms like winning, losing, defense, victory, advantage, and gain suddenly change in the face of nuclear war. Using them to think about nuclear war is like trying to use a rusty old blacksmith's hammer to fix an electronic chip in a new computer—it simply doesn't fit. The antique arsenals in our minds will need to be dismantled before we can dismantle any nuclear arsenals.

Some social scientists see a ray of hope in our thinking gap. Since one of the incentives for going to war in the past was the good payoff in territory or resources, they hope that as nations begin to realize there are few goodies to come out of nuclear war, they might sincerely try to avoid it. Such scientists are optimistic that people will understand the consequences of nuclear war and work to prevent it. Any glimmer of hope sounds good, but people are slow to give up old cherished notions of winning and losing. More importantly, the fact that government officials seem to use the antique language as much as anyone doesn't help to close the thinking gap. They encourage the gap in order to convince people to support defense spending. President Reagan recently conceded that there could hardly be any winners in a nuclear war, but in the next breath he talked of nuclear superiority. Closing the thinking gap might erode public support for our military institutions.

IT'S NOT MY FAULT

There is another eerie force that fuels the arms race. People don't seem to feel any moral responsibility for what they are doing. They are just doing their job. They're just a tiny link in the deadly chain, and they don't want to accept moral responsibility for their small part. This comes from our growing job specialization. Each of us has a miniscule role in the overall scheme of things. We worry about our specific jobs and often don't care how they plug into the larger system. We just obey orders. Somebody else has to worry about moral responsibility, we say. When millions of people say that, who looks out for our common and collective good? There is a diffusion of moral responsibility; it's spread around so thin that few people are willing to be accountable for the tiny bit of evil they contribute to the larger system.

Take the 400 employees at a local company in my home community. They are nice people—friendly, neighborly—just good, down-to-earth people. But every day they work in a company that makes fuses and timing devices for bombs and missiles. Each employee has a small task. Probably no one makes a whole fuse. Most of them never see the completed fuses. They don't see the missiles and bombs that carry the fuses they make. When a bomb explodes in the Middle East or in Central America, they don't hear the cries of pain or see the dead bodies. Because they are removed several steps and thousands of miles from the death and destruction, they don't feel responsible. Employees pass the buck of responsibility to their boss, to the company president, or to the Defense Department—it's always someone else up the ladder that has to answer.

And so moral responsibility gets spread around very thin. It's nice to pass it around, but it's not right. We all hold part of the moral bag. Those who make even a tiny part of a fuse are responsible. I share in the responsibility when I pay my taxes. All of us need to scan our connections with the death industry, and we need to shoulder the responsibility for our part. If that small part is not consistent with our Christian convictions, we need to unplug ourselves.

Some folks have stopped passing the buck of moral responsbility. They are drawing the line and walking away from jobs in the nuclear weapons industry. Roman Catholic Bishop Matthiesen of Amarillo, Texas, encouraged his parishioners working at a Pantex nuclear bomb plant to find other work. Bishop Hunthausen of Seattle, Washington, has set up a fund to help people find other jobs when they resign from military employment. High Technology Professionals for Peace established an employment agency to help engineers find nonmilitary jobs. These are exciting signs that more and more people are willing to draw the line—even if it hurts financially and professionally—and stop passing the buck of moral responsibility. The church could be a supportive sanctuary for those who have the courage to shift occupational gears.

THE MILITANT CHURCH

In an earlier chapter, I suggested that the silent church must bear some responsibility for the arms race. The militant church also bears responsibility. As we all know, with a little effort we can usually find a Bible verse to support anything. I even found one in the previous chapter to support God's laughter! Some Christians and churches sprinkle sacred blessings over the nuclear arms race. They believe that peace will come only if the U.S. flexes tough military muscles. They believe that governments have the right to do almost anything—even to lead us toward the brink of nuclear war. They are caught in the trap of antique thinking, and they use Bible verses to argue that God himself wants the U.S. to have a strong military. They suggest that America needs growing nuclear forces so that the gospel of Jesus Christ can be preached throughout the world and thrive at home.

It's a surprising twist of logic to say that the growth and life of the body of Christ depends on ugly instruments of destruction. It seems like a perversion of the truth to say that the gospel of Jesus Christ, which emphasizes the forgiveness of sin and love for God and neighbor, can only survive if it's protected by piles and piles of nuclear bombs. This is a case of modern profanity when the gospel itself is used to support the preparation for nuclear war. Bible verses and sweet religious phrases used in this way cheer the race along by giving it the appearance of having God's smiling blessing.

A PINCH OF FAITH

Despair, hopelessness, and powerlessness hang heavy in our spirit. What can anyone do in the face of such powerful forces? The issue is so big, the forces so strong, the government so unresponsive, the people so calloused. Maybe the game really is playing us, and there's not really anything we can do.

That fear is the most devastating one of all. It numbs us and paralyzes us. It freezes our emotions. We can't move and we live in dread. There's something nice about being emotionally and spiritually paralyzed. It means we don't have to feel anything. We don't have to act. Our paralysis becomes a nice excuse for doing nothing.

Duped

But in our paralysis we are deceived. We are being taken across by the principalities and powers. Their first seduction is to work quietly behind the scenes—hoping we don't detect them. But once identified, they try to dupe us into believing there's nothing we can do.

> Powerlessness is always a sign of being duped by the principalities and powers. They want us to feel helpless; that is their best means of constraining us.[13]

If they can trick us into believing that there's nothing we can do, then they really have us. If we *think* there's nothing we can do, then we certainly *won't do anything* and the principalities and powers become lord. They reign supreme. We have sold out our souls to their rule when we say it's a hopeless situation. The nuclear freeze movement is a symbolic statement that we the people are still in charge and that we can stop this race.

What we think *is* important. If we all believe that nuclear war is inevitable, it will come to pass. If we say, "Nothing can be done," then nothing will be done and our worst fears will come true. Our spiritual numbness speeds up the process of death and actually helps to bring it about. A self-fulfilling prophecy is at work here. We get what we expect. The church dare not give up and cry hopelessness until we have put as much effort, resources, research, and time into preparations for peace as we have for war.

If Christians have anything to say to this issue, it's a word of hope—a word of faith. If Christians lose faith, then things are bleak indeed. Jesus said a tiny pinch of faith, a tiny mustard seed, is all that's necessary.

Dreamers

Faith means that we dream new dreams. We visualize in our minds how things in God's kingdom could be. Thoughts do become actions. If we submit to hopelessness and despair, we will act that way. Physicians have long told us about the mind's tremendous power over the body. Our minds influence our behavior. We do become what we think. Be careful what you think—it just might come true.

Christian faith is more than mental gymnastics of positive thinking. It's the realization that God is a living presence among us and that over the long haul his truth will prevail. It's the belief that the future peaceable kingdom is already here among us—it has already broken in.

> Have faith in God. Truly, I say to you, whoever says to this mountain, "Be taken up and cast into the sea," and does not doubt in his heart, but believes that what he says will come to pass, it will be done for him.
>
> *Mark 11:22-23.*

When we affirm God's presence among us, we begin thinking his thoughts. We dream his dreams. We redefine the situation and begin practicing the future now. We begin loving our enemies now. We refuse to work in death industries now. We practice peacemaking now by unhooking ourselves from the nuclear war machine. We work for reconciliation now. We witness to his peace now.

If millions of Christians throughout the world had just a tiny bit of faith, if they started loving enemies, if they witnessed against the forces that propel the nuclear locomotive, if they heaped good on top of evil, if they witnessed to the gospel of peace, if they dreamed God's dreams and acted on them now—they could move mountains, even mountains of nuclear arsenals.

We must begin dreaming now of millions of Christians in the body of Christ standing up and giving a public witness for Christ against the use of nuclear weapons.

We must dream of tens of thousands of Christians around the world walking quietly in candlelight processions.

We must dream of millions of Christians writing to their legislators about this threat.

We must dream about an international day of prayer for peace.

We must dream about tens of thousands of Christians refusing to pay at least a part of their taxes that go for war preparations.

We must dream about preachers boldly proclaiming the gospel of peace in their pulpits.

We must dream about thousands of Christians leaving their jobs in military industries.

We must dream about average, everyday Christians boldly witnessing to their friends and neighbors that their faith is in Jesus Christ, not in nuclear weapons.

We must dream. And we must begin *acting* our dreams now—before it's too late. We aren't helpless. We aren't completely powerless. We have choices. There are things we can do. Walter Wink puts it this way:[14]

We can today choose faith or paralysis. Which we choose may well determine the future of the earth.

In the words of the Old Testament,

I have set before you life and death,
blessing and curse;
therefore choose life,
that you and your descendants may live,
loving the Lord your God,
obeying his voice,
and cleaving to him.

Deuteronomy 30:19b-20a.

QUESTIONS

1. Are these "principalities and powers" that propel the arms race real forces? In what ways do you feel their push?
2. In what ways does the nuclear arms race run us?
3. Can you identify additional "undercurrents" that push the race forward?
4. What images of the enemy come to mind when you think about Russians? Does "loving enemies" mean getting along with them?
5. Can you identify other examples of "gaps," "white lies," and "sanitized hate"? How do these encourage the nuclear arms race?
6. In what ways do you get caught in the trap of antique thinking? Will junking our antique thinking slow down the race?
7. How do you respond to the notion that using the bomb to keep the world free for evangelism is profanity?
8. Compare the responses of the "silent" and the "militant" churches. How have they both accelerated the nuclear arms race?
9. Where do you draw the line on your personal moral responsibility? Are you involved in any way in the nuclear arms race?
10. How have the principalities and powers duped us when we say there's nothing we can do?

6

RUMORS OF PEACE

THE GOSPEL OF PEACE

Throughout this book I've tried to forge some links between faith in Jesus Christ and the nuclear arms race. In this chapter we'll look more directly at the gospel of peace. Our basic understanding of the role of peace in the gospel will influence where we come out on the question of nuclear weapons. Thus, I think it's essential to pause for a bit and consider the basic relationship of peace to the gospel. I will highlight some of the key reasons why the Christian gospel compels me to be a Christian pacifist. I won't bore you with a lengthy argument for Christian pacifism; that would take a whole book, and there are plenty of such books around.[1] Then in the next chapter we'll pick up the nuclear weapons issue more directly.

But first, a frank word of orientation. You may already be a persuaded Christian pacifist, you may be seriously struggling with this whole issue, or you may be sure that you could never be a thoroughbred Christian pacifist regardless of what anyone says. Certainly God's children won't ever all agree on this question. Could we, however, stop squabbling over the smaller details and at least meet each other halfway at nuclear pacifism? I am a convinced, 500-percent, dyed-in-the-wool Christian pacifist, but I won't bicker over the details of that stance if we can agree to meet each other halfway and give a united Christian witness that rejects the holding and use of nuclear weapons. If you're already a thoroughbred conscientious objector who would never pull the trigger—even if your mother was assaulted—can you stretch your understanding of Christian peace to the big question of our time? Today's issue is not pulling the trigger; today's issue is whether Christians will support the manufacture and possession of nuclear weapons. Can God's children at least get together on the issue of nuclear pacifism?

The Peace Caboose

For many Christians peace has been a caboose on the gospel train. It's nice to have a caboose around, but it's not really essential. You can take it or leave it. Peace is a nice luxury, an accessory like shutters on a house or icing on a cake, but it's not really at the heart of the matter. Peace for many Christians is something that you tack onto the gospel, a debatable fringe issue that's fun to argue about but one that's not basic to Christian faith.

As Christians we say that salvation in Jesus Christ brings peace with God. But the peace we often talk about is a narrow, warm, fuzzy version that only refers to cozy feelings in our hearts. When we're in a right relationship with God, we will have a deep sense of calm and a peace that passes all understanding. But that's only the beginning of God's peace. It's much more than a caboose of warm personal feelings.

A Peaceable Core

Discussions of Christian pacifism often begin with Jesus' teachings *about* peace. That makes it easy to slice off a few of his lines here and there and end up with a fighting Jesus by asking, "Is that really what he meant?" or by saying, "We probably don't understand the setting of his words." Since I am proposing that peace is at the core of the gospel itself, we will begin with the life, death, and resurrection of Jesus and then come back later to what he said about peace. If it's true that peace is at the heart of God's revelation in Jesus Christ, we should find some rumors of peace in the incarnation itself.

Hindsight sheds more light on what God was doing in

Jesus Christ than the immediate event itself. The shepherds really didn't know the whole story at the manger in Bethlehem, and even the disciples thought God had shut down his shop at the cross. We must look at Jesus from this side of the empty tomb and from this side of Pentecost. The apostle Paul is our key interpreter of Jesus on this side of the resurrection.

Jesus Is Our Peace

Paul writes about the centrality of peace in our salvation in his letter to the Ephesians:

> But now in Jesus Christ you who once were far off have been brought near in the blood of Christ. For he is our *peace*, who has made us both one, and has broken down the dividing wall of hostility, by abolishing in his flesh the law of commandments and ordinances, that he might create in himself one new man in place of the two, so making *peace*, and might reconcile us both to God in one body through the cross, thereby bringing the hostility to an end. And he came and preached *peace* to you who were far off and *peace* to those who were near; for through him we both have access in one Spirit to the Father [italics mine].
>
> *Ephesians 2:13-18.*

Paul doesn't beat around the bush here. Jesus himself made peace and is our peace. In his death he broke down the walls of hostility between us and God and between enemies. In context, this peace is more than just the peace of God in the believer's heart. It refers specifically to the bitter relations between Jews and Gentiles. Jesus' death didn't mysteriously extinguish Jew-Gentile hatred. Rather, it meant that both Jews and Gentiles who accepted God's forgiveness in Christ could begin loving and forgiving each other. As Jews and Gentiles repented of their sins and fellowshipped with God, the Holy Spirit empowered them to forgive even their enemies, thus crumbling the walls of hostility.

Paul later urges the Ephesians to stand firm, with their feet "shod with the equipment of the gospel of peace" (Ephesians 6:15). Peter describes God's message as the "good news of peace by Jesus Christ" (Acts 10:36). Paul sums it up this way:

> For in him [Christ] all the fulness of God was pleased to dwell, and through him to reconcile to himself all things, whether on earth or in heaven, making peace by the blood of his cross.
>
> *Colossians 1:19-20.*

God's Peaceful Triad

God's "triad of peace" has three levels. First, Jesus' death brings peace with God to all who repent of their sins. Second, believers from all backgrounds are joined together in peaceful relations in one community of faith. And third, forgiven disciples of Jesus are now empowered to love even their enemies—an unthinkable act apart from God's spirit. God's "comprehensive peace plan" goes far beyond the first and easy step of warm feelings; it calls his disciples to follow their Lord in peacemaking efforts involving real enemies.

This biblical notion of "comprehensive peace" stands squarely rooted in the Old Testament idea of shalom. The Hebrew understanding of peace was a broad concept that touched all aspects of life. The word "shalom," which appears over 300 times in the Old Testament, didn't mean just the absence of armed conflict; it meant spiritual and material well-being in all areas of life, and it bubbled up when people lived in right relationships with each other and with God. John Driver describes shalom this way:

> Not mere tranquillity of spirit and serenity of mind, peace had to do with harmonious relationships between God and his people. . . . It had to do with social relationships characterized by justice. Peace resulted when people lived together according to God's intention. Peace, justice and salvation are synonymous terms for general well-being created by right relationships.[2]

The Messiah's Business

Jesus as the Messiah fulfilled the Old Testament vision of shalom. His life and death demonstrates the shalom of God's kingdom and makes it possible for others to live in shalom. In Jesus Christ we have God's announcement of his

will for the human community. Jesus clarified the nature of
God's love and peace for all time. Even in the prophetic announcement of his coming, the Messiah was said to be the
one who would save us

> from our enemies, and from the hand of all who hate us;... give
> knowledge of salvation to his people in the forgiveness of their
> sins, through the tender mercy of our God,... [and] guide our
> feet into the way of peace.
>
> *Luke 1:71,77,79.*

Jesus in his life, death, and resurrection is the prince of
peace, who brings salvation from our enemies, salvation
from our sins, and who leads us in the way of peace. Peace in
its many dimensions is what the Savior's business is all
about. To slice off peace from the gospel is to lose the gospel
itself. If peace were possible without the gospel, we would
need no gospel; and if the gospel does not bring peace, we
have no gospel. Salvation means that we live in right relationship with God and with *all* persons—even our enemies.

THE HOLY RHYTHM

So much for Paul's quarterbacking. Now let's take a
closer look at Jesus. A narrow view of Jesus starts and stops
with the cross. In abbreviated form it goes something like
this: "God sent Jesus to die on the cross for our sins, and all
we have to do is believe he did it and we'll have eternal life."
Such a narrow view ignores Jesus' life and resurrection and
gives us the impression that all God needed to do was to have
Jesus die somehow so that everyone could be saved.

The entire story of the incarnation is important. The
cross is not the beginning and end of Christian faith. It's the
middle beat in God's holy rhythm—not the first or the last
one. The basin, the cross, and the empty tomb form this holy
rhythm. The basin, symbolic of Jesus' life of service, comes
first.

The Basin

The basin is the sign of Jesus' ministry of peacemaking
and servanthood. God sent Jesus to demonstrate a new way

of living. A careful examination shows that his life was devoted to crumbling the walls of hostility between Jew and Gentile, Jew and Samaritan, male and female, Jew and Roman, rich and poor. In case after case Jesus is *already* our peace, breaking down the barriers of antagonism. The unthinkable happens. Hated enemies, tax collectors, and zealots walk together with him. Salvation visits the life and home of rich Zacchaeus and others who repent, share their goods, and follow Jesus. In a parable about eternal life, a Samaritan crosses forbidden lines and surprises us by caring for an enemy.[3]

The basin is the *one* symbol of Christian faith that Jesus voluntarily selected himself. He deliberately took the basin and the towel and washed the disciples' feet as a sign of his life of service. Throughout his life Jesus made peace. He was peace. He invited others to "come follow." His peace is not merely warm, fuzzy feelings; it is a state of shalom, in which salvation, justice, and peace merge as broken relationships with God and others mend. God revealed who he is and what he is about as Jesus walked the paths of Galilee and the streets of Jerusalem. "In these last days he has spoken to us by a Son" (Hebrews 1:2). In Jesus, God unwrapped his package of divine revelation and gave us a good view of his peaceful nature and style.

Reverse Fighting

Jesus was a peacemaker, but he wasn't passive. He absorbed hatred, but he wasn't quiet. Jesus called for reconciliation in downtown Jerusalem, not in the desert by the Dead Sea. He preached peace and it got him into trouble. His basin ministry of teaching, healing, serving, and loving enemies cost him his life. His assertive love, healing on the Sabbath, talking with Samaritans, caring for Gentiles, eating with sinners, hosting tax collectors, and his strong criticism of rich folk and pious Pharisees provoked a lot of anger and eventually led to his death. Preaching God's love and inviting others to follow him threatened the religious and political authorities, and they tried to wipe him out.

The cross, the Roman bomb, sprang into action. It's

clear in the Scripture that Jesus' basin ministry triggered the cross. The cross wouldn't have come about if Jesus had prayed quietly out in the hills all his life. The cross was a vicious attempt by men to stamp out this threatening peacemaker once and for all. It was the basin, symbolizing Jesus' assertive and bold peacemaking efforts, that brought about the cross. The ruling powers in typical fashion tried to smother this voice for peace by getting rid of, or killing, him. That's how men usually deal with their enemies.

Now Jesus could have bypassed the cross. He could have stayed in the quiet hill country and avoided it. He could have called down a legion of protective angels. He could have armed the disciples. He could have fled when he saw Judas leave. But he didn't. He took it on the chin. The Scripture suggests that these detours were real options. The decision of whether to run or face up to the cross was so tough that he sweated drops of blood.

There are several layers of meaning to our understanding of Jesus' death on the cross. On this side of Pentecost we see how his death was an atonement for our sins. He became the sacrificial lamb that died for the sins of the world. He stood in our place and suffered on our behalf. We can appreciate this in retrospect. But at the time there was a real sense in which he voluntarily displayed nonresistant love as a demonstration of God's peaceful will.

It isn't easy to practice peace in the face of an ugly cross. Only after intense struggle did Jesus decide to obey the Father's will and commit himself to living the way of peace even in the middle of the violence that was just around the corner. His willingness to say, "Not my will but thine be done" was not merely another way of saying "Okay, Father, you want me killed, so I'm ready to throw in the towel and die." Far from it! Doing the Father's will meant quietly and firmly demonstrating how God copes with evil. Jesus wanted to run. He wanted to call down all those angels. He wanted to hike it back to Nazareth—quickly. But God was pleading for him to face up to the enemy and to love the enemy in public—showing once and for all that God's arms are long enough to reach around the meanest enemies.

This was God's opportunity to show how he deals with evil. He doesn't run away from it, nor does he fight it with its own power tactics and cruel weapons. God fights evil with love. He fights in reverse.[4] He fights evil with goodness and compassion. That's how he wanted Jesus to fight. And that's how he calls us to fight. So when Jesus said "yes" to the Father's will, he was, in effect, saying,

> Yes, I will continue to demonstrate your love, your compassion, your peaceful ways even in the middle of this violence. Yes, I'll keep on performing my basin ministry knowing full well that I'll get strung up on that cross. I won't resort to violence and I won't run away. I'll just keep right on doing your will, washing those dirty feet in my basin, even the dirty feet of those mean Roman soldiers pounding the nails into my body.

That's what was going on when Jesus said "yes." And that's different from saying, "Okay, Father, if you have to kill me somehow, I'm ready." God's plea to Jesus was, "Please keep on being my kind of peaceful person now, even when they accuse you falsely and pound you onto that painful cross. Don't give up our basin ministry now. Show them that my love is big enough to handle the trickiest Sadducee and the cruelest Roman soldier."

And Jesus said "yes," he'd stick with the basin ministry even when the heat was turned up. And he did. As the last nails were tearing through his body, his words were, "Father forgive them." He was absorbing their hatred. And that kind of defenseless fighting made peace. This is the scandal of the gospel, of God's love, and it's still hard to accept and follow today.

The reverse fighting shocked those around him. God's peace was irresistible. They repented and joined the peaceful kingdom. A robber hanging beside him, and even a Roman centurion, ringleader of the violence, turned around and believed. But to most people the battle was over. The terrible Roman cross had indeed wiped out Jesus' basin ministry. The principalities and powers had whipped God and beaten him badly. Evil prevailed. The drama was over and nastiness had won the day, or so thought the disciples as they dejectedly turned and headed north toward Galilee. Violence was victorious, or was it?

God's Last Word

This was just an intermission. God had a surprise Act III. He took the evil cross, turned it upside down, and used it for good. God took advantage of a bad situation and used it for the salvation of the world. The empty tomb was God's last word. It was God's way of telling us that in the long run his truth prevails! The resurrection is God's message that at the end of the game he will be victorious even over the principalities and powers. The resurrection embarrassed the ruling powers and left them with red faces. They thought they had eliminated this troublemaker, but suddenly he was running around preaching peace again.

Like the disciples, we look at things in the short run, from the foot of the cross, and things often look bad from there. The resurrection reminds us that God is in charge, and although the game is tense and violent, he will triumph over the long haul. That is the message of the book of Revelation; Jesus has already been victorious. The game is already won, even though it's still being played. This hope is the taproot of our Christian faith. Such hope gives God's people the strength to be faithful now even under the threat of nuclear war. This hope gives us courage to live and speak peace even in the midst of nuclear violence, because we know that death, even our own death, isn't the last word. God's victory is around the corner.

We have trudged through all this to make a point—and it's a big one. The biblical notion of shalom is at the core of God's revelation to us in Jesus Christ. Peace is not something we can take or leave. It's not a luxury that we can tack onto the gospel when it's convenient. It is the gospel. When we slice peace from the gospel, we have lost the very gospel itself. If the gospel doesn't reconcile, if it doesn't bring enemies together, if it doesn't break down walls of hostility between us and God, and our antagonists, then it's not the gospel. The gospel of our Lord Jesus Christ at its very core is that kind of gospel.

In capsule form the "holy rhythm" goes like this. The basin, symbolic of the life and teaching of Jesus, demonstrates God's revelation of true shalom—the peace that comes when broken relationships are healed. Jesus' basin ministry shows that God's peacemaking is not weak or passive. It persistently speaks out and *makes* peace even when such moves threaten the status quo, even to the point of triggering a cross.

Evil forces frantically used the cross to crush God's peacemaking efforts. Most importantly, the cross shows how God fights in reverse—he fights evil with good. He fights hate with love.

The empty tomb and the risen Jesus witness to God's ultimate victory. They show how God turns the worst of evil intentions to his glory. The empty tomb is our enduring emblem of Christian hope.

LOVE THOSE ENEMIES

There are three early witnesses to the gospel of peace: the words of Jesus, the writings of the apostles, and the testimony of the early church. Peace is a central theme in the New Testament with over a hundred specific references to the word itself.[5]

God is frequently called the God of Peace.
Jesus is called the Lord of Peace.
The Holy Spirit is the Spirit of Peace.
"Peace" was the early Christians' greeting.
The gospel is often called the gospel of peace.

In Jesus' words,

Love your neighbor as yourself.
Blessed are the peacemakers.
Love your enemies.
Do good to those who hate you.
Bless those who curse you.
Pray for those who abuse you.
Be merciful even as your Father is merciful.

Forgive seventy times seven.
They that take the sword die with the sword.

In Paul's words,

Bless those who persecute you.
Repay no one evil for evil.
If your enemy is hungry, feed him.
Overcome evil with good.
Owe no one anything except love.
Let the peace of Christ rule in your hearts.
We are ministers of reconciliation.

The Early Church

The evidence is clear that the early church for the first 300 years refused to participate in military service.[6] Historical records show it was rare to find a Christian soldier until about AD 170-180. Over the next 100 to 125 years there were a few isolated instances of Christians joining the army. Both the teaching of the church fathers and the practice of the average Christians overwhelmingly supported Christian pacifism in the first 300 years. After the emperor Constantine "Christianized" the government in the fourth century, the peace witness of the Christian church began to crumble.

BUT GOD FOUGHT IN THE OLD TESTAMENT

But didn't God fight in the Old Testament? How can we oppose war if God himself commanded war in the Old Testament? Let me summarize a few key issues related to warfare in the Old Testament.[7]

Different types of Old Testament warfare emerge in the exodus, the conquest, and the Davidic kingdom. Sometimes God fought for his people, and other times he used foreign nations to fight against Israel. So when we say, "What about war in the Old Testament?" we must be clear about which type of war.

The holy wars that God fought for his people were quite different from our ideas of war today. God was the ruler and king of Israel. Miracles in the form of crumbling walls, hornets, hailstones, and flooding rivers were God's weapons of war. God deliberately kept the armies of Israel small and weak, making it obvious that any victories were won by his miracles, not by the people's military prowess. Repeatedly God made it clear that he would miraculously "give the enemy into Israel's hand." He was the hero, not the troops of Israel. He was their king, savior, and liberator. His way of fighting was different from that of the other kings and nations surrounding Israel.

The Hebrews soon tired of this kind of fighting and wanted a king (Saul) and an army to do their own fighting. They wanted to be tough like other nations. After getting their king they gradually strayed again from God's ways, and he eventually used the armies of other nations to punish them.

It is true that even in God's style of holy war, people were massacred. How can this be reconciled with the image of God we find in Jesus Christ? There are several ways to grapple with this gap between the Old and New Testaments. If we see the Bible as a "flat" book in which God's revelation doesn't change, then it's difficult to resolve inconsistencies and contradictions between biblical authors. A "flat book" approach doesn't give us an internal key or guide for interpretation.

On the other hand, we can view the Bible as God's progressive revelation, which culminates in Jesus Christ. When we look at the Bible this way, the New Testament becomes a fulfillment of the Old. In the New Testament and particularly in Jesus Christ, we have a clearer and updated picture of God's nature. More importantly, Jesus becomes our key to interpreting *all* Scripture. In other words, Jesus is the authoritative yardstick by which we evaluate other teachings of Scripture. Jesus introduced a higher ethic or way of living that supersedes some practices in the Old Testament, such as killing, murdering witches, polygamy, stoning stubborn children, owning slaves, oppressing women, and hoarding wealth.

Anyone who uses warfare in the Old Testament as a crutch to support war today must also be ready to advocate these other practices found in the Old Testament. There are sharp differences on some ethical issues between the Testaments, and if we accept Jesus as God's final revelation, then he becomes our authoritative guide for interpretation. The theme of God's kingship as liberator and savior is central to both Testaments.

Now even if you don't buy the idea of progressive revelation, there is still no logical way that holy war in the Old Testament can be used to support nuclear war today. A consistent application of holy war practices for American Christians would mean a deliberate *reduction* of our nuclear forces so that any victory would obviously result from God's miraculous intervention and not from our nuclear superiority. We would declare that God is our president and would expect him to fight *for* us and *not through* us. We would literally need to stamp "In God We Trust" on our bombs and submarines. In short, a consistent application of holy war to our situation would require American Christians to urge radical disarmament by our side. We'd need to fall way behind the Soviets so that God could be our miraculous hero and take the credit for any victory. Sounds ridiculous, doesn't it?

Any honest attempt to use Old Testament holy war to justify nuclear war fails. Those who use Old Testament warfare to justify the nuclear arms race today haven't read their Bibles carefully or, if they do, aren't willing to accept its implications of radical disarmament.

BUT DIDN'T JESUS SAY . . . ?

Christians who advocate participation in war sometimes point to things that Jesus said or did to justify their position:

> And making a whip of cords, he drove them all, with the sheep and oxen, out of the temple.
> *John 2:15*

> I have not come to bring peace, but a sword.
> *Matthew 10:34*

> [Jesus praised a soldier,] "Truly, I say to you, not even in Israel have I found such faith".
> *Matthew 8:10*

"Let him who has no sword sell his mantle and buy one...."
And [the disciples] said, "Look, Lord, here are two swords." And
he said to them, "It is enough".

Luke 22:36-38

Other verses are also used to justify force, but these four
are the most often quoted ones. Any specific teaching of
Jesus must be interpreted in its own context, as well as in
the setting of Jesus' entire life and other teachings. To lift
one obscure reference out and use it to demolish the central
thrust of Jesus' life and teaching is a careless and irresponsible way to use the Bible. Anyone can find a single Bible verse
to prove anything!

These texts, taken in their context, can hardly be used
to make Jesus into a warrior. There is no textual evidence
that Jesus ever hit anyone with a whip or threatened to kill
the merchants in the temple. When he said he brought not
peace but a sword, he was referring to the word of God. The
context suggests that obedience to the word of God does
sometimes create divisions even in families. In his response
to the centurion Jesus applauded the soldier's faith, not his
profession. His instruction to buy a sword must be understood in a figurative sense as he described their preparation
for his death. Certainly two swords were not enough to
defend twelve disciples, and a short time later Jesus
condemned Peter for cutting off a man's ear. Or perhaps
Jesus was testing their understanding when he told them to
buy a sword. "It's enough" was a sigh of exasperation when
he realized that the disciples were taking him literally. When
he said, "It's enough," he was saying in effect, "Okay, you
don't understand, so let's move on."

We do not have space to discuss these passages in detail, and others have already done that well.[8] But let's sup-
pose for a minute that I'm dead wrong in this interpretation.
Let's assume that Jesus did lash someone with a whip in the
temple. Let's assume Jesus really did tell each disciple to buy
a literal sword. Let's assume Jesus was praising the
centurion's military profession. If this was the case, is it evidence that Christians should support nuclear deterrence today? Does it follow that just because Jesus touched someone

with a whip we have the right to threaten massive nuclear revenge? Just because Jesus praised a soldier doesn't give us the right to threaten mother nature and to maim future generations, does it? Regardless of how you interpret these verses, they are flimsy reasons for supporting the manufacture of nuclear weapons today.

BUT THERE WILL BE WARS AND RUMORS OF WARS

"And you will hear of wars and rumors of wars" (Matthew 24:6). These words from the lips of Jesus accurately describe the war gossip we hear today. They easily become an excuse to avoid witnessing for peace. They are often repeated by Christians with a fatalistic sigh that says, "Well, that's how God said it would be, so we can just sit back and enjoy the show." There's a big difference between *describing* what's happening and *approving* of it. Jesus also said we'll always have the poor with us. But that didn't mean he approved of economic oppression or poverty. In fact, he spoke out very harshly against the rich who exploited the poor.

It's one thing to say that something exists, and it's quite another thing to say whether it's right or wrong. Just because rebellious humans have threatened each other with war down through history doesn't make war right or give God's people the right to applaud it. There will probably be rumors of nuclear war for a long time, but that cannot be an excuse for Christians to self-righteously stick their heads in the sand and bury their witness for peace. To applaud nuclear weapons just because Jesus said we will have rumors of war is a sign of a callous and hardened heart—one very different from Jesus' compassionate heart as he cried over Jerusalem, wishing that its citizens knew "the things that make for peace."

BUT AREN'T SOME WARS JUST?

The so-called just-war theory has been the historic bridge over which most churches have traveled from the nonviolent teachings of the New Testament to the battlefield. The idea, based on Greek and Roman thinking, was articulated by St. Augustine in the fifth century and revised several times. It suggests that under certain conditions individual Christians and nations are justified in participating in war. The just-war bridge carried much of both the Protestant and Roman Catholic Church's teaching about war until recently. The key conditions for determining whether a war is just or unjust usually include:

1. The war must be declared and conducted by a legitimate ruler.
2. War is permissible only as a last resort.
3. The purpose of the war must be good—usually defense against an attack.
4. There must be a reasonable chance of success.
5. The good coming out of the war must outweigh the evil (proportionality).
6. The war must be conducted justly with innocent civilians protected (discrimination).

All of these conditions must be met before a war can be considered just. Historically, churches on both sides of a conflict usually thought their cause was just. The just-war bridge groaned under the weight of the Vietnam War and is crumbling today under the heavy burden of nuclear weapons. In the words of Michael Walzer, "Nuclear weapons explode the theory of just war."[9]

How could more good than evil ever come out of a nuclear war? Radioactive fallout drifting hundreds of miles away from the attack, as well as thousands of acres of massive destruction, make it impossible to protect civilians in a nuclear war. Even a counterforce attack aimed at military targets would certainly kill millions of innocent civilians. How can the purpose of fighting back in a nuclear war be considered defensive when in reality it's massive revenge for what an enemy has already done? The idea of a reasonable success hardly fits a war in which both parties lose badly and their societies are destroyed.

A nuclear war would be over before church leaders ever had a chance to sit down and decide whether it was justified. The distance between killer and victim makes it impossible to see whether the war is fought justly. For these and other reasons, it's difficult to squeeze nuclear war into the just-war mold. It's fairly obvious that these six specific just-war yard-sticks could not justify any nuclear war. However, some of the underlying moral reasoning can apply to nuclear war discussions. For example, perpetrating some evil such as threatening nuclear revenge might be justified if that prevented nuclear war.

Since there's little time to talk about the morality of a nuclear war once it's started, the moral questions must be asked *before* the war begins. Is it morally just to threaten to use nuclear weapons? Should the church support government policies of nuclear threat for the purpose of preventing nuclear war? We'll turn to these questions in the next chapter.

BUT THE GOVERNMENT'S ORDAINED BY GOD

Romans 13:1-7 is used sometimes to support nuclear deterrence by saying, "God has ordained our government. The president and Congress are his ministers for our good. We are to obey the government, and if government leaders think that nuclear war policies are necessary, then we should obey and support them." There are some problems with this logic.[10]

First of all, the Romans 13:1-7 passage is sandwiched between two pleas by Paul for love and nonviolence. At the end of chapter 12, he says,

Repay no one evil for evil.
If your enemy is hungry, feed him.
Overcome evil with good.

Next come the seven "meaty" verses about government, sometimes called the "pray, pay, and obey" verses. These are followed by a second slice of love.

Owe no one anything except to love one another.
You shall love your neighbor as yourself.
Love does no wrong to a neighbor.

It's a tragic irony of church history that the seven 'pray, pay, and obey" verses have been used to justify killing in direct violation of the teaching on love in the verses at the beginning and end of the passage. How could the tragic destruction of nuclear war ever be shaped to fit Paul's advice on loving enemies and neighbors?

The original Greek text suggests that Christians are to be "subordinate" to government. Being *subordinate* doesn't mean a Christian *obeys* every government demand. There may be times when the Christian caught between the demands of God and Caesar needs to "obey God rather than men" (Acts 5:29). Being subordinate means that even when the Christian respectfully says "no" to government, he or she willingly suffers the consequences in a nonresistant manner. If the government asks me to kill someone, I respectfully say "no," and I quietly take the consequences even if it means jail or death because I am still in subjection to the government. Obedience is reserved for God alone.

Some translations say government is ordained by God, giving the impression that God stamps his approval on everything the government does. This also implies that a government has the right to do anything it wants to. The original text suggests that God instituted authorities. In other words, God puts authorities in place in a general sense to provide order in society. Without order we couldn't survive. Just because God instituted or set up government in a general sense doesn't mean that a specific leader is God's servant, nor does it mean that everything a government does is right.

The government's job according to the apostle Paul is maintaining order by protecting the good and by punishing evildoers. Government does its job as instituted by God when it protects the innocent and punishes the evil. God lets governments run their own course. If they act belligerent and start punishing good and rewarding evil, they become like the beast of the Roman Empire described in Revelation 13. Eventually they come crashing down from their pedestals of power, tripped by their own folly. God may use their collapse or ruin to teach a lesson or to render his judgment on their evil practices, but that doesn't mean he willed or led them into their stupidity.

Paul is not calling for blind obedience to government. He is pleading for a nonresistant posture, *even* in the face of a tyrannical government. Moreover, in a democracy, with freedom of speech, Christians are part of the political process just because they are citizens. In a certain sense they are the government, and of all people they should be doing whatever they can to influence government in the direction of peace.

Since God instituted governments, they are accountable and answerable to a higher power. Christian witness reminds government that it's not its own boss. Paul implies that a government's power has limits. Does a government have the right to punish good and reward evil? Does a government have the right to kill small children?

As far as nuclear war is concerned, does a government have the right to threaten a war that would kill millions of people? How would such policies ever reward good? Does a government have the right to hold its own citizens and the citizens of other countries hostage to terror? Is government really protecting and defending its own citizens when its nuclear policies can not prevent attack, but only promise massive revenge on the enemy? At what point do a government's defense strategies shift from protecting its citizens to actually endangering them?

Is a government "God's servant for our good" when its military policies threaten to destroy civilization and God's good creation? Who sets the moral limits on a government's behavior? The seven verses on government in Romans 13 dare not be twisted into meek approval of nuclear weapons. The outcome of a nuclear war will certainly punish everyone and reward no one!

One way to think about church and state is to consider them as two separate orders operating under different moral codes. The church exhorts its members to follow ideal Christian teachings but expects less of the government. There are several problems with such a clean division of moral responsibility into two separate bins. If there are two moral codes, then who sets the rules for government and on what ethical foundation are they anchored? Suggesting that there are two standards tends to lower the moral expectations for government and lets it more easily stray from high codes of conduct.

Furthermore, individuals are involved in both church life and government affairs, and a neat separation in our minds doesn't resolve the practical dilemmas that individuals may feel when caught between two standards. Individual Christians who subscribe to the two-ethic doctrine in the area of nuclear weapons, for example, may accept nuclear weapons as citizens but not as Christians. So for all practical purposes they accept nuclear weapons, and their Christian values are irrelevant for their opinions as citizens. The double-standard approach also has the effect of making Christian faith and the church's witness irrelevant for government policy since it's "outside our moral turf." If government is outside the constraints of Christian morality, are all other social organizations also given the license to operate at sub-Christian levels of morality? Certainly governments will not approach Christian principles of morality until the leaders make personal Christian faith commitments. Even if that never happens, is that a reason not to call governments to the high standards of Christian morality?

The government will never act like the church, but then the church doesn't always act Christian either! Should we not call ourselves, our churches, and our government to the high standards of conduct embodied in the Christian tradition? When we make the call for conversion and set high expectations, the church becomes the salt of the earth or the moral conscience of the society, reminding the human community what it could and should be.

LET'S BE REALISTIC

The message of Jesus and Paul as well as the witness of the early church is clear and hardly debatable. Christians of all stripes agree that these teachings set an ideal for Christian behavior. But just how seriously should we take them? They might work in a rose garden, but we live in a violent world. How should Christians deal with a Hitler? Aren't there times when it's better to use force to stamp out evil rather than let it run rampant? Don't some situations justify doing a little bad—say, shooting a Hitler—to prevent a great deal of evil? Aren't there times when peacemakers need to use a pinch of violence to achieve good results in the long run? Is it responsible to look the other way and let evil forces destroy innocent people? Isn't it okay to use force to constrain a killer on a shooting spree?

In other words, even though we prefer to live faithfully by Jesus' teachings, don't we also have social responsibilities to keep evil in check in a real world of violence? In doing our part to arrest evil, even when using a bit of violence, aren't we preserving freedom and protecting the welfare of many others? The church has wrestled with these sticky dilemmas down through the centuries. It's not a matter of force, yes or no. Everyone uses some force. It's a question of where we draw the line on the use of violent force. How many exceptions can we tack onto Jesus' teachings without prostituting them completely? Are we watering down his straightforward instructions the moment we make exceptions?

Love your enemies, except when. . . .
Love your neighbor, except when. . . .
Return good for evil, except when. . . .
Live peaceably with all men, except when. . . .

Drawing Lines

There have been many answers to these tough questions. Some Christians believe these are commands of perfection aimed at a few select disciples. For others, these are ideals which Christians should try to achieve even though they usually won't. Some say Jesus' teachings predict Christian behavior in a future millennium and are not intended for today. Other Christians apply these instructions only to believers in the church and not to the political behavior of Christians as citizens. Some have said that God has two arms or two kingdoms, the church and the government, and each realm has different standards of behavior. Still other Christians think these hard biblical teachings are binding for all Christians except in certain justifiable situations. And finally, some insist that Jesus' words on peace-making and loving enemies apply to all Christians at all times regardless of the situation.

Two Camps

To utterly simplify a very complex issue, we can sort out two major camps in the church. The *Never Ever* tradition insists that the use of violent force by Christ's followers is always wrong and out of step with the spirit and manner of Christian love. The small Never Ever stream has persistently bubbled up throughout the history of the church.

The common practice of most churches we might call the *Sometimes Maybe* camp. These believers also take Jesus' words seriously, but concede that evil situations sometimes justify participation in war, or the use of violent force in order to achieve a greater good. This position doesn't welcome force and only allows it when there's hope of peace around the corner. The Sometimes Maybe people say we are often caught in gray situations where we need to choose the lesser of two evils.

SUMMING UP

There are many intermediate positions between the Never Ever people and the Sometimes Maybe folks. I find myself wading in the historical stream of the Never Ever people, but I realize there are many fuzzy situations which defy easy answers. Let me sum up by sharing some reasons why I'm a Never Ever person.

1. The way of defenseless love is at the center of God's revelation in Jesus Christ. Using violence to stamp out evil seems inconsistent with the whole point of God's message in Jesus Christ. If God loves the world and as his disciples we are to love what he loves, how can we kill?

2. To declare Jesus as Lord means that my allegiance to God's kingdom takes priority over other demands on my life—even those of government. This means that in certain situations I may need to obey the higher law of God rather than the law of man. To say that Jesus is Lord may, in some

rare situations, require that I willingly die for the sake of the gospel. If I use armed force, I'm really saying that Caesar and violence is my lord. And if I'm willing to die for my country, but not for my faith, then who really is my lord?

3. The biblical view stresses the futility of force in the long run. Those who take the sword will also die by the sword. This means that if I resort to the use of violent force, I am stooping to evil tactics that in the long run will only trigger more violence. Only defenseless love can slice through the cycle of violence. The biblical law of sowing and reaping will have the last say. If I sow violence, sometime, somewhere, in some way I will reap violence.

4. Joining the Never Ever people also emerges out of my understanding of the nature of the church. My brothers and sisters in Christ are scattered throughout the world in all nations. Participation in military action that harms a member of the Christian family is unthinkable and utterly wrong. And besides, how can we talk about God's love and invite newcomers into the family of God when we're calling them enemies and threatening to kill them? Participation in military action ridicules both the church— the international body of Christ—and evangelism—God's call to salvation.

5. Being a Christian pacifist doesn't mean I'm a passive weakling or a docile sponge. Turning the other cheek is a strategy of love which disarms opponents. Peacemaking may require intervention in touchy and explosive situations. Forging peace in risky places is often harder than grabbing a gun or looking the other way. Making peace is quite different from keeping peace, and it requires hard work and public witness that may bring harsh ridicule.

6. What would I do if someone attacked a member of my family? I don't know. Sweet theories might shatter in the face of a mean situation. If spontaneous love initiatives—offering a cup of coffee—didn't work, I might use some force. But I'd have to stop at the point of killing someone even if my life or a family member's life was at stake. I'm not sure what I'd do if I knew that by killing one person I could save the lives of hundreds of others. If I had a gun and saw a maniac shooting innocent civilians, I'd probably try to shoot the

sniper in the leg or hand. So where would I draw the line? At the point of taking a life. But any use of brutal force would be a compromise, and I would do it with full knowledge that it might trigger a whole new cycle of violence.

7. Finally, defenseless love isn't always effective, nor will it always work, at least not in the short run. Jesus got killed. Force doesn't always work either. Reverse fighting, however, probably works as often as brutal force. The important question is not whether it works, but whether we are reliable witnesses of the gospel. And although it might look as though it doesn't work at the moment, God may make our foolish witness work in the long run.

I haven't forgotten about nuclear war. If you're a Never Ever person, you're probably yelling "cheers" by now. If you're in the Sometimes Maybe camp, you're no doubt ready to write me off as a dove and are wondering what all this has to do with nuclear war. Regardless of which camp we're in, it's important to sort out our basic convictions about peace before tackling our response to nuclear war.

Peace Through Weakness

Here is the crux of the matter: How do we achieve peace? Everyone wants it! It's precisely at this point that the biblical perspective clashes head on with prevailing American and Soviet policies. The slogan of American foreign policy is "peace through strength." This means that peace is secured or guaranteed through stronger and tougher military might. As we have already seen, God's way of reverse fighting is exactly the opposite. God's method is "peace through weakness." Heaping good on evil, loving enemies, blessing those who persecute you—all of this is a strategy of peace through weakness. Governments contend that weakness invites attack. Presidents claim, "We've never gotten into a war when we were strong."

Beyond saying that this tough approach directly conflicts with God's method of reverse fighting, we must also ask, "What kind of peace is the government talking about?" Is it really peace when millions of citizens on both sides are terrorized by the threat of nuclear war? Is it really peace when nations threaten to blow each other up with nuclear-tipped missiles and hold each other's citizens hostage to fear? Is that peace? What kind of peace is it that threatens to shatter mother nature herself? Surely that is not the biblical notion of peace. Such "peace" is terror covered up with a sweet-sounding Christian term. We must carefully undress such slogans and not confuse them with the biblical notion of shalom. We must also be aware that peace through weakness may bring a cross; it could result in political oppression and domination.

When you believe that peace comes from strength, then you build and prepare a huge war machine that serves as a messiah to usher in peace. And so governments, both American and Soviet, pile bombs higher and higher, believing that they will bring peace. This is what Robert Lifton calls "the logic of madness," the idea that larger arsenals of bombs and tougher and tougher threats will somehow eventually bring peace. No matter where we come out on using force, we all can agree that nuclear war itself would be a terrible tragedy. No one debates that. No one wants nuclear war. We can call it sin, immoral, unethical, or whatever we like. The real questions of the day, however, are these: What is the best way to prevent nuclear war? Is the preparation for nuclear war as morally wrong as actual war itself? These are the tough issues of our day, to which we will turn in the next chapter.

Trade with Peace

Biblical faith and Christian doctrine teach individual responsibility. Western legal systems hold individuals accountable for what they know and do. Jesus described a nobleman who gave his servants different amounts of money, with instructions to "trade with the talents" until he returned. Several servants invested their money. One servant buried his in the ground. When the master returned, he judged each servant's investments. This *isn't* a parable about investing our money wisely! The point of the story is our responsibility to use our knowledge of the kingdom of God wisely. Those who squander their knowledge of God's kingdom will be held accountable for their foolishness. Some day the spiritual bank accounts will be opened, and we'll have to give an account of how we invested our knowledge of God's kingdom.

God's desire and strategy for peace is one of the "talents" deposited in the church's account. This is our treasure. But what will we do with this gem? Will we bury it or will we trade with it and invest it wisely? In times like these, who is responsible to speak out about nuclear weapons? Will we foolishly squander the gem in our heritage? And who will answer for it if we bury our treasure in the sand?

QUESTIONS

1. What is your reaction to the suggestion that peace is at the heart of the gospel?
2. Where do you draw the line on the use of force by Christians? Under what circumstances could you kill someone?
3. Can you think of situations that justify using a "little" evil to achieve a greater good?
4. How seriously should we take the peace teachings of Jesus and Paul?
5. Are there good biblical reasons for not being a Christian pacifist?
6. Did God intend his reverse-fighting style to be a model for his followers? Is it also intended as a model for government behavior?
7. In what ways is Christian pacifism "realistic"? In what ways is it "unrealistic"?
8. Can the moral reasoning regarding "just" wars be related in any way to nuclear warfare?
9. What might happen if the government adopted a policy of "peace through weakness"?
10. Who sets the moral standards and limits for a government's behavior?

7

DARE WE TOLERATE NUCLEAR WEAPONS?

THE MORAL JAM

Can we tolerate nuclear weapons on moral grounds? This is the big question, and you guessed it—my answer is no. Why can't we tolerate nuclear weapons? We may shake our fingers at them and call them sin, but that doesn't make them go away. Our nuclear predicament isn't quite so neat and simple. No matter how much we despise them, nuclear weapons are not likely to fade mysteriously away in a few months. We will have to live with them and tolerate them for some time. But dare we tolerate them morally? Dare we rearrange our ethical furniture to make room for them in our house of moral values?

We are caught in a corner with bombs piled up all around us, and whatever moves we make could bump some off the pile. There's no easy way out of the corner. It is indeed a jam—an ethical situation in which doing some good, like working toward gradual disarmament, might result in terrible evil, like nuclear war. And it's possible that making bad threats to use nuclear weapons might work for good and actually prevent nuclear war. U.S. military policy is rooted in deterrence—the idea that threatening to use nuclear weapons in massive retaliation is the best way to keep an opponent from ever making the first move. By making nuclear snarls and threats we hope to prevent nuclear war.

Decision-making involves thinking about our *acts* and their *consequences*. It's nice when good acts bring good results. But sometimes there are sticky situations in which doing bad may bring good results. Our acts and their results are pulled apart in this nuclear jam. It's hard to bless threats of massive destruction, and yet we fear the terrible possibilities of nuclear war if we don't make some threats. Do the ends justify the means? Can we threaten to use nuclear weapons in order to prevent nuclear war? Are we morally justified in threatening immoral actions if the threats bring about good—in this case averting nuclear war? Is there a moral difference between threatening to use nuclear weapons and actually using them? Is it all right to threaten to kill people in order to save them? Threatening to destroy the Soviet Union may save American society, but blasting them to pieces will surely destroy us also. Do we need to sacrifice doing right (disarmament) in order to prevent the terrible evil of nuclear war? This is a *very* sticky ethical mess indeed![1]

We will briefly look at four ways of coping with this dilemma. These four options hinge on our answers to three critical questions:

Is it wrong to manufacture and possess nuclear weapons?
Is it wrong to threaten to use nuclear weapons?
Is it wrong to use nuclear weapons?

Snarl and Bomb

Snarl and Bomb advocates believe the only way to protect freedom is to make terrible nuclear threats and to be willing to carry them out if necessary. Some in this camp think that only small nuclear weapons should be used in selected ways against strictly military targets. The purpose of making bad threats and intending to carry them out is to save people, prevent war, and protect freedom. But what if the threats fail? Millions of innocent civilians would certainly be destroyed. The official policy of both the U.S. and the USSR appears to be Snarl and Bomb.

Snarl and Bluff

Snarl and Bluff folks argue that in order to prevent nuclear war it's okay to threaten to use nuclear weapons as long as you just bluff and never actually intend to use them. The only purpose of nuclear weapons is to make sure that nuclear weapons are never used. This way you can have your cake and eat it—you prevent war and you don't need to explode any weapons. There are some difficulties with bluffing. It involves lying both to the enemy and to your own military people. You must deceive both of them into thinking that you really mean it when you don't. Is it permissible to lie in order to avoid murdering millions? To make believable bluffs that aren't a joke, real weapons must be ready to blast off at any minute. What if they go off by accident or because of an error? And what if your enemy calls your bluff? What about the enormous cost in dollars and terror to your own people of keeping your nuclear guns loaded?

Hold and Bluff

Countries could simply hold nuclear weapons without threatening to use them. This policy according to some military thinkers would be enough to scare off attackers. The simple knowledge that country X has the bomb might frighten away any aggressor even if country X never made a nuclear snarl. Country X could keep everyone guessing by saying nothing about when or how it would get the big stick out of the closet. Such a snarless policy should lower the "ante" and be less likely to scare other countries into a frenzy of bomb building.

Never Ever

The most radical ethical solution is simply to say that nuclear weapons are immoral, period! Such a Never Ever position contends that if it's morally wrong to use a nuclear weapon, then it's also wrong to threaten to use one, to hold one, and to make one. In other words, it's not morally tolerable to possess something that is wrong to use. Unlike a knife that can be used to peel an apple or to kill someone, nuclear weapons can only be used to make threats of destruction or to destroy. Neither of these purposes can be reconciled with basic Christian values of love, peace, reconciliation, and forgiveness. Simply building a bomb makes its use possible and thinkable even if it's carefully handled. Since exploding it accidentally or deliberately could bring terrible destruction, which might trigger even worse terror, the Never Ever folks say it's immoral to build a bomb in the first place. The fact that the nuclear bomb *is*, makes its use possible, thinkable, and more importantly it initiates new cycles of violent threats from opponents.

Christian pacifists condemn exploding nuclear weapons, but they are divided on whether it's okay to snarl and bluff with them. When we make difficult decisions, we usually consider moral principles as well as the consequences of what we do. Some folks stress the rules and apply them across the board, while others focus on what would happen. The Never Ever nuclear pacifists stress the moral principle of nonresistant love and say that even building a nuclear bomb contradicts the very notion of Christian love and compassion. The Never Ever people insist on the rule of nonresistant love regardless of what might happen *even* if dismantling nuclear bombs might ignite a war.

Snarl and Bluff Christian pacifists stress the consequences of the act more than the rule of love. Snarling and bluffing in order to prevent war is better than burying bombs and risking a nuclear war. According to these folks it's better to do a little bad (snarling) for good consequences than make a terrible nuclear mess by doing something good (disarming). According to this position Christians should be willing to *tolerate* the possession of nuclear weapons even though they don't "approve" of them. And thus Christians should be willing to support a government policy of deterrence.

It should be obvious by now that I'm a Never Ever nuclear pacifist. If that's not clear, you haven't been paying attention! I am a Never Ever nuclear pacifist for several reasons:

1. The biblical perspective stresses the application of moral principles over consequences. Christian faith asserts

that intentions are the same as acts. Desires, intentions, plans, *and* behavior are linked together in an inseparable chain of morality. Moreover, the deception required in bluffing is not a Christian virtue.

2. Neither the consequences of making nuclear threats nor the consequences of nuclear disarmament are known or predictable.

3. The underlying assumptions of nuclear threats are incompatible with Christian values.

4. Nuclear threats may not actually work as well as we think they do.

5. The consequences of making nuclear threats are already affecting us today in spiritual, economic, and psychological ways.

We'll look at each of these issues, paying special attention to the consequences of nuclear threats that already touch us since these are often skipped over in discussions of nuclear pacifism.

IS TOLERANCE THE SAME AS APPROVAL?

It's not too hard to call nuclear war sin. But what about possessing nuclear weapons? Can Christians tolerate holding nuclear weapons if their purpose is to prevent war? Ted Koontz points out that since nuclear war happens so fast there's no time for ethical reflection after it starts. Thus we need to think through the ethical issues carefully *before* the war begins. Our moral reflection must focus on the *plans* to fight and prevent nuclear war. According to Lloyd J. Averill, we must set the moral limits *before* nuclear war begins. We will hardly have the time or communication facilities to do it after the first mushroom cloud rises. And if the decisive moment comes, average people won't be asked, and the Senate and House won't have time to vote. The only chance we have to speak is ahead of time. We must decide in advance how much power to give our leaders, and in Averill's words "tolerate no more than we are prepared to approve."[2]

Is there a difference between *tolerating* and *approving* nuclear weapons? Can the church tolerate the possession of nuclear bombs if governments are seriously working at arms control and initiating steps of disarmament? If governments don't slow down the race and begin disarmament, should moral toleration turn to disapproval? Some church leaders propose tolerating nuclear weapons for a short time because in their view holding the weapons might prevent war while taking steps toward disarmament could trigger a war.[3] Even if we won't bless nuclear weapons, will we put up with them until a better solution is found? Such thinking is based on the shaky assumption that gradual nuclear disarmament is more risky than continuing the arms race.

Does tolerating nuclear weapons give advance approval to their use? To tolerate them makes their use thinkable and possible. A biblical perspective leaves little room for tolerating nuclear weapons. Manufacturing and holding nuclear weapons, as well as preparations to fight a nuclear war, cannot be morally divorced from nuclear war itself. Jim Wallis puts it this way:

> The willingness to produce, possess and use nuclear weapons must be named for what it is: the chief manifestation of human sinfulness and rebellion against God in our age.[4]

Why can't we divorce preparations for nuclear war from the war itself? Jesus said we can't divorce our intentions from our actions. Our thoughts are real and they lead to acts. The Scripture suggests that looking lustfully at another person is the same as committing adultery; hating a brother is as bad as killing him (Matthew 5:22, 27-28).

The act simply reveals what's *already* in one's heart. Nuclear war would merely unwrap the billions of tons of hate that are already packaged up in our collective hearts. Nuclear war is not a "maybe" down the road sometime; it's already here *now* in our spirit when we support the holding of nuclear weapons. Hatred is already here *now* in our intentions if we support the possession of nuclear weapons. The Bible links attitudes and behavior together. Christians can not neatly assume that the sin only begins when the first bomb explodes. The sin comes when we decide to begin building a bomb in the first place.

As in most fuzzy ethical issues, the question here is where to draw the line. Do we draw the line at manufacturing, holding, threatening, or using nuclear weapons? Moral acceptance of nuclear weapons at any point is a serious compromise of basic Christian values and allows a gradual moral slide toward nuclear war. The powerful forces of government will always stretch and strain at the church's moral reins. If Christians agree to tolerate nuclear weapons, the moral constraints will gradually be stretched in the direction of their use. Once the church gives consent to the existence of nuclear weapons, we have little moral control over their use. As we have seen, technological rather than moral concerns shape military policies and will likely determine how nuclear weapons are used. One of the reasons we have gotten so close to the nuclear brink is that the church has quietly tolerated nuclear weapons for so long.

Nuclear disarmament is the logical policy outcome of a Never Ever ethical position. Obviously that will not happen overnight! If we were starting over in a new world without nuclear weapons, a Never Ever pacifism would mean not making nuclear bombs in the first place. But since we don't live in such a world, we need to start from where we are. So while the long-term goal is the abolition of nuclear weapons, we could begin with small and gradual steps of nuclear disarmament. And while it may take years to reach the goal, such a turn would be a major shift from current U.S. and Soviet policies.

RISKY RESULTS

A second reason for rejecting nuclear weapons is the risks they nurture. Christian pacifists who are nuclear bluffers emphasize the positive, long-term results of making nuclear threats. Nuclear threats and bluffs, while not nice, are intended to prevent nuclear war. A Never Ever approach, the bluffers point out, might trigger a horrendous nuclear war. The flaw in this argument is that No One really knows what the consequences will be *either* way. We can't predict what would happen if one or both superpowers took gradual steps toward nuclear disarmament. And no one knows what will happen if one or both sides keep on snarling.

The policy of deterrence certainly has not slowed down the arms race. Making threats and bluffs encourages the enemy to do the same thing and only stimulates the arms race. The risk of war by mistake or sabotage will be real as long as the bombs are around. Christians who condone threats and bluffs also have no way of knowing whether the government is bluffing. We can hope the president is bluffing, and we can hope he will never give the ultimate command, but we never really know. It's entirely possible that threats and bluffs could fail and directly or indirectly trigger a nuclear war.

If the U.S. slowly removed half of its nuclear bombs over several years, what's the worst that could happen? We'd still have plenty of bombs to blow the Soviets to bits. Why would the Soviets launch a direct attack on the U.S. mainland? What would they gain by blowing us up? On the other hand, gradual nuclear disarmament might send signals of weakness that invite attack or reduce the nation's leverage at the bargaining table. One of the rules of nuclear war is that the more secure your opponent feels, the less likely he will strike you. The more you threaten the other guy, the more likely he'll attack you. Gradual U.S. steps toward nuclear disarmament might make the Soviets feel more secure and might make them less likely to attack. Or such steps might encourage the Soviets to act more boldly.

The choice is not simply between speeding up the arms race and immediate nuclear disarmament. There is a continuum of choices ranging from immediate nuclear disarmament to preparations for fighting and winning a nuclear war. But it's impossible to predict the risks of any of these options. Bluffers usually assume that the risks from gradual disarmament would be much worse than the risks from threats. No one knows! The risks that come with nuclear threats might be just as bad, if not worse, than those accompanying gradual disarmament. If that's true, then tolerating nuclear weapons might turn out to be a choice of the greater evil. Since it's hard to estimate which is the greater evil, we're caught in a dilemma.

Someone has said that if we're going to go down burning in the fiery furnace either way, we should decide whether
we want to burn in the name of peace or in the name of war.
If we have to gamble, why not gamble on goodwill instead of
threats? Certainly the Christian perspective calls for heaping love on threats rather than making bigger and bigger
threats.

EIGHT PROBLEMS OF DETERRENCE

A third reason for not tolerating nuclear weapons lies in
the conflict between nuclear threats and Christian values. In
addition, deterrence has some weak spots of its own.[5] We'll
consider eight "threats" to nuclear deterrence:

1. Deterrence is based on the manipulation and ex-
ploitation of fear. It hopes to avoid violence by threatening to
apply it in horrendous ways. Deterrence as practiced by the
superpowers assumes that massive threats to destroy the
enemy are the primary way of preventing war. Fear is not a
Christian tool.

2. While the threat of punishment for aggression
doesn't necessarily belittle others, nuclear threats tend to
degrade the opponent to subhuman levels by assuming that
the enemy only responds to the promise of brutal violence. It
dehumanizes the enemy, simplifies his intentions, appeals
to his lower motives, and attributes to him the worst possible
traits. They are "madmen who only understand violence.'
This is certainly not the way to love enemies.

3. Deterrence depends on a funny contradiction
between terror and rationality. We want to scare the tar out
of the Soviets, and at the same time we say our own survival
depends on their rational choice not to use nuclear bombs.
We say they are ruthless aggressors, madmen; yet we place
our future on their coolheaded calculations. For deterrence
to work we need opponents who are smart enough to realize
the consequences of being international outlaws. But what
about a maniacal dictator? Would nuclear threats work with
him?

4. Deterrence cultivates salvation by threat. If we really
believe that our threats save us, then we pay little attention

to serious efforts at reconciliation and mediation. We are experts at making threats but are amateurs when it comes to peace offers. Deterrence assumes that violence or the threat of violence is the primary way that nations solve problems. Christians specialize in peace offers, not threats.

5. Deterrence blocks serious disarmament efforts because it requires a balance of bombs between the parties. Any moves toward gradual disarmament are seen as rocking the present stability. Yet by its very nature the system of threat spawns all sorts of nuclear weapons. The whole idea of deterrence is to scare your opponents. To do a good scare job you want as many weapons as possible. So in the long run, deterrence feeds the growth of bombs and prevents serious gestures of disarmament.

6. The most dangerous assumption behind deterrence is that nuclear weapons will never be used. Of the thousands of arms races historically, only a few have not ended in war. Will the nuclear arms race be different? If Japan had possessed nuclear bombs in World War II, would that have prevented the destruction of Hiroshima and Nagasaki? The supporters of deterrence abhor nuclear war, yet their whole argument rests on the fine thread of hope that nuclear bombs will never be used. Is the chance of nuclear weapons ever being used greater if we threaten to use them or if we vow never to use them? Even common sense suggests that if we play with nuclear matches long enough we will eventually strike up a war.

7. If deterrence fails, millions of ordinary Americans or Soviets who had little responsibility in waging the war will be killed by the bombs. Average citizens probably would not want their leaders to start a nuclear war, nor could they prevent them from starting it—yet deterrence will kill millions of such innocent people if it fails.

8. Deterrence only works if you act like you really mean it. It must be credible enough to actually scare the enemy. You can't act as though you're just teasing. The U.S. must convince its own generals and the USSR that it really means it. Military leaders are caught in the dilemma of not wanting to use nuclear weapons, but acting as though they certainly

will. The danger is that either side's generals or leaders might believe that they really mean it and might act that way in a moment of crisis and push the button. Deterrence keeps the weapons in place that make a nuclear war thinkable.

Alan Geyer sums up his critique of deterrence by saying,

> Ultimately the issue is not what kind of nuclear weapons we need, nor how many of them: It is how best to overcome the demonic myth that our security requires nuclear arms at all . . . it must open up a third way which recognizes that weapons of mass destruction are massively irrelevant.[6]

DO NUCLEAR THREATS WORK?

One reason for continuing the present policy of nuclear threats is the notion that deterrence works. By threatening the Soviets with terrible revenge, we have prevented nuclear war for nearly forty years. Or have we? We've made it safely through these years, but no one knows why! There is simply no way to prove that nuclear threats have prevented nuclear war. Even *if* deterrence worked, we don't know why it worked, and we don't know whether it will work in the future. Frankly, we don't know what secured our safe passage. Was it deterrence, God's grace, economic factors, lack of interest in fighting, or the uncertain effects of nuclear war? Probably it was a combination of these and other factors. If nuclear weapons have been our salvation, we don't know why or how they did it. We don't know why the superpowers haven't attacked each other. Was it because they never intended to? Were they afraid of each other's weapons? Or did other factors stop them?

It's possible that nuclear weapons have prevented a conventional war on the scale of World War II, but again we don't know for sure. Nuclear weapons did not spare the U.S. from humiliating defeats. They did not stop Soviet expansion in Hungary, Cuba, Vietnam, Czechoslovakia, or Afghanistan. Nuclear deterrence didn't prevent a humiliating American retreat from Iran. Nuclear weapons have not eliminated small conventional wars, which have killed millions since 1945. That nuclear weapons haven't been used to squash these events is an honorable testimony to our reluctance to use them. But then what good are they? If we can't justify using them to stop small wars and if we say we would never actually use them for massive destruction, what good are they? Are they only good for building up our diplomatic muscle and our national prestige?

There is one way that deterrence does work. The nations that threaten to use nuclear weapons become the most likely targets of nuclear war themselves. The weapons designed to prevent attack are the same ones that might provoke an attack aimed directly at them. This is the frightening way in which deterrence does work. And so we must not only ask whether deterrence works, but we must also ask what kind of world deterrence has created for us. Is this the kind of world we want to pass on to our children?

TERRORIZING OURSELVES

There is an even more compelling reason why nuclear weapons cannot be morally tolerated. On what moral or ethical basis can we justify holding ourselves, our children, and other citizens of the world hostage to terror? Such terror vaporizes hope in young children and adults alike. Do we understand what we are doing? Do we understand what it means to yank the rug of hope out from under an entire society? Stifling hope kills the spirit of a people.

Smothering Hope

As we watched a television news report on the danger of nuclear war, my young daughter with anger and fear in her eyes said, "Dad, you're lucky because you're an old man [I'm only 36], and you're soon gonna die. It's not fair because I probably won't even get to live my life because of this terrible stuff." John Mack, in a study of the psychological effects of nuclear war on children, says, "Children are aware of the threat and live in fear of it."[7] Some parents report children asking, "Why should we work hard to make good grades in school if the world's going to blow up?" This emotional load is heavy enough for adults to carry, let alone young children. We can try to insulate them from the threat, but they soon catch on. When young children think their 36-year-old parents are lucky because they will soon die, we have smothered the spirit of hope—an atrocity of the highest order.

Physicians report counseling young married couples who are afraid to raise children in a world filled with nuclear bombs. Recently, a 45-year-old college student, after reading extensively about the arms race, stopped by my office and pleaded, "Just tell me one word of hope, just one word of hope. I need to hear it so bad." What have we done? What have we done by smothering hope? Have we not already begun destroying life?

A Jittery World

Living a few miles from Three Mile Island, we occasionally hear special emergency sirens being tested—often without warning. More than once, some of my friends have jerked up at the sound of the first blast, asking, "Is this an attack?" A neighbor recently woke up in the middle of a thunderstorm, thinking it was a nuclear attack. After reviewing data from a study of "psychological fallout" among the bomb generation born between 1940 and 1950, Michael Carey says, "We have created a world of victims who think no matter where you are, it [the bomb] will get you."[8]

When youngsters are afraid they won't live to grow up, when adults hesitate to have children, and when folks jump at the sound of a siren, we are in danger of extinguishing hope. We are stamping it out. The threat of the bomb has injected death into the nervous system of our society. Smashing hope strangles life itself. Is there any greater crime than gagging the spirit of life, crushing joy, and smothering hope? What does it mean to raise children in a jittery world?

Stifling hope breeds an ethic of "eat, drink and be merry for tomorrow we die." No wonder everyone wants an immediate "high" from sex, alcohol, drugs, or leisure. Why is it that in the last decade we saw an enormous interest in death and dying? Books, courses, and seminars galore on death and dying greet us everywhere. Haven't we known "how" to die for many centuries? Why are we suddenly so preoccupied with dying? Has the bomb's terror already invaded our subconscious in subtle ways? Could it be that our subconscious fear of the bomb's threat oozes out as concern for our own individual deaths? It's impossible to say for sure, but I suspect there's a connection.

Dying Now

Even if a bomb never explodes, people have already begun to die. The spirit of hope has already been scorched. The dreams of many are already tortured. This is not the first time the shadow of death has hovered over a society. People have coped with extermination before. But we are the first generation ever to live with images of massive social suicide haunting our minds. We are the first generation capable of annihilating our civilization and God's garden.

There's simply no way of knowing how this nuclear blight will affect the soul of our society in the long run. The threat of nuclear war, like a terminal cancer, eats away at life-giving hope. We can't see it and we can't always feel it, but it's there and it nibbles away at our souls.

On the surface we're a nation of shiny missiles, sleek submarines, and powerful bombs, but underneath all the sophisticated weaponry our spirit is wilting. We're like a shiny red apple that's rotting at the core.

The prophet Isaiah said that when there's no vision the people perish. What happens when the vision is a nuclear mushroom cloud? What happens when images of human suicide dominate the landscape of our minds? Do you hear? Do you understand? People are already dying. We are choking the spirit of life now. And what the murder of hope will mean over the decades remains unknown. It's for this reason, because of the funeral that's already in progress, that we cannot tolerate nuclear weapons.

WRECKING THE ECONOMY

Nuclear weapons account for about 15 percent of the military budget, but since it's difficult to isolate their economic effects, we will look at the economic impact of the entire U.S. military budget. Conventional wars in the past usually lasted several years, giving nations time to build up their military production gradually. Nuclear wars last a matter of minutes and hours. Even large conventional wars today would be brief, leaving little time to crank up the production of arms. This means that nuclear countries must have all their guns loaded all the time. Their military production must stay at full tilt, resulting in a permanent wartime economy, which places a heavy burden on our pocketbooks. If nuclear weapons were abolished, the cost of conventional weapons would probably increase if the U.S. wanted to maintain a large military presence around the world.

According to MIT economist Lester Thurow, the present U.S. military buildup will wreck the economy.[9] There is evidence that Soviet military expenditures are also grinding down their economy. President Reagan's Council of Economic Advisors reported that the Pentagon's enormous bite will have "adverse economic effects" on the U.S. economy. Contrary to the popular myth that military spending is good medicine for the economy, recent studies show that it's a virus which produces economic ills. How does military spending wreck the economy?

Eating Bombs

Although not the only cause, high military spending does jack up inflation. We can't eat bombs, wear missiles, or drive submarines. When we work, we produce goods or services that can be sold in the marketplace. We then take our wages and use them to buy products that we need. The normal balance between the demand for goods and the supply of goods is disrupted by high military spending because military production doesn't put toasters and basketballs on the shelves of Sears and Roebuck. Tanks and missiles sit on Pentagon "storage shelves" until they're obsolete. Massive amounts of natural, industrial, and human resources are sunk into products that no one can buy. At the same time, employees working in the armed forces and for military contractors get wages which increase their purchasing power. So in the end there's more demand chasing fewer goods, which means higher prices and more inflation. A *Wall*

Street Journal article, "Burning Up $1 Trillion," capsulizes the burden of military spending:

> Defense spending, in this sense, is the worst kind of government outlay, since it eats up materials and other resources that otherwise would be used to produce consumer goods.[10]

Military spending gobbles up raw materials, technicians, factories, and capital which would normally be used to manufacture cars and dryers. Since military contracts often work on a cost-plus basis, they can pay almost anything to get what they need. This forces private industry to pay more for employees and raw materials, and this in turn inflates prices for all of us.

Choking Production

Intensive military production chokes the industrial output of our economy. A recent study of thirteen major industrialized countries found that those spending a smaller share of their economic output on the military generally experienced faster growth, greater investment, and higher productivity.[11] The countries with the heaviest military burdens had stagnating economies and lower production. Japan is an example of what happens when a country devotes its full attention to industrial growth and spends a small amount for defense. Datsun and Sony threaten our economic health as much as Soviet missiles. U.S. production has been dropping, and some of that slump is a result of using billions of dollars, millions of people, and huge amounts of raw materials to make bombs that collect dust on Pentagon shelves.

Uncle Sam's Red Ink

Military spending is one source of the growing red ink in Uncle Sam's budget since World War II. The national debt has been steadily growing, with Uncle Sam going into the hole nearly 100 billion dollars a year. President Reagan cut taxes, stepped up military spending, and ended up with a very red budget. Like most of us, when Uncle Sam spends more than he takes in, he goes into the hole. The huge jump in military spending pushes the nation further into debt and makes life worse for all of us. When Uncle Sam loses money, he has to borrow it from banks, and that drives up interest rates and leaves less money for the rest of us to borrow. The U.S. has been borrowing almost $1 billion a week for years. High levels of military spending tighten the economic screws on all of us.

Stealing Jobs

A final zinger in all of this is the theft of jobs. Contrary to rumor, military spending doesn't increase jobs. But if we cut military spending, wouldn't some people lose their jobs? Certainly, military spending does provide jobs, and those jobs would be lost, depending on where the cuts hit. However, investing money in civilian industry produces *more* jobs than military spending. In fact, Marion Anderson has shown that over several years every time the military budget went up $1 billion, 10,000 jobs disappeared in the U.S.[12]

For example, Anderson shows that for every $1 billion spent on the MX missile 17,000 people will be hired, but the same $1 billion spent in other industries would produce many more jobs: apparel manufacture (28,000 jobs), hospitals (48,000), education (62,000), and retail trade (65,000). According to Anderson, $1 billion spent on civilian industry produces about 27,000 jobs, whereas $1 billion spent on military production creates 18,000 jobs. Thus on the average, across all types of military and civilian spending, about 9,000 to 10,000 jobs are lost for each $1 billion jump in military spending.

Military spending steals jobs in two ways. It requires highly automated technology and very expensive raw materials. Money is used to buy sophisticated production equipment rather than to hire people. Military production generally requires more machines than people in contrast to civilian production. Second, the goods and services produced in the civilian sector have a "ripple effect"; their sale produces more jobs. Unlike cars, bombs don't make additional jobs for "bomb dealers," "bomb mechanics," "bomb attendants," or "used bomb dealers." Certainly some "ripple" jobs are created by military production, but not nearly as many as in civilian production.

Wassily Leontif, Nobel prizewinning economist, summarizes the economic drag of military spending:

> Huge jumps in military spending will mean higher inflation, a worsening balance of payment gaps, a drain on productive investment, soaring interest rates, a debased currency and in the long run more unemployment.[13]

Military spending helps a small number of companies and their employees, but it bites the rest of us severely. About 300 of the nation's 435 congressional districts get the short end of the Pentagon stick each year.[14] They pay more in taxes than they receive back in contracts or wages. Several studies have shown that the average American would be much better off financially if military jobs were converted to civilian enterprises.[15] Growing military expenditures drag down the economy and make the U.S. a weaker and poorer nation. Senator Chiles of Florida, in response to Pentagon requests for more money, asked, "What good is a strong national defense if we don't have a strong economy to defend?"

Robbing the Poor

In 1953, President Eisenhower—sounding like a biblical prophet—said, "Every gun that is made, every warship launched, every rocket fired signifies in the final sense a theft from those who hunger and are not fed, those who are cold and are not clothed." That robbery is taking place now. The poor get shot from both sides in this battle. With the federal budget transfers from human services to deadly services, millions of low-income elderly, handicapped, and disadvantaged people lost financial support. There is mounting evidence that Reaganomics favors the rich and hurts the poor. Few tidbits are trickling down from the rich. I'm not an advocate of government handouts to freeloaders, but there is a place for helping those who through misfortune or a poor choice of mothers are caught in a jam. Federal aid could be

218,   *Facing Nuclear War*

given to churches or private social agencies, which might administer it more efficiently than the government. Aiding the rich through tax breaks and yanking federal supports out from under the working poor for the sake of increased military spending is a travesty of justice that God will not wink at.

Besides having aid snatched away from them, the poor are also the first to feel the bite of inflation. They are the first fired as jobs disappear. They are the first to do without as prices rise. They are the ones who really get hit over the head in a recession because they have few savings, little income cushion, and shaky jobs. After leveling off, the poverty rate is now climbing again in the U.S.[16]

As federal cutbacks in social services hit the road, there was a rapid jump in the number of street people in American cities. These are beggars who live and die on the street. These are the ones who slipped through the president's "safety net." Physicians report a rise in child malnutrition. The poor, the disabled, the children, the elderly, and the unemployed— these bear the painful brunt of the outrageous increases in military spending. Even if the bomb never explodes, people are dying now. They are hungry now. They are jobless now. The bomb's effects have already hit us. Our commitment to the bomb is already killing people in a literal sense. Refusing to budge on his 1983 defense budget when it produced red ink, President Reagan said,

> I must accept a large deficit if that is what it takes to buy peace for the rest of the century.

The president is buying peace. The price is high. The poor are paying for it. They are dying for it now. What kind of peace is this that economically strangles the innocent? It is actually expensive and risky hate, and we are all paying for it now.

STARVING THE WORLD'S POOR

We live in a global military prison. Buying and selling weapons is a spreading and contagious disease. Virtually all the developing counries are plunging their scarce resources into arms at the prodding of the giants and at the expense of dire poverty among their own people. Guns, tanks, and bombs are seen as the solution to most problems. The blossoming world arms budget of at least $550 billion annually will only breed more violence and trample the world's poor deeper into the dust of poverty.

The numbers tell their own story without comment.[17]

Global arms budgets exceed $550 billion a year (nearly $1.5 billion a day), which is equal to the annual income of the poorest half of the world's population. About $100 billion of this annual military budget goes for nuclear weapons.

Eight hundred million people live in dire poverty.

Five hundred million are starving or hungry and a billion more suffer from malnutrition.

The number of starving and severely malnourished may double to one billion by the year 2000.

The 35 poorest nations, with one fourth of the world's population, hold a wretched 3 percent of the wealth.

The 140 developing nations hold 75 percent of the world's population and 20 percent of its wealth.

The world spends 2,300 times more for military activities than for international peacekeeping.

Between 1960 and 1980 the number of armed troops in developing countries rose from 8.7 to 15.1 million.

Throughout the world, military budgets are double the size of food growing budgets and five times greater than housing expenses.

Between 1960 and 1980 the military budgets of the developed nations increased by $320 billion, fourteen times higher than their foreign economic aid.

In August 1981 the Reagan administration withdrew $28 million in foreign aid from twelve poor countries.

The Soviet Union has the worst record of foreign aid assistance among the high military spenders.

The U.S. military budget in 1982 was about $200 billion, while foreign economic aid totaled about $8.2 billion.

Military spending is widening the great divide between north and south in the world. Figure 7.1 shows some of the gaps.

	Developed Countries	Developing Countries
Population	1.1 Billion	3.4 Billion
GNP per Person	$6,468	$597
Life Expectancy	72 Years	56 Years
Literacy Rate	99%	52%
Educational Expenses per Person	$286	$18
Military Expenses per Person	$300	$29
Public Health Expenses per Person	$199	$6.50

SOURCE: Overseas Development Council, reported in *Newsweek*, October 26, 1981.

Figure 7.1. The Great Divide

In his introduction to the 1980 report of the Independent Commission on International Development, former West German Chancellor Willy Brandt made the connection between world militarism and international development.

1. The military expenditure of only half a day would suffice to finance the whole malaria eradication programme of the World Health Organization. Even less would be needed to conquer riverblindness, which is still the scourge of millions.

2. A modern tank costs about $1 million. That amount could improve storage facilities for 100,000 tons of rice and thus save 4,000 tons or more annually. The same sum could provide 1,000 classrooms for 30,000 children—just one tank's worth.

3. For the price of one jet fighter ($20 million) one could set up about 40,000 village pharmacies.

4. One-half of one percent of one year's world military expenditure would pay for all the farm equipment needed to increase food production to the level of self-sufficiency in the world's food-deficit countries by 1990.[18]

We can dream about arms merchants feeding the world's poor, with their annual $550 billion, but it probably won't happen. Throwing money at world poverty won't take it away. A deliberate and radical shift from military aid to long-term economic development is the only possible hope for world misery, and that is probably hoping against hope. What can Christians do? What does it mean to be a member of the family of a God who loves the whole world? Many of our brothers and sisters in Christ are on the other side of the divide. We can at least begin to realize that the military policies of our governments are robbing the world's poor now. Of course there's no magic guarantee that a drop in military spending would increase foreign aid.

Converting the world garden into a prison and allowing millions of deaths from starvation must be an outrage to a God who loves the whole world. National commitments to militarism are killing people *now* around the world, even if triggers are never pulled. We can live simply ourselves and support church and government programs of international aid. That's not much, but it's better than blindly condoning national policies of militarism.

A SHADOW OVER THE CROSS

The mushroom cloud casts a gloomy shadow over the cross. A Japanese journalist was asked, "Why after so many years of missionary work, especially by large numbers of Americans after World War II, have only about one half of one percent of the Japanese become Christian?" After giving several reasons the journalist responded, "There is another factor; for many of us the cloud of the atom bomb still hides the cross of Christ."[19]

One of the sad ironies of modern history is that "Christian" America has led the nuclear arms race. Uncle Sam, an international symbol of Christian faith, is also the mightiest merchant of military force. America sings "God Bless America," imprints "In God We Trust" on its coins, pledges to be "one nation under God," and holds presidential prayer breakfasts. American presidents describe the nation's "mission" and worldwide "destiny" with religious words. Flag and cross blend together in a common patriotic fabric. What's American is Christian and what's Christian is American—at least that's the impression touted at home and abroad. In a recent Christmas message President Reagan reminded the world that America is a nation that celebrates the birth of the babe in the Bethlehem manger. Keeping tradition with other presidents, Mr. Reagan in his 1982 State of the Union address described the special destiny of the United States:

I have always believed that this hemisphere was a special place with a special destiny. I believe we are destined to be the beacon of hope for all mankind. With God's help we can make it so.[20]

How is it that the one nation who calls itself Christian became the chief steward of the atomic bomb? The religious icing on the American cake gives the impression that even God himself smiles warmly on the bomb. What greater profanity, what greater distortion of the gospel, can there be than to stamp the blessing of a loving God on the bomb?

The bomb shadows the cross in two ways. The American people are deceived into believing that the bomb goes hand in hand with Christian faith. And the world perceives that even Christian nations will do the unthinkable if they have to. Calling itself Christian out of the one side of its mouth and threatening to use the bomb out of the other side, America tells itself and the world community that

the Christian faith supports the threat of nuclear violence,
the Christian God blesses the holding of nuclear arms, and
the Christian way is peace through military might.

The dark shadows of these messages blur the cross. Who will embrace such a gospel? What kind of good news is this? Is the biblical God really a God of love? With its seal of approval on the bomb, the cross loses its call of radical obedience to God's will. It becomes religious window dressing.

LET'S MEET HALFWAY

I've contended that preparation and planning for nuclear war cannot be morally divorced from war itself. Terrorizing ourselves, robbing the poor, blurring the cross, and threatening to use nuclear weapons can not be justified by the Bible. As a Christian I cannot condone the production, holding, or use of nuclear weapons. If it's morally wrong to use a nuclear weapon, is it not also wrong to build one? The moment we begin building a bomb we have crossed the threshold from the unthinkable to the thinkable. Even though we say that holding the bomb is necessary to prevent war, we open the door to its possible use the instant construction begins. Supporting deterrence pinches us three ways: it compromises basic Christian values, it may fail and destroy us, and it's already blighting our lives today. Christians who support nuclear deterrence today confer God's blessing on military solutions in the same way that the just-war theologians did in the past.

As Christians of all stripes, can we join together in a unified witness of nuclear pacifism? Can we agree that on the basis of our common faith in Jesus Christ we renounce the making, holding, and use of nuclear bombs? Can we meet each other halfway at this middle ground? Can Never Ever and Sometimes Maybe folks join in a common chorus of Never Nuclear?

Never Ever Christians will need to stretch their Christian pacifism a bit. Historically, conscientious objectors have been trigger refusers. Too often their emphasis has focused on trigger refusing instead of on peacemaking. Individuals, we say, must own the moral responsibility for what happens when they pull a trigger. Are we not just as morally responsible if we endorse government policies which lead toward nuclear war? The urgent question for the Christian pacifist today is not "Will you pull the trigger?" but "Will you quietly condone government policies based on nuclear threats?" In a democracy blessed with free speech, silence is a form of consent. Christian pacifists who refuse to pull triggers and who say nothing about nuclear weapons *are* silently supporting the arms buildup. Such quiet Never Ever folks must bear some of the moral responsibility of the ugly effects of the arms race which are already among us. And silent trigger refusers will also hold part of the moral buck if nuclear mushroom clouds ever rise again.

And what about Sometimes Maybe Christians, who believe that the followers of Christ can participate in military force in certain situations? Can you also stretch a bit and agree that no circumstances could ever justify holding and using nuclear weapons? Can you also come halfway and be Never Nuclear—against possessing and using nuclear weapons? Can you affirm that the lordship of Jesus Christ makes these hideous instruments of destruction intolerable?

In a 1981 papal message Pope John Paul II called for an "immediate reduction and ultimate elimination of all nuclear weapons undertaken simultaneously by all parties through specific agreements."[21] Approximately thirty U.S. Roman Catholic bishops in early 1982 signed a statement declaring that it was wrong to possess nuclear weapons.[22]

Regardless of our brand of Christian faith and religious background, isn't it about time that we come together on nuclear pacifism? Can we stop bickering over other differences and agree, on the basis of our confession that Jesus Christ is Lord, that we can not support making, possessing, or using nuclear bombs

> that destroy millions of humans indiscriminately,
> that twist God's creation permanently,
> that contaminate the genetic pool of future generations,
> that devastate thousands of acres of land and property,
> that threaten the existence of civilized life itself,
> that leave unthinkable horror, terror, and suffering.

Can we forge a consensus around nuclear pacifism and say that making such weapons is immoral, intolerable, and inconsistent with Christian faith?

TWO HATS

Christians wear two hats. We are Christians and we also are citizens. Sometimes we get squeezed between the demands of God and the demands of Caesar. Nuclear weapons cannot be justified by the standards of Christian faith. Even Christians who justify making nuclear threats usually agree that nuclear weapons should be abolished when evaluated *solely* by the principles of Christian faith.

On the one hand, as followers of a man who didn't retaliate in the face of the cross, Christians can hardly tolerate nuclear weapons. Yet on the other hand, we don't want to be irresponsible citizens who botch up the security of our fellow citizens while sincerely trying to do good. So we tend to compromise by saying that although we can't *as Christians* approve of nuclear weapons, we can tolerate them *as citizens* since a lot of earthly wisdom seems to think they are necessary. Or we may say that as Christians we won't condemn the government's right to hold nuclear weapons, but we cannot conscientiously join the armed services and help to keep the weapons in place. But what if as citizens we think that threatening to use nuclear weapons is a risky policy that might eventually lead to nuclear war? Do Christians have the right to impose their views on the government? Can we tell government what to do?

In a democracy or republic we participate in the government! We not only have the right, but we have the responsibility to contribute our opinions and insights. Voicing our opinions is not telling the government what to do; it is simply being the government. A representative government reflects the ideas of all kinds of people with all sorts of religious and political beliefs. The chief job of a democratic government is to develop middle-of-the-road policies that reflect the majority of public sentiments. Christians, as well as those of other persuasions, feed their beliefs into this process.

When Christians tolerate nuclear weapons, they are for all political purposes blessing the nuclear arms race. The government can go on its merry way and doesn't need to worry about the church since the church politely agrees to be quiet. If many American churches joined in the call for nuclear pacifism, they might at least pull government policies back toward the middle of the road even though the government would likely not adopt the churches' position.

Personally, from under my two hats I view the Christian/citizen tension this way:

1. As a Christian I cannot tolerate the making, possession, or use of nuclear weapons, and I call for them to be abolished. I say this publicly, pointing out that my opinion on this matter is shaped by my Christian values.

2. Through public witness I inform my legislators and fellow citizens of my opinions, and I suggest that a policy of

gradual nuclear disarmament would be a wise and prudent one for the nation to pursue. Such a process makes as much sense and may be as realistic and as safe as the present madness.

3. I realize that my voice is only one of many voices in a pluralistic society. I don't expect everyone to agree with me. I only hope that my voice will be joined by similar voices and that our chorus may help to slow down the nuclear race, and nudge it toward disarmament.

4. I'm fully aware that the outcome of my actions can't be predicted. I don't know what would happen if everyone took my position. I can only remind those who support holding nuclear weapons that they can't predict the outcome of nuclear deterrence either. And while my position may risk their lives, their position also may risk my life.

SOWING AND REAPING

The thread of sowing and reaping weaves its way through both the Scripture and our experience. We reap what we sow. We get what we pay for. Our sins do find us out. We can sweep evil under the rug, neglect our friends, waste our money, and cheat on deals and relationships. We can get away with it for a while. But someday, somehow, often in unexpected ways, the evil sprouts and comes back to haunt us. Eventually we pay for our foolishness. In the long run we do reap what we sow. And so it is with nuclear war.

If a nation invests its brightest minds in military research, spends enormous funds building weapons, whips its economy, feeds its natural resources to military factories, terrorizes people, and throws its best efforts into preparing for war—sometime, somehow, somewhere such a nation will probably be involved in a war unless it bankrupts itself financially first. In the biblical perspective those who sow hate reap war. Those who sow threats reap more threats. Those who build bombs are destroyed by bombs. Those who plant forgiveness reap hope. Those who plant understanding reap respect. Those who sow kindness reap peace. Be careful what you plant; it may sprout and grow up to greet you again somehow, somewhere, someday.

QUESTIONS

1. Is a government justified in making immoral threats in order to prevent war? Are nuclear weapons required in order to maintain international stability?
2. Is threatening to use nuclear weapons as immoral as actually using them?
3. Is there a moral distinction between approving and tolerating nuclear weapons?
4. Are there other ways that the preparation for nuclear war affects us now? How do you feel some of the effects?
5. What might be some long-term effects of smothering hope in a society?
6. Which of these statements comes closest to your own beliefs?
   a. It is a sin to build a nuclear weapon.
   b. Governments have the right to hold nuclear weapons.
   c. Governments may threaten to use nuclear weapons if they are only bluffing.
   d. Governments may use nuclear weapons if necessary, but Christians cannot participate in nuclear armed services.
   e. Governments may use nuclear weapons if necessary, and Christians may participate in nuclear armed services.
7. Can you support the idea of Christian nuclear pacifism? In what ways can you or can't you?
8. What kinds of nuclear military policies would decrease the risks of war?
9. Are we morally responsible for nuclear war when we quietly give consent to nuclear war policies?
10. In what ways is the bomb a shadow over the cross?

8

YOU CAN DO SOMETHING

A PEACEMAKING WITNESS

In exasperation we all beg to know, "What can I do?" This chapter focuses on the doing, but it's not a how-to manual. We all would like a bag of quick do-it-yourself gimmicks for local peacemaking. Specific ideas are helpful, but they're not as important as the conviction and courage to act.

Scenarios of nuclear havoc soon wear out. Yes, the church carries the treasure of peace in its bosom, but what in the world can we do about all of this? None of us wants a nuclear war. But what *can* we do? The fear that we really can't do anything and the dread that anything we do won't make a difference is the most deadly enemy of hope. It's probably true that we can't do much and what we do probably won't matter that much. But does that mean we do nothing?

The motivation and technique of our peacemaking witness is just as crucial as the act itself. Before looking at specific programs of action, we must carefully consider the roots of our witness. Why? How? What?

The Roots: The Fellowship of Peace

A witness is some bit of evidence that points to someone or something else. It's an act, a word, a symbol, or a gathering of people that stands for or represents something

228

else. Our peacemaking witness is a two-way street as it reflects the love of God and points others to Jesus Christ, the prince of peace. Christian peacemakers are living reflectors that transmit God's design for peace in the world now. And the process of peacemaking points to the lordship of Jesus Christ in the church and in the world today. We are not only witnesses *to* Jesus, but we are witnesses *with* Jesus as we join his peaceable kingdom today. Our acts break forth as signs of God's love and also as identification tags which confirm our membership in his grand peace movement.

Our witness is rooted in two things, in a personal fellowship with Jesus Christ through the Holy Spirit and in our fellowship with our brothers and sisters in the body of faith. The murmur of the Holy Spirit's voice along with the corporate prompting of fellow disciples inspires and shapes our peace ministry. Our witness in local settings will have its own unique character forged in the crucible of our relationship with Jesus Christ our lord; and flowing out of the deeper recesses of our spirits, the witness will be tempered and polished in our life together with brothers and sisters who also confess Jesus as Lord.

While we will often be tempted to throw in the towel and give up, our ministry will be rekindled and revitalized again and again in moments of worship, in sharing the Lord's supper, and in quiet words of affirmation spoken by other brothers and sisters who care.

And so our witness is squarely anchored in God's saving acts of holy history. The timid bits of witness we contribute may direct others to God's peacemaking activity and become the public markers of his peaceable kingdom today. Our witness is rooted in his program through the inner witness of the Holy Spirit as well as in the outer witness of brothers and sisters who share the Eucharist and words of counsel and good cheer.

The Reason: Setting the Record Straight

Many factors spur us to action in the face of nuclear war. We may act because we're scared. Fear propels us. We don't want to be fried alive in a nuclear furnace. If we live in a high-risk area, we might act out of personal interest to protect our property and the historical sites dear to our community. Or perhaps our action reflects genuine care for the welfare of millions of others who would melt if a nuclear inferno touched down on their homeland thousands of miles away.

These are all sensible reasons for acting to prevent nuclear war, but they bypass the taproot of Christian action. Why do we act even in the face of hopelessness? Why do we respond in the midst of despair? We act simply because we are called to be witnesses to the gospel of Jesus Christ. We are compelled to speak and tell the truth regardless of the consequences. For us it is a matter of spiritual integrity, an issue of spiritual honesty. Will we tell the truth in times like these? Will we clarify God's peaceful vision?

Our witness sets the record straight in two ways. It clarifies in the public record God's peaceful purposes in Jesus Christ and in the world. Our witness removes God's blessing from warmaking and announces that God's way is reverse fighting— heaping good on evil. In making this pronouncement we set the record straight so there's no doubt or question about God's peaceful purposes and means.

Second, we also set our own record straight. Our peacemaking witness is a personal declaration of exactly where we stand on the question of possessing nuclear weapons. It brings us out of the closet. We can't enjoy the luxury of being ambivalent, vague, or wishy-washy. It's easy to nod politely and say "Yes, that's interesting" to folks on both sides of this emotional issue and cover up our real convictions. A peacemaking witness of word or action strips off any polite cover-ups and reveals exactly where we are on the question. It sets our personal record straight so that there can be no doubt about our convictions. The reason for our witness is spiritual truth-telling—telling the truth about God's peaceful intents and erasing any ambiguity about our personal opinions.

A German news report of the docudrama *Holocaust* shown on television a few years ago described the reactions of German children as they learned for the first time of Hitler's atrocities against the Jews. The report said the children asked their parents two kinds of questions: "Where were you when this happened, and what did you say and do? Where were the churches and the Christians, and what did they say and do while this was going on?"[1]

Those same questions get to the heart of our spiritual integrity today. Moreover, compared to Germany, churches in the United States today have time, freedom of speech, and access to information. If we make safe passage through these turbulent nuclear years, what will we tell our children or grandchildren some years down the road when they suddenly glance up from their history books and ask, "What did you say and what did you do in those times when they were making all the nuclear bombs? And what did other Christians say? And what did the church do?" What will you say then? How will we answer our children and our grandchildren?

And if our worst fears should be realized and we are the survivors of a nuclear holocaust, what will we say when the children ask, "Where were you when they were preparing for nuclear war? What did you do and what did you say? Where was the church and what did it say? And what about the Christians, what did they do?" These are the questions of our time that cry out for Christian witness.

As for me, I want the record crystal clear. I hope there's no shadow of doubt nor one bit of uncertainty as to where I stood and what I said if my children and grandchildren ever get around to asking what I was doing as the nations prepared for nuclear war.

A third aspect of setting the record straight relates to the myths about the arms race that abound across the land. Alan Geyer suggests that a key ministry of the church in these times is uncovering the lies about security, gaps, defense, and nuclear superiority which governments perpetuate about the arms race.[2] Spiritual truth-telling involves debunking and shredding the lies of propaganda and pleading for governments to set their own records straight and tell the truth.

A Secondary Reason: Effectiveness

I've proposed that spiritual integrity—truth-telling—motivates our peacemaking witness. But shouldn't we be concerned about results? Shouldn't we be trying to save the world from destruction? Shouldn't we be trying to organize the most effective political campaign to change military policies? We easily fall into the trap of American pragmatism and worry about effectiveness and results. We're inclined to do "what works" and junk the rest.

From a Christian perspective an effectiveness approach can err on two counts. First, it takes our focus off God's peacemaking ministry and puts it on our program, and we soon lose sight of his. We soon become all wrapped up in our own organizational efforts and forget that this is really God's enterprise and not ours. We soon take ourselves too seriously and begin protecting and guarding "our program" sometimes in ways that are not very peaceful. An effectiveness strategy usually ends up emphasizing "our good works" rather than the saving works of God in Jesus Christ. Furthermore, the "Will it work?" approach puts so much emphasis on the outcome that it becomes easy to use some rather forceful means to get the results we want.

The *primary* purpose of our peacemaking effort is not to change specific government policies. It's not to produce effective results. It's not to organize programs that work. Our job is spiritual truth-telling. Our calling is to be faithful witnesses. If our focus is on spiritual honesty and integrity, it will always be clear that the peace witness is God's and not ours. It will be obvious that we are joining in God's worldwide witness and not trying to get him to bless our provincial program. This doesn't mean that we shouldn't pay attention to effective strategies. A truth-telling witness and an effectiveness orientation aren't necessarily in conflict with each other. Often we can tell the truth and work for specific policy changes at the same time.

A focus on strategy gives the impression that we know exactly what God is up to. It suggests that we think we are going to usher in his kingdom in its fullness here and now. Rather, we should give the witness and then let the chips fall where they will, knowing that God in his own way will put all the pieces of his puzzle together in his own time.

Now just because our primary Christian agenda is spiritual truth-telling and not political strategizing doesn't mean we shun political involvement. Many public acts of truth-telling by Christians down through history have been very political in their consequences. Most public deeds have political consequences when they address a common concern. Although our peacemaking witness is not designed around effectiveness, it may bring political results. If 10 million Christians told their congressmen once a month that on the basis of their Christian faith they prefer to live without nuclear weapons, that would make an enormous political impact. If 15 million Christians refused to pay part of their income taxes because they felt the use of their taxes for warmaking was inconsistent with their prayers for peace, wouldn't that make a political difference? If 10,000 Christians in every major American city joined twice a year in public candlelight processions, that certainly would have a political impact.

Just because our witness is based on spiritual truth-telling doesn't mean it's not public or political in nature. Its political impact increases directly as the number of witnesses grows. But the moment the *primary* purpose of the witness becomes political effectiveness, its ownership becomes ours instead of God's. Our primary call is to spiritual faithfulness, not political effectiveness. We give the witness regardless of whether or not it's effective in changing policies. We give the witness not because it works, but because it's true. We also realize that the witness may lead to a cross; it may not appear to be successful by most standards. And we realize that God has that uncanny ability to turn our ineffective efforts into effective ones for his purposes.

We give the witness not to change the world, but to keep the world from changing us. And if we have no witness, then the world has already changed us. We give the witness as a matter of clear conscience. We speak the truth not because it will change everything or usher in the millennium, but simply because it is the truth. We know God turns crosses into resurrections, and we witness in faith, believing that in ways unknown to us he will take our frail gestures and turn them into gains for his kingdom.

The Message: Shalom

The message of the witness is fairly simple, even though we say it in a lot of different ways. God wills shalom—wholeness, justice, and love—for the human community. The Scriptures and Jesus Christ reveal God's will for peacemaking. They show that God's method is reverse fighting. God invites all people to join in reverse fighting so that they can enjoy the rich blessings of shalom. The gospel of Jesus Christ mediated through the Holy Spirit gives us the strength to heap love on evil. All peoples and nations are invited to accept the call to salvation and join the witness of peace.

The Method: In Tender Love

The method of our peacemaking witness is as crucial as the message. The method in a real way shapes the message. If we storm and stomp around in a conversation, insisting that peace is God's will, it quickly becomes obvious that we haven't experienced a very peaceful peace. Emphasizing truth-telling instead of effectiveness makes it clear that this is God's peacemaking ministry and dissolves our need to defend it, protect it, and expand it to guarantee its survival. When we witness to the truth, the truth speaks for itself and demonstrates that over the long run it doesn't need our help to protect it. We can relax and give a gentle witness since the truth looks out for itself.

Again and again I see it happen in classrooms and discussions. A debate emerges around the need for a strong military policy based on nuclear weapons. The lines are drawn, people choose sides, and they go after each other. Too often the peace advocates use verbal weapons that push the two sides apart, sowing animosity instead of reconciliation. The same forces that keep nations apart are also at work in our own lives, and peace proponents easily alienate themselves from others in their verbal fights for peace.

The apostle Paul teaches us to speak the truth in love.

We must speak the truth about the gospel of peace. We must speak it boldly, publicly, and firmly, but we must always say it gently, tenderly, and in love. Our best tool for disarming opponents is the gentle touch, soft word, and honest tactic.

The message of peace is jeopardized and dealt a severe blow whenever the means are not peaceful. Peaceful ends don't justify nasty means. Those who deny government the right to make nuclear threats for the cause of peace dare not succumb to verbal threats in making their witness. Peaceful techniques and gentle ways in mean situations become themselves the message of peace. Tender acts in the midst of snarls say it all. More so than with most other issues, the method here *is* the message. This doesn't mean we avoid the hot spots. Christians will be involved in public demonstrations, they will be in the midst of tough political battles, they will be in the middle of controversies, they will be involved in civil disobedience, but in all these involvements we forfeit the witness of peacemaking the moment we heap hate on hate. We will lose control and botch things up at times, but those sorry moments also provide opportunities for reconciliation, new chances to heap good on evil.

The technique must always be nonviolent, loving, nonresistance that cares for enemies even when the enemies are members of our church, our community, or our government. We cannot insist on peace or try to make it by force. Peaceful relations emerge from voluntary choices. They are not shoved down throats. Using verbal might or intellectual wit to force peace on others is no different from the government's "peace through strength" tactic that we decry. We welcome, we invite, but we never force the peace stance on others. We employ the reverse fighting method at all levels of our witness, in personal conversations as well as in organized political efforts. And we do it with the real awareness that reverse fighting isn't always successful.

The Place: Everywhere
The witness is shared everywhere from the church's sanctuary to the public political stage. The gifts of peacemaking are distributed in a variety of ways throughout the body

of Christ. Some of us will work primarily within the church, teaching the ways of shalom to children and converting Christian adults from the bomb to the cross. Others will share their witness through special peace organizations within and beyond the church. Some will be directly involved in traditional political action, and others will make their witness in quiet and personal ways. All of these efforts are valid and welcome.

The Holy Spirit touches each of us in different ways and uses all sorts of vehicles to get the job done. Individually we may look lopsided, because some will work entirely within the church and others almost exclusively outside the church. The variety of ministries is a God-given balance to the body of Christ. Although lopsided in our individual efforts, when taken as a whole these diverse gifts complement each other and provide a rich mix. Our mutual respect for each other's peacemaking gifts is utterly essential for the welfare of Christ's body. Tearing down each other tears down the whole body. There are many avenues of peacemaking, but there is one Lord. Our job is to be faithful to the gifts he has given us. He blends them together into his own colorful fabric.

The Label: Sometimes

Whenever possible we remind folks that our witness is done in the name of Christ. He motivates our witness and receives the glory from it, and we should freely say so. But we don't make a big deal about it. We remember that the truth is big enough to stand alone without the help of religious props. Jesus himself was reluctant to announce that he was the Messiah. He didn't use all sorts of religious clichés to prove his messianic identity. He told inquirers to look around and see what was happening and then urged them to make up their own minds. We are so eager to stamp a religious blessing on our efforts as though we fear they need defense and can't stand on their own feet. We should say that our witness is in the name of Christ, but we shouldn't make a big scene over it, and when it's not appropriate to say anything, we know the truthfulness of the witness will carry its own weight.

Sometimes we join others in special peace efforts even though they're not necessarily doing them in the name of Christ. Even though our motivations are different, if the cause is just and the methods are gentle, we happily join in. Doing so provides an opportunity for dialogue and a chance to witness not only for a peaceful world order, but to Jesus as the source of our peace. Jesus himself said that those who aren't against us are for us. Our witness isn't watered down or diluted just because it doesn't have a religious nametag on it or just because non-Christians of good cheer also walk along with us. God's truth doesn't need a slick advertising agency to plaster his name on everything; his truth is capable of standing on its own merits.

THREE STEPS OF INTEGRITY

There are three steps of spiritual integrity in peacemaking. The first step involves our beliefs. What exactly do we think and believe about the bomb? At this first stage we gather information, sort out convictions, and sift through our attitudes. How serious are we about peacemaking? Are we willing to make a serious commitment to public witness? Do we really believe that peacemaking is central to the gospel? What exactly should we say about the arms race? These questions require prayer and reflection.

At this stage the discipline of prayer is especially vital. Moments of prayer and meditation are not chances to twist God's arm; they are times to clarify our own spiritual allegiance. Who is our lord? Under which banner do we march? In what ways have we strayed from God's truth? In moments of reflective prayer God's spirit helps us sort out these critical questions. Prayer that purifies and refurbishes our spirits lies at the heart of our peace witness.

And then as the Spirit prompts us, we own the convictions that emerge. In this instance the integrity of peacemaking means confessing our inner feelings of suspicion, toughness, and coolness which clash with the fruits of the Spirit. Moreover, it means clarifying exactly what we believe about nuclear arms. This first step of study, prayer, and reflection is the cornerstone of our peacemaking, for in it we refine and polish our inner convictions and commitments. Without the strength of the Spirit's inner witness, our peacemaking efforts will wilt in the heat of the battle.

The second step involves our speech. Are we willing to say what we believe? With polite nods and graceful smiles we can easily avoid putting our witness on the line in public. Among friends and relatives who disagree, it takes courage to tell the truth, but tell the truth we must if our witness is to have integrity. Believing the right thing in our hearts isn't enough. Spiritual honesty requires that we translate our convictions about nuclear weapons into words.

In the third step of spiritual integrity our beliefs and words hit the road in specific acts. Ideas and words aren't enough; they both must be translated into concrete acts of witness. Writing a letter, attending a meeting, tacking up a poster, organizing an event—all of these acts are statements of our inner commitment to peace. Spiritual integrity consists of a harmony among attitude, word, and deed. To smother or hide our witness at any of the three levels is spiritual dishonesty. The Holy Spirit empowers our witness and gives us courage to proclaim it in word and deed.

THE PARADOX OF TENSION

Life is made up of many contradictions and inconsistencies. Often the truth is found in the middle of a paradox. It's hard to live with the ambiguity of paradox. Most of us want to pound our stakes in solidly on one side or the other of an issue. Although that makes life easier and simpler, we may miss the truth in the process of pounding. There are a bundle of paradoxes in the witness of peacemaking, and we need to learn to enjoy them. If we swing sharply to one side or the other, we forfeit the truth. These issues may sound like contradictions and they are. We must learn to embrace them at the same time and enjoy the incompatibility. We need them both in the same instant. If we cling only to one, our witness becomes lopsided and narrow.

Push and Pull

Facing up to the threat of nuclear war pulls us inward,

back to the roots of our faith. Worship, prayer, and meditation take on new meaning in the face of this monster. The
enormous evil in the belly of this demon forces us back to a
new reading of God's Word. His truth comes into clearer
focus than ever before. His bidding for peace makes more
sense than ever. But there's also a push outward in all of this.
We sense a fresh mandate to speak out and to speak out
boldly. The witness of God's spirit and the urgency of the
hour demand creative responses. We can't sit idly by and live
with a clear conscience. We are propelled outward. This is a
good and healthy tension which pulls us back—listening
quietly for God's word—and pushes us outward—doing
things we've never done before. We must cultivate the tension, for without it we become either pious recluses or se-
cular activists.

Depending and Doing

There is also a tension between depending on God and
doing his work. We know that in a real sense we are utterly
dependent on him for the outcome of this whole thing. In the
final analysis our life, our security, our future lies in his
hand. He pushes the big button, and we can only trust in his
sovereignty. But there is also a real sense in which we do his
work, and he depends on us. We are his agents of peacemaking. He does his work through us as his ministers of reconciliation. And so we lean heavily on God, knowing that he
also leans heavily on us. We wait for God's initiative, knowing
that he also waits for ours. We cherish the presence of his
Spirit, we seek his direction, we respect his sovereignty, and
we go about doing his work even though we aren't always
sure how close we are to the end of the game or what the next
play is. But we do know whose side we're on, and so we keep
on playing. This is a healthy and important contradiction,
saying at once that we depend on God and that he depends
on us.

Dream and Despair

We dream about the abolition of nuclear weapons, for
we know the gospel compels us to call for their elimination.

We follow the dream and work persistently to rid the planet of such nuclear nuisance. We call for nuclear disarmament as a policy that's consistent with our understanding of the Christian gospel. Yet realistically we know it won't happen quickly. Modern nations aren't about to lay down their nuclear swords. Moreover, if one nation disarmed independently, it might push us even closer to nuclear war.

The dream seems so far from reality that we easily fall into despair, for that seems like a more realistic response. But we know if we accept things the way they are and allow the dream to be dashed into the ground, we've given ourselves over to the powers of death. And so we dream unthinkable dreams even when they seem like fantasy—even in the midst of despairing realities, for if no one offers a vision of hope we will all surely sink into the pits of despair. We know our dream won't "work," but we act on the gospel's mandate anyway, giving a testimony to the prince of peace and hoping to restrain the galloping nuclear horses a bit before they break through the fences of reason.

Joy and Outrage

We also need a balance of joy and moral outrage. In some ways the arms race is so silly that we join God in laughing at it. We pun and poke fun at all its ironies. We play and go about our business as usual, knowing full well that we can't change a thing. We'll never dismantle a bomb. Our meager witness certainly won't turn this race around. And so we plant flowers, we laugh, and we hope against hope that somehow the whole thing will turn out all right. We go about our work with joy, living in the hope of the resurrection, knowing that we worship a God who can turn the worst situations into good ones for his glory.

But we are also angry. We are morally outraged at the thought of taking reckless chances with God's creation. We are irate over the hideous waste of money and resources in bombs, while humans starve. We are incensed at the lies and myths perpetuated in the name of truth by governments. We take this whole thing very seriously as a slap in God's face by his creatures. Such folly will not go unnoticed, and such stupidity will most certainly be paid for. And so we take this nuclear bull by the horns and curse it in the name of God. But we also laugh.

ON WHICH BANDWAGON?

If we agree that manufacturing and possessing nuclear weapons is irreconcilable with Christian faith, what specifically do we say to our government? Which bandwagon do we hop onto? Which political initiatives do we support? Which program do we rally behind? A nuclear freeze? START (Strategic Arms Reduction Talks)? Arms control? Disarmament? Nonviolent national defense?

Arms control treaties are aimed at stabilizing levels of armaments. Treaties such as SALT I put a lid on the numbers of certain nuclear weapons, reduced others, and permitted the development of some new ones. In contrast, nuclear disarmament refers to specific steps of weapon reduction until a country has eliminated all its nuclear weapons. Multilateral disarmament involves mutual steps by two or more countries which reduce their nuclear weapons together. In unilateral initiatives a country voluntarily reduces some of its weapons without any guarantee that its opponent will follow.

Any specific treaty for arms control such as SALT, START, or a nuclear freeze is a complicated process of political negotiations and technical details. The specific shape of such treaties is hammered out at the bargaining table with the opponent and with political forces back home. We should stay informed about such treaties, but we don't need to know them in detail in order to support them. We can speak up without having our own special disarmament plan. The job of Christian citizens is not to develop a detailed disarmament package and try to shove it down the government's throat. In some cases Christians working in government may be in positions where they can have a direct hand in shaping specific policies. The vast majority of us, however, will stand on the sidelines expressing our views, without direct involvement in the construction of foreign policy.

So what do we say? The goal of Christian nuclear pacifists is quite simple: the abolition of nuclear weapons. In the same way that slavery became outlawed because of its immorality, we work today toward the elimination of the heavy burden of nuclear weapons. Only when they too are outlawed can we rest. That may be an impractical political goal. It will sound like utter fantasy to the many who say, "One of the facts of the modern world is nuclear weapons, and we'd better learn to live with them since they won't mysteriously fade away."

As Christian witnesses we insist that such weapons are incompatible with the values of Christian faith. We state our goal clearly, and then we support *any* particular treaty or arms control agreement that moves in the direction of eliminating nuclear weapons. We support a nuclear freeze simply because it halts the arms race and gives us a chance to breathe. We support START negotiations because they may limit some weapons and reduce others. So we jump onto any bandwagon that promises to nudge the whole process closer to the goal of abolishing nuclear weapons.

But we remember that a nuclear freeze or a START agreement is only one small step in the right direction. We dare not fall asleep after one treaty is signed. The Christian witness to abolish nuclear weapons will not be easy or quick. It will require a great deal of persistence over the long haul. But once our motivation—the love of Christ—is firm and our goal—the abolition of nuclear weapons—is clear, we will support any specific treaty or agreement that moves us in that direction.

There are three rules of thumb for our support of specific arms control or disarmament treaties:

1. We will support any platforms that move us toward the long-term goal of abolishing nuclear weapons.

2. We will carefully examine any agreements. Do they in fact slow down the arms race? Or are they showy public-relations rituals which merely eliminate a few obsolete nuclear weapons and permit the development of new ones?

3. We will remember that any single agreement is *only* a small step in the right direction, and so we will continue to call for sharper reductions and new treaties.

In mid-1982 President Reagan, under considerable heat from the nuclear freeze movement, called for START negotiations with the Soviets, and he proposed a mutual one-third reduction in the total number of bombs carried by missiles. President Brezhnev said the call for negotiations was "a step in the right direction," but he repeated his call for a nuclear freeze on all nuclear weapon production. President Reagan's proposal was a welcomed beginning point in arms negotiations, but it appeared unfair to the Soviets for two reasons. First, the Reagan proposal allows the U.S. to continue developing its new generation of weapons: cruise missiles, the MX missile, the B-1 bomber, the Trident II submarine, and the neutron bomb. It also does not limit warheads carried by bombers, in which the U.S. has a large advantage. Second, since the Soviets have nearly three fourths of their bombs on land-based missiles, a one-third cut would hit them twice as hard in their prime area of strength. Likewise, the Brezhnev proposal for a freeze was unacceptable to the U.S. because it would have shut down production on the new generation of U.S. weapons and eliminated their use as chips at the bargaining table.

The Christian call to abolish nuclear weapons will often sound like a radical voice crying in the wilderness, and it will not be welcomed by the prevailing powers. The abolition plea has integrity with our faith in Jesus Christ and *is* useful in the political process. A public call to abolish nuclear weapons may help to tug the whole political process closer to our goal. The plea for abolition is not only biblically sound; it's also an effective political posture in turning the arms race around. A moderate, middle-of-the-road approach compromises the Christian message, encourages the political status quo, and does little to slow down the arms race.

DO SOMETHING

Throughout these pages I have pled for a Christian witness for peace in the age of the bomb. A witness in the final analysis must act. So what do we do? All of us are wondering that. What can we do? We'd like to be handed a blueprint for peacemaking in the nuclear age that spells out the details.

We aren't experts at this. Many of us are newcomers to the peace witness. Where do we begin?

May I be inconsistent for a moment and speak out of both sides of my mouth? On the one hand I will argue that anyone who really cares will find something to do. Begging for a bag of tricks can be an excuse for not doing anything. But after making that point I'll turn around and offer a few suggestions for peacemaking that will perhaps stimulate ideas of your own.

Doing something is an eloquent statement of our hope in the risen Lord and in his future. This hope is not the same as an optimistic outlook on life that's cultivated by exercises in positive thinking. Christian hope is anchored in God's ability to turn crosses into resurrections and to triumph ultimately. Apathy, despair, and indifference are signs that death has infected our moral nerves. By doing nothing we put our blessing on things as they are.

When we act, we plant a tree of hope, and it's the most precious gift we can ever give to our children. When we sit idly by in the face of this ultimate threat, we mock the preciousness of life itself and consign ourselves over to death. Our act may not be effective, it may not make a difference, but it is a sign of hope in the midst of a hopeless situation. It is a way of teaching hope, of nurturing hope, even in the face of despair. Our act is an affirmation of life itself—a sign that we have chosen life—and most importantly it's a sign that God's spirit is alive and well in a dark world. To do nothing when we know the facts is to be duped by the powers of death and darkness. Our act also brings spiritual therapy and cleansing. In it we declare our identity with the kingdom of God and his purposes. So step out and act; do the Father's will now in the middle of the night of despair, even as Jesus did in Gethsemane. Act in the hope of resurrection.

Those who care and those who are moved by compassion will act. They won't need a blueprint for action. They won't need a list of things to do. In each community, in each parish, in each small fellowship, the Holy Spirit will provide insight, direction, and ideas. The local conditions vary, the gifts of individuals are unique, but the Holy Spirit will provide the proper mix and direction for action. More than ideas for action, we need courage, spiritual boldness to do and say what we already know is right. So follow the leading of the Spirit, heed the impulses of your heart, and do something. Do it kindly, gently, and with respect, but *do* something.

Now having just said that we should follow our hearts and not yearn for detailed do-it-yourself manuals, let me offer some suggestions for a peacemaking witness.

SEVEN RULES
Don't Reorganize Your Community

We're often tempted to create a new community organization to cope with each new issue that comes along. Don't do it. Work within existing networks, groups, and organizations. Our communities are already organized. We are already members of civic groups, church fellowships, occupational and professional organizations. Share the peace witness with local groups such as the Rotary Club, the PTO, the senior citizens, the den mothers, and the band parents. Utilize these existing opportunities where you already have a foothold. There are times when a new organization is needed, but be careful not to rush into hatching one and lose all your energy setting up new bureaucratic machinery that simply drags people to more and more meetings. Work with what you have. If you aren't careful, the peace witness will be smothered by frantic organizational activity.

Think Small

Start with specific acts. Don't develop a crusade. Don't launch a campaign blitz filled with slogans. Take small, natural steps where you are now. Think about all the people and groups you are a part of now. Take tiny steps with those natural contacts. If you are on a program committee or if you can offer program ideas, suggest a film or a speaker that could deal with the arms race. Take some modest steps in your natural setting.

Keep It Simple

The arms race is complicated. Keep your remarks and

suggestions down to earth. Too much information too fast can confuse. Say whatever you are saying in everyday English. Translate the technical jargon of the arms race into plain English.

Keep It Local

Ties with national organizations provide helpful information and keep us in touch with national trends. It's important to join one or more national groups to keep up-to-date, but the focus of our witness should be in our own backyard. It's easy to run off to a big national demonstration in Chicago, San Francisco, or New York. It takes more courage to organize one at home among the people we know. Nuclear weapons will not be abolished until average men and women in average communities in several nations are convinced of their immorality. Work at home. Stay at the grass roots.

In and Out of Church

Some of us will find the coolest reception to a peace witness in our own churches. That's not the way it should be, but that's often the way it is. Don't give up on the church. For some the church will be the major focus of their witness. For others the witness will be a public one in the world's marketplace. Both witnesses are needed and both are valid. Do whatever is natural for you.

Be Persistent

It will be a long uphill struggle. One freeze, one START treaty, one demonstration, one American-Soviet summit conference, one sermon, one elective course will not be enough. Develop some peace habits, and stick with them on a regular basis. Allow them to become good ruts in your life. We already have monthly routines of bill paying. Is it asking too much to send a postcard to our congressional representatives each month? Could we have a peace parade every Memorial Day? Why not sponsor a peace essay contest every Valentine Day? Could the July 4th Sunday become a traditional time for a peace sermon in your church? These are good traditions. Establish them. Faithful disciples need the prompting of good traditions as well as the spontaneous urging of the Holy Spirit. Our family joins the annual ten-mile peace walk from Nazareth to Bethlehem, Pennsylvania, each year. It's a good rut to be stuck in.

Find Fellowship

Peacemaking can be a lonely venture even in the church. It's easy to lose hope and fall into despair. A warm smile, a word of encouragement, a brother or sister's zeal warms our hearts and gives us stamina to go on. We need each other. We are members one of another. We are God's people in this together. We need to find each other and share together in both informal and formal ways.

STARTING POINTS

Here is a list of some things you might want to try. The ideas are not listed in order of priority or importance. You will need to adapt them to your own circumstances. Hopefully they will stimulate more brainstorming that will break out into action. Again let me underscore the need to do what fits and makes sense in your own community. Names and addresses of organizations are listed in Appendix 4.

Get the Facts

Learn more about the arms race. Gather information so that you know what you're talking about. Read additional books and brochures. Join one or two national peace organizations to keep up-to-date as the facts change. To be informed takes time and effort, but it's essential. Purchase books dealing with peace issues for the church library. Print reviews of them in your church's newsletter. Pay special attention to children's books. There are some excellent ones on the market.

Learn more about your church's teachings on peace. Write to your denominational office for recent statements or a list of books. Discover what your church teaches about war and peace—you might be surprised! If your denomination has a peace group or newsletter, join so that you can keep in touch.

Find a Friend

Get together with a friend who you think might also be interested. Reach out and find at least one other person to lean on. Share ideas. Brainstorm together about activities that you might begin in your community. You may eventually want to invite others, but at least start with one. If others are interested, you might want to form a peace advocates group in your congregation or community. Share your convictions. Pray together. Keep in touch.

Spend Money

Important things usually cost money. If you are serious about participating in a peace witness, be prepared to spend some money. There are a whole host of good peace activities which don't cost a thing, but books, subscriptions, postcards, speakers, and films usually do. Consider your total personal budget. Is it really asking too much to devote a small portion of it toward peace? Peacemaking takes more than good intentions! It costs something in time, effort, and money.

Contact Legislators

The senators from your state and the representatives from your area are your link with the government. Let them know how you feel about nuclear disarmament. If you are quiet, they can only assume that you approve of what's going on. Send them postcards or letters on a *regular* basis. One letter is not enough! Is it asking too much to spend a dollar a month for postcards? The message doesn't need to be fancy or long. Write your own personal message. If you don't like to write, call them at their local offices or in Washington, D.C. They are as close as your telephone. If they aren't available, speak to a legislative aide. One way or the other, let them know on a regular basis how you feel about militarism and other related issues. Better yet, go to their offices and speak to them personally. Invite them to come and speak to your church or club. After a major speech or news conference, write or call the White House to let the president know your opinions on the subject.

Group Study

Organize a group in your church to study and share together on the Christian response to the nuclear threat. Perhaps this could be an elective church school class. You might utilize existing groups or set up a special, short-term group. If this doesn't work, try a weekend retreat. A concentrated time of group study and reflection can be very effective in establishing a local base of support.

Films

There are excellent films available which dramatically portray the nuclear threat. Arrange to show one at your church, club, or community organization. They are effective discussion starters and may stimulate more serious study of the threat of nuclear war. Check your denominational head-quarters for a list of film titles, or use some of the films listed in Appendix 5.

Mass Media

The peace witness can be shared effectively in your local news media. Write letters to the editor in response to news stories, and raise issues regarding your local congressional representative's position on nuclear arms. A letter to the editor about your congressional representative will get much more visibility than a private letter sent directly to the representative. Express your views on radio talk shows. Urge your local television station to show films dealing with the nuclear arms race. Suggest news stories to the newspaper or television station of unique individuals working for peace or of a special out-of-town visitor speaking at a local conference. Purchase space in the newspapers for peace ads or statements at special times of the year.

Speakers

Invite special speakers to address your class, club, or fellowship group. If possible set up a debate—it's more exciting and gives fair exposure to both sides of the issue. Physicians are especially effective and convincing when speaking about the medical effects of nuclear war. Ask a local physician to speak to your group. It will be a good chance for him or her, if not already familiar with the medical effects of nuclear war, to learn about them. Call the national office of Physicians for Social Responsibility to identify local doctors who might help. Many folks start taking nuclear war quite seriously when they hear physicians say it's not good for their health. Ask your family doctor whether he or she has joined Physicans for Social Responsibility. Encourage your doctor to join. Give him or her a copy of *The Final Epidemic*, a book of easy-to-read essays on nuclear war written by physicians.

Traditions and Holidays

Establish some annual peace traditions around special days on the church calendar or national holiday schedule. Consider Christmas, Easter, Pentecost, Mother's Day, Memorial Day, July 4th, or the anniversary of the Hiroshima and Nagasaki bombings (August 6 and 9). A peace walk, a meal, a sermon, a day of fasting, a poster contest, tree planting—these or other events could become annual peace traditions related to any of these days. Become involved in traditional church or community events, parades, fairs, picnics, or festivals. Include a peace float or a peace display as a regular part of one of these events. Develop a traditional Peace Sunday with the entire worship service—mass, liturgy, sermon—and perhaps a fellowship meal focusing on the gospel of peace. Give an annual Peacemaker of the Year award to a member who made special contributions to peace during the year. Traditions are important reminders that help to keep the dream and the witness alive.

Special Events

Create special peace events in your church or community. These fun and educational events could be once-and-done occasions, or they too might become annual traditions. Sponsor an essay-writing contest on a peace theme for youth. Ask local businesses to contribute toward the award. Perhaps a poster contest would meet the needs of younger children better. Give children's peace books for prizes. A youth group could release gas-filled balloons with messages to track how far radioactive fallout would drift as it's blown by the wind. Organize a "run for your life" race. Runners depart from a selected "ground zero" and see how far they can run in thirty minutes—the amount of warning time before a missile attack. Write Physicians for Social Responsibility for details.

Conduct a mock draft-board trial, and interrogate youth regarding their convictions as conscientious objectors. Hold a mock arms-negotiation session between the USSR and the U.S. Encourage youth or adults to write a short play dealing with the arms race, and present it to a group as a discussion starter. Games, role playing, and simulations are helpful peace-education activities.

Corporate Public Witness

Public witness such as peace vigils and processions can take on many forms. Such public activities are an important aspect of a peace witness when done in an orderly and respectful fashion. We shouldn't see them as some sort of low-down, last-ditch effort that smacks of dishonorable anarchy. When organized and orchestrated with dignity, public witness in streets and parks is an appropriate peace witness in a democracy. A candlelight walk or vigil incorporating many of the churches of a community can be an important symbol of the unity of Christ's body as well as a call to peace.

You may want to join public demonstrations planned by others, or perhaps your group could initiate one on the local level. Public demonstrations can be used effectively to commemorate special events or to send messages of concern about public policies to government leaders. Public witness at nuclear arms manufacturing sites or at the corporate offices of military contractors is an effective way of reminding the community of the military's presence as well as raising ethical questions with employees and the general public. A prayerful presence needs to be established at these centers of militarism as a witness to God's peace. Participation in some form of public witness encourages us to declare our Christian convictions in the civic arena. It takes courage. Churches could become staging grounds for public demonstrations that carry the banner of Christian faith.

Political Action

The laws and policies of our government are made by elected representatives. Long-term changes in government policy will depend on the people we elect to office. Christians working for the abolition of nuclear weapons will want to vote for candidates who favor arms reductions. We may also offer to work in the campaigns of such candidates or make financial contributions. Such traditional political activity will, of course, never usher in the kingdom of God. Nevertheless, we should vigorously do everything in our means through political avenues to express our opinions. Our primary efforts should focus on a peace witness under the banner of the church, but we will also use our voices, our influence, our ideas, our resources, and our votes in the democratic process to reduce nuclear arms.

Taxes

Taxes are a direct way in which most of us support the military policies of our governments. Can Christians who pray for peace also pay for war with their resources? It's a hard question, and there are good arguments on both sides. There are some excellent study guides available on the war tax issue. If you haven't thought about it carefully, read some of the helpful materials that are available, or better yet, gather some friends together for a series of discussions.

The single statement by Jesus, "Render ... to Caesar," is wide open for interpretation (Matthew 22:21). It doesn't settle the question of who decides what is God's and what is Caesar's. Does Caesar or does the church? Nor does it clarify how much is Caesar's? Besides, what happens in a democracy when the citizens are Caesar? I suspect that Jesus deliberately left the statement open-ended so that Christians down through the centuries in many different political settings could respond in appropriate ways to their particular Caesars.

Withholding some war taxes is certainly not an effective way to reduce military spending. The IRS will eventually collect most of the funds that are due. And as long as only a tiny minority of people refuse to pay part of their taxes, legislation won't change. So tax resistance is a matter once again of a clear conscience, of spiritual integrity. Personally I find it quite inconsistent to say I love my enemies and then turn around and offer my resources to kill them. Roman Catholic Archbishop Hunthausen in Seattle, Washington, withheld half of his 1981 personal income tax as a protest witness against "our nation's involvement in the race for nuclear arms supremacy."

Our local congregation has developed a 777 plan, in which members are encouraged to withhold a symbolic amount of their taxes such as $7.77 or $77.77. The numbers were selected for their biblical significance. Seven is the biblical symbol of perfection, and Jesus asks us to forgive 70 times 7. The money that is withheld is given to a peace fund held by the church until the Internal Revenue Service collects it.

It's important to send a cover letter along with your tax forms, with copies to your senators and congressional representatives, explaining why your Christian commitment requires you to withhold some of your taxes. If it's too scary or if you feel uncomfortable withholding a small symbolic amount, you can at least send a letter of polite protest when you pay your taxes. I feel that Christians who pay taxes without a letter of protest are directly condoning and supporting the government's military efforts. The number of tax refusers is growing as more and more Christians find it impossible to reconcile conscientiously their prayers for peace with their payments for war.

You can also support the World Peace Tax Fund. This is a bill in the U.S. Congress which would allow conscientious objectors to direct the military part of their tax money toward peaceful purposes. The World Peace Tax Fund address is given in Appendix 7. Write your representative and senators, and urge them to support the World Peace Tax Fund bill.

Effects of Nuclear War

One way to bring the realities of nuclear war down to earth is to describe the effects of a nuclear attack on your home area. It's an effective educational tool, which starts people thinking and talking. With the help of a local science teacher you can easily calculate the effects of a nuclear attack on your community. It makes a good youth group or class project. The local newspaper might be interested in publishing your description, and you might consider distributing copies of your report to the public. You could also present your report in a slide show that could be shown to other groups. See Appendix 6.

Military Contractors

If it hasn't already beeen done, you might want to identify military contractors in your area. What products are being manufactured? How much money enters and leaves your area in the form of military taxes and military contracts? Your report might be of interest to the news media as well as to other church or community groups. Tips for getting started are given in Appendix 6.

Follow Your Heart

There is nothing earth-shattering in these suggestions. Common sense, the guidance of the Holy Spirit, and courage are the most important ingredients. Perhaps some of the suggestions will ignite some vision and witness in your life. Follow your heart, follow the Spirit, pray for courage, and do something. Even if it's a tiny gesture and even if it seems irrelevant, try it, for in doing so you will join with Christian brothers and sisters around the world who are also planting hope.

QUESTIONS

1. Do you agree that spiritual integrity is the primary reason for the Christian peace witness?
2. How do political effectiveness and spiritual truthtelling complement or conflict with each other as two motivations for witness?
3. Should the goal of the Christian peace witness be the elimination of nuclear weapons or the prevention of nuclear war? Might nuclear weapons be required in order to prevent nuclear war?
4. Imagine your children or someone else asking you twenty years from now, "What were you doing and saying during the nuclear arms buildup?" What would you say? Would your response be any different if you were a survivor of a nuclear war?
5. Are there times when we need to obey God rather than man, even if that means civil disobedience?
6. Does the urgency of the nuclear war threat call for more radical forms of witness than traditional political activity?
7. Is it inconsistent to pray for peace and pay for war? Why or why not? Who decides what and how much is Caesar's in a democracy?
8. Someone has said that "little acts of resistance such as tax refusal are the real signs of hope." Do you agree? Why or why not?
9. What specific peacemaking activities are appropriate in your setting?
10. Are you willing to commit yourself to one specific public act of witness over the next week? What will it be?

9
RUNNING AWAY FROM NUCLEAR WAR

We have arrived at the last chapter. By now you know that it's not easy to face up to the issue of nuclear war. It's complicated, depressing, and scary. It's much easier to run away from it. You may be thinking of all sorts of reasons for doing nothing. In this chapter we'll look at some ways of running away from nuclear war. These are detours around the issue, which we conveniently use in order to avoid facing up to it. In an earlier chapter we scanned some of the emotional reactions to the threat of nuclear war. These too can become escape routes from action. In this chapter we'll focus primarily on religious beliefs and everyday folklore that sound like good reasons for running away from nuclear war.

PIMPLES AND CANCER

Pimples are easier to detect than cancer, and we can usually do something about them. Cancer hides, spreads, evades detection, and it's terribly dangerous. When asked about the danger of radiation from nuclear power plants in contrast to the threat of nuclear war, George Kistiakowsky replied, "That's like worrying about a pimple when you're dying from cancer."[1] Kistiakowsky, who worked on the original bomb project and served as President Eisenhower's science advisor, graphically underscored the supreme urgency of the war threat. His statement struck me particularly hard, living only six miles from Three Mile Island, where many of my neighbors fear radiation leaks, but seem oblivious to the threat of nuclear war.

The threat of nuclear war and the control of nuclear weapons is the chief moral issue of our time. And yet in spite of its promise of annihilation we have been slow to face up to it. The church has historically spoken out on other moral issues: slavery, alcoholism, abortion, civil rights, child abuse, materialism, adultery, honesty, and pornography. These are important moral and ethical issues that the church should properly address, but they almost seem like moral pimples in the face of nuclear war.

We endlessly debate the origin of the world, trying to understand in retrospect how God's creation relates to scientific studies. There's not much we can do about creation now! What about evolutionary changes in nuclear technology that might destroy God's creation? Why are we so disinterested in how the world might end?

We work to protect endangered wildlife species—seals, eagles, and other rare animals—but what about a military buildup that endangers humanity? We protect the right to life of babies before birth. But what about their right to life after birth? We are concerned about addiction to alcoholism, but what about addiction to nuclear superiority? We deplore child abuse. But what about murdering millions of innocent civilians with nuclear bombs? We condemn smut peddlers, who pollute the minds of children, but what about nuclear peddlers, who pollute the genetic pool of future generations? We preach against drunken drivers who recklessly kill others, but what about reckless nuclear policies that threaten to massacre millions? We decry chemical pollution of streams and land, but what about nuclear pollution that permanently disturbs the harmony of nature? We spend thousands of dollars for medical care to extend the life of one terminally ill patient, but devote virtually no funds to peace and research that might extend the life of humanity.

We must be consistent in guarding God's precious creation against abuse. If we focus only on the pimples and forget the cancer, we will surely die. If we neglect the cancer, pimple picking will be useless.

In the face of nuclear war other moral pimples fade. Why protect the environment if it will soon be destroyed? Why care for malnourished children if they will soon die anyway? Why invest billions in education if youth will never grow up? Why bother to study in school if you'll never get a chance to use the skills? Why work for prison reform if the prisons will soon be blown up? Why protect the wilderness areas if they'll eventually turn into radioactive wastelands? Why do any of the good things that we are doing if they'll be undone in a few years?

Don't misunderstand. We *should* care for human life and God's good garden. We should be doing all these things. But if we really care about human life and the natural creation, we will also work persistently for the elimination of nuclear weapons, for they are the gravest threat of all to God's creation. They are the hidden cancer that threatens to terminate life. We dare not stop at pimple picking. We must eradicate the cancer as well as the pimples.

It's easy to run away from the nuclear war issue because it's so big, so complicated, so hidden, and so far away. We see the child abuse, we smell the chemical pollution, we hear the cries of accident victims, we talk with prisoners, and we read abortion advertisements. These issues are all close at hand. They beg for our attention. It's easy for us to respond to specific things that we can see and do something about.

RELIGIOUS EXCUSES

There are many excuses for turning away from nuclear war, even some good ones. In the biblical story of the good Samaritan, the priest and the Levite saw a badly beaten man, and they passed by on the other side of the road. They had some good religious reasons for running away. According to religious law, if their shadows merely touched a corpse, they would be defiled and need ritual purification. Not certain whether the man was dead or alive, they conveniently passed on. It was the traditional enemy, the Samaritan, who was moved by compassion and faced up to the situation. Religious excuses are quite tempting because they sound "spiritual" and give the impression that God blesses our running away from issues. After all, who can challenge God's apparent blessing? And yet these religious detours around nuclear war are diabolic because they twist the good news in such a way that God ends up blessing apathy and hopelessness.

God Won't Let It Happen

One way to shrug off responsibility is to say that God would never let such a terrible thing like nuclear war happen. Since God would never permit such horrendous tragedy, we really don't need to worry about it. Surely he would never allow such massive death and suffering to come to pass. Sorry, but history and the biblical record are not on the side of this excuse. God has permitted some very nasty things to happen in the past. About 20 million Soviets and 5 million Jews were killed in World War II. Millions and millions of people have been killed in the folly of war down through history. God doesn't necessarily intervene and stop our human stupidity. To say that God would not let nuclear war happen lays the responsibility for the whole thing squarely on him and neatly pardons our responsibility as sinful humans. There is no reason to suspect that God is suddenly going to step in and stop us from doing even terrible things to ourselves and his creation. Creating us with free wills meant that God took the chance that we might make some tragic choices.

It's God's Will

Another related excuse for doing nothing is to pass this big nuclear buck off on God's will. Passing the buck is nice. It puts the heat on someone else. In fuzzy situations all of us are tempted to toss the responsibility off into someone else's lap. Passing the big buck to God goes something like this:

> If God wills a nuclear war, we'll have one. If he doesn't, then we won't. It all depends on his will, and all we have to do is sit back and see what happens.

We wash our hands, walk by on the other side, and pretend that it's not our responsibility. When we dismiss this whole issue by saying that it's up to God's will, we confuse God's sovereignty and human free will. These must stay in healthy tension. God created us with the ability to make choices. We make decisions and are responsible for what we do. And there are also things beyond our control that only God keeps tabs on.

To pass nuclear war off on God's will is utterly unfair to God and irresponsible on our part. Who made these weapons in the first place? It wasn't exactly God's idea, was it? Who decides to push the button? If humans choose to murder, kill, and rape, do we say that they aren't responsible and it's just God's will? Since God created us with free choice, perhaps he needs to share some of the responsibility when we choose to do destructive things. But it's not fair play to blame our foolish behavior on him. If a nuclear war comes to pass, it will come to pass because humans deliberately *decided* to build and explode bombs, not because God wanted it. We can't excuse ourselves from responsibility by blaming our mistakes on God's will.

A second confusion lies in thinking that God might will a nuclear war to render his judgment on sinful nations. We may be tempted to say, for example, that since nuclear war might be God's way of rendering his judgment on moral decay in American or Soviet society, we should not interfere with his plan by witnessing against nuclear war. There's a sharp distinction between God's *intention* to commit an act and his *use* of human folly for his glory after the fact. While God does not will or plan a tragedy, he may use it to teach us a lesson.

In the Old Testament, God used the warfare of other nations to teach Israel some lessons, but that is very different from saying God deliberately concocted the wars himself. God sometimes takes the stupid things we do and uses them to teach us or others a lesson. Rape and murder are not God's will. The destruction of God's people and his creation is *not* his will. His will as revealed in Jesus Christ is for salvation, shalom, wholeness, and justice. God does use evil to serve his purposes *after* we have made our choices, but we dare not twist this fact around and say that he *plans* and justifies the evil. If a nuclear war comes to pass, God may use it to teach us some hard lessons, and it may be his verdict of moral outrage on our warmongering, but that doesn't mean that he planned it, willed it, or pulled the trigger. He allows the law of sowing and reaping to work, and when we trip into our own trap he may use our fall to teach us some lessons.

Consider an analogy. I teach my children not to play with matches. But we do buy and store matches in our home. If one of our children plays with matches and burns down our house, that will be a terrible lesson for all of us. I will use the tragic experience to talk with all the children about disobedience and responsibility. But using their mistake to teach them a lesson is quite different from saying that I purposely wanted to burn down the house.

If we pretend that a nuclear war is God's will, what will the Christian survivors say after the war? Will they preach a God of love to other survivors? Who will believe in a God that does these kinds of things? Will the Christians themselves lose faith? In Billy Graham's words,

> I cannot see any way in which nuclear war could be branded as being God's will. Such warfare, if it ever happens, will come because of the greed and pride and covetousness of the human heart. But God's will is to establish his kingdom in which Christ is Lord.... Is it his will that resources be used for massive armaments which could otherwise be used for alleviating human suffering and hunger? Of course not. Our world has lost sight of true values and substituted false gods and false values.[2]

Signs of the End Time
There's a widespread temptation to sidestep the issue by saying that the rumblings of nuclear war are signs that the end of the world is near. We see nation rising up against nation, terrors and great signs in the heavens, famines and pestilences. Famine and pestilence would certainly follow in the wake of nuclear war. The apostle Peter, in describing the coming day of the Lord, says, "The heavens will be kindled and dissolved, and the elements will melt with fire!" (2 Peter 3:12).

Images of destruction in the book of Revelation which used to sound like remote fairy tales, suddenly take on possibility in the face of nuclear war. "A third of the earth was burnt up, and a third of the trees were burnt up, and all green grass was burnt up. . . . Then from the smoke came locusts on the earth, and they were given power like the power of scorpions of the earth" (Revelation 8:7, 9:3). Might such biblical descriptions come to pass in the aftermath of a nuclear war? What should we make of all this? How do we read the signs of the time? Is the end near?

We need to remind ourselves that Jesus himself said even he did not know the exact time of the end (Matthew 24:36). For many centuries faithful believers have thought the end was near. Every generation searches to discover whether the end is just around the corner in their own lifetime. It's easy to latch onto fixed schemes based on biblical passages and try to predict a play-by-play account of God's last inning. Our human imaginations are intrigued by the challenge of forecasting the number of acts in God's holy drama.

We must say in all modesty that if Jesus didn't know the day or the hour, we certainly can't know it either. Our generation might be different or it might not be. Perhaps God is beginning to pull down the curtain on history, or maybe he's not.

Our attempts to predict and act as though we really know the details of the end betray our arrogance, our hankering to be like God. When we act as though we know how everything is going to pan out, we are playing God's role. We should pay attention to the signs of the time, but we dare not become know-it-all forecasters. In all humility we must remember that we are the creatures and not the Creator, and we can never say for sure when the Creator will pull his curtain.

Even if the end is near, it is no excuse for Christians to self-righteously applaud it. In describing the last days Jesus said, "Men's love will grow cold" (Matthew 24:12). Our love and compassion have indeed grown cold when we run away from the potential suffering of nuclear war by piously saying,

"It's just a sign of the end times," thus cheering on the process that will lead to terrible anguish in a molten furnace. Regardless of whether the end is near, Jesus calls for a patient and faithful witness that endures to the end. In his words, "he who endures to the end will be saved" (Matthew 24:13).

Hard and callous hearts run away from nuclear war saying, "Aha, the end is near." Faithful Christian disciples witness to the gospel of peace, especially in the midst of rumors of war, regardless of how near the end is. If a faithful peace witness was ever needed, it is needed now! Not because it will turn the world around or slow down the coming of the end, but simply because it is the true witness to the gospel of Jesus Christ.

The End of the World

Some folks assume that a major nuclear war would automatically end the world. So why speak out about it? A major nuclear war is not likely to shut down the world, at least not immediately. An all-out nuclear war would be an unprecedented catastrophe, but the scientific evidence suggests it would hardly be the end of the world. Even an all-out exchange might leave 100 million or more American survivors. Until southern-hemisphere nations have the bomb, the destruction would be primarily limited to the northern hemisphere.

To be sure, it would be a very different world. It's impossible to predict the long-term consequences. The resulting devastation could lead to epidemic disease, famine, and economic collapse, which might kill millions more in the years after the attack. The long-term effects of radiation are unpredictable. Worst-case scenarios might lead to the breakdown of civilization some years after the attack. In any case, a nuclear war won't bring the immediate end of the world. There will be survivors. It's a grave mistake to think that God will just end the world someday with a big nuclear bang. If a nuclear war comes, it will come by accident or because humans have decided to fight one, and it will not be the end of the world, at least not right away.

The Lord Will Return

There is a widespread belief that, according to biblical teaching, the rapture will provide an escape hatch for Christians. The Lord will return and take the saints out of the world before a nuclear war begins. Thus Christians will be safe with God and need not worry about the horrors of nuclear war. Surprisingly, many Christians who hold this view also promote the use of nuclear arms as a security measure against communism. They are sure that God will bail them out safely through the rapture, and at the same time their support for nuclear arms shows a complete lack of trust in God's providence. They endorse the use of nuclear weapons, which may hasten the day of the fiery furnace for everyone else, but are sure they'll escape without a singed hair in the rapture.

It is crass and demonic to promote the very nuclear policies that invite war and then to glibly say that God will bail the Christians out while everyone else is scorched in the nuclear fire. In such a scenario, unfaithful Christians who preach peace through strength and help to trigger the war are rewarded by God with an early trip to heaven.

As before, we must say with all modesty that even the most devout believers can never say for certain how things will end. These are things that God alone keeps tabs on. Belief that the rapture will end all worries for God's people becomes twisted into an excuse for avoiding the issue of nuclear war. Faithful Christians who anticipate the rapture can do so expectantly and still witness to the peaceful gospel of Jesus Christ. It's a cheap and uncompassionate hope that awaits the rapture while smugly applauding the pending torture of millions of others. With genuine hope, true disciples affirm the triumph of God in the long run and persist in a faithful Christian witness to peace, realizing that only God knows the details of the end times.

It's a Political Issue

Frequently Christians shrug off any responsibility for thinking about nuclear war with the comment, "It's a political issue, not a spiritual one." We sort issues into boxes labeled "spiritual" and "political" and say it's the church's job to worry about the spiritual ones while the government looks after the political ones. In other words, nuclear war is none of the church's business. The church should stick with the gospel and not meddle in politics. Such thinking is a slick way of running away from the issue of nuclear war. Moral issues can't be categorized so neatly into spiritual and political boxes. There are numerous biblical examples of people like Isaiah, Jeremiah, and Micah who showed that so-called political issues were truly spiritual ones.

Would we say it's only a political issue if the government required children to read *Playboy* in elementary school? If the government forced parents to give all of their children into government custody at birth, would we say that's just a political issue? How can we say it's not a moral and spiritual issue when millions of citizens of both superpowers are held hostage to terror? When governments pursue policies that might lead to the deaths of millions, is that merely a political issue?

Are not spiritual values at stake when natural and human resources are used to make bombs while millions of children die from starvation? Is not the root cause and remedy of nuclear militarism spiritual in nature? How can we neatly avoid an issue with such vast ethical implications by flippantly saying that it's just a political issue the government should deal with? If nuclear war is not a moral and spiritual issue, what is? If the church has nothing to say on this question, then we'd better shut down the shop! Billy Graham says,

> The nuclear issue is not just a political issue—it is a moral and spiritual issue as well. And because we live in a sinful world it means we have to take something like nuclear armaments seriously.[3]

Archbishop John Roach, president of the National Conference of Catholic Bishops, put it this way,

> On a global scale, the most dangerous moral issue in the public order today is the nuclear arms race.[4]

Preach the Gospel

Other folks respond to the threat of nuclear war by saying the church should preach the gospel as never before and not get sidetracked into irrelevant social issues like nuclear war. The proclamation of the gospel *is* at the center of the church's mission, and it should stay there. But we must ask what kind of gospel the church is preaching. Is the church preaching the gospel of Jesus Christ that calls for conversion to a life in which all things become new, even our attitudes toward enemies? Are we preaching a gospel that calls for allegiance to Jesus Christ above nationalistic demands? Are we preaching a gospel of personal salvation which also transforms our social relationships? Or are we preaching a gospel of warm feelings that doesn't touch our attitudes toward militarism?

Dale Aukerman has noted that if all Americans were converted to the gospel that is preached from most pulpits, the mass conversion would hardly make any difference on the nuclear arms race, since the gospel that is typically preached has nothing to say about war.[5] A gospel that says nothing about the central moral issue of our time is not gospel. So while the church ought to be preaching the gospel, we must also ask what kind of gospel is being preached. Does it address the chief expression of sinful rebellion in our day? Or does it call for both spiritual conversion and tough military threats in the same breath?

A Problem of the Heart

In a recent conversation with me about nuclear war, a friend sighed and said, "Well, it's a problem of the heart, and so there's not much we can do about it." Such a statement is a step forward because it does recognize that nuclear weapons are indeed a spiritual issue and not just a political problem. Some Christians say that the arms race is only a symptom of a deeper spiritual disease and nothing will ever change until the basic disease is cured. They believe that protesting nuclear arms is a waste of time since it misses the spiritual point completely.

The clamor for nuclear superiority does reflect greed for

power that flows from rebellious hearts. And while it's correct to say, "It's a problem of the heart," that statement often ends the conversation, since it assumes the arms race won't stop until the leaders of both superpowers are converted and change their policies. Depending on what kind of gospel they hear, their conversion might not even make any difference on their nuclear policies. Since it's not likely that leaders on both sides will suddenly accept Christian pacifism, we're inclined to throw in the towel and go about our business as usual.

There are several problems with this excuse. There are many other situations flowing out of sinful rebellion which we do something about, even though the issue is most certainly a spiritual one at the core. If no laws prohibited drunken driving and a splurge of alcohol abuse resulted in several fatalities in our community, would we simply sigh and say, "Too bad, it's a problem of the heart," and let the drunken drivers keep on killing innocent victims? Of course not. Even though the alcoholism resulted from rebellious hearts, we would quickly pressure local authorities to enact stricter drunken driving laws. These laws wouldn't address the spiritual problem, but they would be responsible steps to protect innocent victims. We might also develop ministries for alcoholics aimed at the spiritual problem in their hearts, but we certainly wouldn't sit back and glibly say, "It's a problem of the heart," while drunken drivers killed innocent victims.

We support laws against child abuse even though we know full well that such laws will not cure the spiritual disease. We endorse legislation to control the flow of pornography even though it doesn't get at the spiritual problem of the vendors. We do whatever we can to constrain evil, not because such efforts eradicate sinful hearts, but simply because we care about the innocent and can't responsibly let evil run wild. Of course such laws are short-term "fixes" which don't get to the heart of the spiritual problem, but that isn't an excuse for doing nothing while evil runs wild. Using this reasoning, we might say that the purpose of nuclear weapons is precisely this—to stop evil from runnning wild.

We can't shift gears quite so easily! It's one thing to support legislation to constrain evil, and it's quite another thing to try to rein in evil by killing people. Besides, in our zealous passion to thwart nuclear evil we have ended up endangering ourselves and millions of other innocent citizens.

So while laws, arms control agreements, and public pressure won't cure spiritual diseases, we still support them, *not* because we think they address the basic problem, but because we care about innocent victims. We restrain a violent criminal not because it will change the person's heart or address his basic spiritual need, but because we care about the people who might be victimized next. And so we work for the elimination of nuclear weapons not because that deals with the basic spiritual issue, but because we care about the millions of people who might be killed if the race runs on.

And whenever possible we work on both levels, addressing spiritual needs and doing everything we can to reduce nuclear arms. The irony of the excuse that the arms race is a problem of the heart is that it's often a problem of the heart of those who use the excuse. Their hearts are so calloused to the possible suffering and tragedy in a nuclear war that they can turn away and do nothing without even feeling guilty. It is a problem of the heart, but whose heart? And while the arms race has spiritual roots, that dare not excuse us from working to control it on other levels.

Too Busy Doing Good

When confronted with the urgency of the nuclear threat, it's easy to respond by saying, "I'm already involved in good projects and I just can't drop my work and jump on this bandwagon, so stop making me feel guilty for doing nothing." The call for urgent action is not a call for all people to drop their present jobs and/or ministries of goodwill. Some people will change jobs and devote full time to peace ministries, and others will shuffle priorities and schedules as they join in a peace witness. The urgency doesn't demand an either/or of dropping everything we are presently doing and suddenly jumping on the nuclear protest bandwagon or doing nothing.

Most of us will continue our present work and juggle some of our fringe activities. We may need to resign from some committees and refuse to help on other projects or drop some recreational fun in order to devote more time to peace efforts. We can tamper with fringe activities. It's important to keep on doing our constructive work since it's a sign of hope and a candle in the darkness. These good ministries transform our peacemaking efforts into more than just curses at the darkness. But the good work we are doing dare not become an excuse to do nothing for the cause of peace. All of us can find *some* time and *some* ways to witness for peace either on top of or alongside of our present work. If we care, we will find time. We must find time, for the hour is late and the danger is near.

EVERYDAY EXCUSES
I'm Not an Expert
There are also everyday excuses for doing nothing. These don't carry the weight of religious blessing, but they are also powerful detours around action. A common one is this: "I'm not an expert," or "It's too complicated." That's a pretty good excuse since this topic *is* very complicated. The arms race is a scholar's gold mine teeming with all sorts of interdisciplinary issues and implications: technical, political, economic, historical, psychological, moral, and theological.

Although the issues surrounding the nuclear arms race are complicated and complex, there is also a somewhat simple choice between two options. It's ironic how some very sticky situations can hinge on fairly simple questions. The arms race is at once complicated and quite simple. We can either pursue our present aggressive arms buildup, *or* we can stop the production of new nuclear weapons and embark on a program of arms reduction. Each path has its own risks, and we'll need to decide which ones we're most willing to live with.

On the one hand we can embrace a huge defense buildup and frantically produce bigger and better weapons as a way of making sure that a holocaust never comes. Along this path we'll search for the big technological breakthrough—the superweapon that will finally put us far ahead and provide a threat beyond challenge. We'll continue believing that there's something to gain in nuclear war and that a nuclear war could be won. We'll continue thinking that our security increases as the arsenals get larger and larger. If we choose this option, we will try to maintain "superiority" and "a margin of safety." We will intimidate our enemies with the most threatening weapons. Our massive military buildup will hopefully bleed the economy of the other side to death. Such a policy asserts that more and bigger clubs will provide more security.

The other path to international security takes quite a different route. We will choose this alternative if we believe that the bomb "has changed everything except our way of thinking." Moving in this direction requires a change in our traditional ideas about war. We will realize that nuclear weapons make war obsolete, that there are no longer winners and losers, and that there's nothing to be gained by nuclear war. We will understand that superiority is meaningless with our present overkill capacities. We will realize that, in contrast to the past, our security today becomes more fragile as the weapons pile up.

Following this road means we will not assume that what's good for the Soviets is automatically bad for the U.S. We will erase our image of the Soviets as heartless scoundrels bent on conquering the world by force, and will realize that the superpowers have mutual interests - that what's good for them may also be good for us. We will realize that cooperation is in everybody's best interests.

These are the two roads and both are lined with risks. Pursuing superiority will surely perpetuate the spread of bombs. As the arsenals throughout the world grow, we will move closer to the brink of war. As more nations place their hands near the button, the likelihood of war will grow. We can enjoy the prestige of having the biggest arsenal, being number one, as long as we are also willing to accept the real risks of increasing the chances of a nuclear exchange.

If we follow the second route toward a stable peace, and

gamble on some goodwill initiatives, there are also risks. Taking the lead to halt the race may be seen as a sign of weakness and invite aggression. Freezing nuclear arms production and moving toward arms reductions may bring national embarrassment and humiliation. This route may dampen our national pride and esteem. It may shrink America's international base of power. A safer and more secure future may require such concessions. We don't have to be experts to make the choice.

But either way we turn, the risks and the costs are high. We will need to decide whether trying to maintain a number one image is more important than reversing the arms race. We'll need to decide whether preparing to kill the enemy is more important than increasing our security. We will need to consider whether a false sense of superiority is worth the possible cost of nuclear war. And we will need to decide whether anything is worth increasing the chance of nuclear war. Regardless of our choices, we now at least have some idea of the consequences of such a war so that we can decide whether we want to pay its price.

Now I realize this is simplifying things, but it doesn't take an expert to see that our present policies are leading us closer to nuclear war. One reason we are in this nuclear quagmire today is that we have left this whole thing up to the experts entirely too long. We dare not plead innocent on this question and shove it aside as "out of our area of expertise." The issues are straightforward enough for most of us to understand. The grave threat of nuclear war touches all of us, and we dare not toss it into the laps of preachers, weapon designers, and politicians. We dare not leave it up to them. The danger of nuclear war falls into everyone's turf regardless of professional expertise.

I Don't Have a Solution

Of course you don't have a solution and I don't either. No one else has been bright enough to come up with one, or we'd be out of this nuclear jam by now. A perfect solution to the problem isn't a required license for speaking out. There are no final or permanent solutions to complicated problems.

Until nations beat their bombs into solar collectors, there will be no final solution—and that's not likely to happen in the near future.

Many forces combine to shape the response of governments to the nuclear threat. A government's final position results from negotiation, bargaining, and compromise among its own political leaders as well as with opponents.

We don't need a solution in order to speak out. Christians along with everyone else feed their ideas into the hopper of public opinion and hope they contribute to a better final result. Our primary concern is to tell the truth, not to offer perfect solutions. Not having a workable solution dare not be an excuse for running away from truth-telling.

I Can't Make a Difference

A related excuse is, "What I do won't make a difference." Probably it won't. One person isn't going to change the world. None of us is going to turn the arms race around alone. However, if everyone uses that as an excuse, the sum of thousands of shrugging Christian shoulders indicates wide-scale support of the nuclear arms race. It's true that one person can't make much of a difference. But it's also true that a million shrugging shoulders do make an enormous collective indifference, while a million letters to legislators might change things drastically. The arms race will never turn around as long as Christians of all persuasions sigh deeply and say "It's just too bad, isn't it?" and go about their business as usual.

The whole problem with saying "I can't make a difference" assumes that the point of a Christian witness is to make something happen. That is *not* the primary reason for our witness. The purpose of Christian witness is to tell the truth rather than to worry about the consequences. If five million Christians stood up and told the truth about the gospel of peace, that would make an enormous impact on government policies. But the major purpose of the witness is to tell the truth, not to make something happen. It doesn't matter whether our acts make a difference or not; what does matter is whether we're willing to tell the truth about the gospel of peace. And who knows, our truth-telling may light some fires under others and compel them to tell the truth as well.

What Will Be, Will Be

Others say, "Let's be realistic and realize that what will be, will be, and there's not a whole lot we can do about this thing." It's certainly true that we can't change a lot of things and we do have to take some lumps and live with them. But such a philosophy taken to its extreme is certainly not Christian and borders on a pagan philosophy of determinism. Do we believe that we are only puppets with no strings of our own to pull? When we say, "What will be, will be," we make chance our lord. We deny our God-given ability to make choices, and we reject God's role in shaping history. To put our faith and hope in fate is a sorry rejection of Christ's lordship over history. Making chance our lord denies God's creative work in the Holy Spirit and leaves us worshiping at a pagan altar of fatalism.

But I'm Not Responsible

It's also easy to get off the hook by saying, "I'm not responsible." I don't design weapons. It wasn't my idea to build a nuclear bomb. I haven't supported the arms race. I wouldn't press the button on the Russians. I don't work in a bomb factory. My record is pure. My hands are clean. So why should I have to clean up the moral junk that other people scatter around? This excuse is especially tempting for Christian pacifists who have consistently stood in the peace tradition. If anyone's hands are clean, certainly theirs are since they argued for peace before the bomb was ever built. But this excuse is used by many others who are not directly involved with the bomb.

I've already made the case that all of us *are* involved as taxpayers and as citizens in a democracy with the privilege of free speech. Beyond that, it's a question of who picks up the trash. Because we are God's people, we care about his world as he does. We have compassion. We care for God's good garden as well as for our fellow citizens, who are created in his image and who share the garden with us. Even though we haven't dumped nuclear trash all over his garden, we help to pick it up simply because we care as he cares. We love as he loves. We are moved to compassion as he is. We help to pick up the nuclear litter not because we carelessly dumped it here, but because we care deeply about the garden and the other folks in the garden. As stewards of life in the garden we cannot turn our backs on moral trash. And so even though we don't work in a bomb factory, we tend the garden as best we can because we are God's people and we are the stewards of his garden.

I Don't Know What to Do

There's not a "right" thing to do. Don't expect a special trick that works miracles. There aren't magic formulas. If you truly care, you'll find ways to share your witness publicly. The Holy Spirit charts the course of action for those who care.

Those who say, "I'm concerned about the threat of nuclear war, but I can't think of anything to do," really don't care. Remember the old saying "If there's a will, there's a way"? When people truly care about something, they do find ways to respond to it. If we heard that the government was planning to conscript our children into the armed forces at the age of ten, we would do *something* about it; and we would act without a blueprint that spelled out all the details. People who genuinely care will act, and they will find ways to express their concern even if they don't know all the ropes.

The "I don't know what to do" alibi simply doesn't wash. Most of us can think up better excuses than that! Our stalling for action is often not so much a problem of not knowing what to do as it is a problem of finding courage. We know what to do, but we're afraid to do it. We're afraid of what others will say, afraid that we might look foolish. So let's at least be honest, and if we're scared, let's admit it instead of blaming our inaction on not knowing what to do. Those who care will find the courage and the way.

WHO WILL BLOW THE WHISTLE?

There are times when someone has to stand up and

blow the whistle. Blowing the whistle is a way of saying "That's enough!" or "It's time to stop!"

Who blows the whistle on government in a democracy? Who has the moral responsibility to say, "Enough is enough; it's time to stop!" When government works for the public good, there is little need for whistle blowing. Are there, however, circumstances when God's people might need to stand up and say, "Here's where we draw the line"? Or should Christians always grant an elected government the right to do anything it pleases? Are there any conceivable situations that merit respectful protest? Is there a time for righteous moral outrage?

What Will It Take?

What will it take before we blow the whistle? Are there any scenarios that would prod us to action? If our government developed plans to exterminate all illegal aliens as a way of discouraging illegal immigration, would we care enough to protest? If the government decided to poison fish in streams throughout the country to curtail the need for environmental protection of fresh waters, would we say anything? If a democratic government initiated legislation to forbid services in church except on Sunday evening, would we blow our whistles then?

If the government required every child to subscribe to *Playboy* magazine, would we care enough to speak out? If our local municipalities held open hearings on the possibility of requiring a $100 per capita tax at the time of church baptism, would we go to the meetings and speak up? If the federal government set in motion plans to exterminate any child born to a couple after their first two children to control population growth, would we stand up and blow our whistles then?

If the government constructed weapons that could destroy the earth and contaminate it for unknown generations, would we speak out? If the government pursued dangerous nuclear policies that threatened by accident or design to murder millions of people, would Christians blow their whistles then? If the government already had at least 26,000 nuclear bombs and planned to make 17,000 more in the next decade, would we cry out, "That's enough"? What will it take to spur us to witness?

If a nuclear bomb exploded accidentally in a training flight and killed 300,000 people in Omaha, would that be enough to wind us up? If two Middle Eastern countries in a border spat reached for the big stick and swatted one million people in the process, would that be enough to get us moving? What will it take? What will it take for God's people to reach for their whistles?

Under what conditions will we intervene and blow the whistle? Only if our occupational and economic interests are at stake? Are personal interests the only thing that will move God's people?

Consider two of your neighbors. They live side by side in separate houses across the street from you. They are bickering over their property line. The dispute grows into a legal battle, and finally one evening you see your neighbors carting automatic rifles and pistols into their homes. The basements become arsenals loaded with hand grenades, ammunition, and dynamite. In the early evening there is target practice on the back lawns. A concrete wall is built on the property line, and guards are hired for 24-hour surveillance. The outcome of this buildup is clear—someday, somehow, something will trigger a fight which will certainly destroy your neighbors and their homes.

As observant neighbors across the street, what would we do? Would we sit back and pass the buck to God by saying, "If he wants them to have a fight, he'll allow it. After all, he's in control, and the neighbors can't do anything that he doesn't allow." Is that what we would say? Would we toss it into God's lap, shrug our shoulders, and go about planting shrubs and fruit trees on the back side of our garden so that we didn't have to think about it? Would we say that since we didn't start it and since we aren't in the middle of it, the fight's none of our business? If children were playing with matches, surrounded by spilled gasoline, would we also quietly sit by and watch?

Or might we think that Christian responsibility begged

us to venture across the street and offer to mediate between our hostile neighbors? Would we understand that the children of God—the peacemakers—do whatever they can in whatever ways possible to promote reconciliation? If we were afraid of walking across the street, would we at least call the police or the crisis intervention center? Would we make any moves or do anything to stop the fight? The only difference between this example and the growing threat of nuclear war is that we happen to live in a room in one of the houses threatened by nuclear conlict. Our home is at stake. And even so we shuck off responsibility.

Piling up weapons of catastrophic destructiveness paves the way for devastation. If in such conditions God's people politely give their consent to government policies, does it mean that we would never under any circumstances stand up and blow our whistles? What could be worse than the threat of civilization as we now know it being snuffed out? Will we quietly give government the right to lead us toward collective suicide?

If the trend toward nuclear holocaust runs its natural course, will the hands of peace-loving Christians who haven't touched their whistles be pure and clean? If Christians, of all people, the lovers of peace, those of good cheer and goodwill— if even the peacemakers stand idly by without blowing their whistles, who will? Has the time not come for us to blow our whistles loud and clear? John Stoner has said,

> If a nuclear holocaust comes about, it will only come because millions of Christians have quietly given consent to the preparations for it.[6]

The Sin of Silent Consent

There are sins of commission—doing evil by acting— and there are sins of omission—doing wrong by doing nothing. In a democracy, quiet consent is a sign of support. Those who say nothing and do nothing about preparations for nuclear war are themselves helping to propel the race forward by their silence. Billy Graham, in describing his change of heart about nuclear arms, says,

> We cannot wash our hands of our responsibilities. What some
> people do not see is that failing to oppose something may at
> times actually be condoning it.[7]

Doing nothing is a sign not only of consent, but also of death—a sign that death has so infected our culture and our lives that the will to live is gone. Indifference is a yes to death—a yes to the forces that dull our moral nerves. Doing something—just anything—is a testimony of exactly where we personally stand on this question, and it's also a sign of hope. Doing something is the most tangible clue to our children and to those around us that our hope has not vanished in the face of this terrible threat. Our tiny acts are signs that we believe God was victorious over death.

The Buck Starts with Me

It's easy to pass this big buck off to God or to our denominational peace groups. It's hard to face up to the fact that each of us as individuals holds part of the nuclear war buck. As one poster says, "In a democracy we all push the button." The nuclear threat will not fade until common people from all walks of life begin holding this buck. It's easy to push the buck off onto others. Why doesn't my pastor or priest preach about it? If only our peace and justice committee would do something about this. Why don't church leaders speak out more boldly? Why aren't the young people tackling this one? Why doesn't the government do something?

These are good questions, but the *most* important question in all the pages of this book is a simple one. It's the ultimate question, one that requires courage to answer. It's easier asked than answered.

What are *you* doing about it?

Are *you* doing as much as *you* can?

This is the "me" question, the only one that matters. It doesn't matter what your pastor or priest says. It doesn't matter whether the peace committee does its job. It doesn't matter whether your denomination is slow to respond. All that matters is whether *you* are doing everything that *you* can.

As God's people we hold the treasure of peace in our hands. What will we do with it? What will you do with it? Will we bury it or will we invest it? The world waits to see. The King waits to see. And the King will return to find out.

PROMISE, HOPE, AND DREAM

As we ponder our "me" question, it's helpful to recall a promise, a hope, and a dream. The promise is from the Old Testament. We already noted the relevance of Psalm 23 to the arms race in an earlier chapter. The promise provides us comfort as we walk in the valley of the shadow of death.

> Even though I walk through the
> valley of the shadow of death
> I fear no evil;
> for thou art with me;
> thy rod and thy staff,
> they comfort me.

The promise is simply that God walks with us even in the dark valley of death. There are no miraculous promises here to kill off wild lions, no promises to mysteriously bring an early dawn, no promises to magically remove the mountains, no promise to dumbfound robbers—*only* the promise of his presence. And that's enough. For it brings us comfort and dispels our fear. The promise still holds in the face of nuclear war. No promises to mysteriously bail us out. No promises to miraculously dismantle the nuclear arsenals. No promises to shoulder our responsibility. *Only* the promise that he is with us and that he understands. He has been through this before. And so the ministry and witness of his spirit brings comfort and joy. And that comfort and that joy enable us to be faithful witnesses unto the end of the age.

The hope is a New Testament theme that threaded its way through the somber lines of this book. Looking into the face of nuclear war is like standing at the foot of the cross.

Things look bleak. The outlook is dark and the future is uncertain. Our hope lies in the empty tomb—that sign of all
signs that God is at work behind the scenes. The risen Lord
is our glorious hope that God can use the terror of men to
his glory. We look through a dark glass. We can't see ahead,
but we rest in the hope that God again will ultimately
triumph, even over the evil powers that hold sway in a nuclear age. As he did in the resurrection, so he will again
disarm the powers and call their bluff. And so we live joyously
in this hope.

The dream emerges today around the world. In the face
of a truly international holocaust that threatens life in the
East and West, under socialism and capitalism, in free and in
totalitarian societies, there is *one* world body that links humanity together across political and ideological barriers.
There is *one* fellowship around the globe that rises above national, ethnic, and political ties in its common confession
that Jesus is Lord.

The dream grows out of this fellowship, a dream of
Christian brothers and sisters standing up in the East and
the West with candles of peace in their hands. The future is
in our hands. The issue is here and the time is *now* for the
body of Christ to join hands in a worldwide peace witness.
This is the moment for the church to be the church, to proclaim the good news that God is no respecter of person or nation, to say that in Jesus Christ there is no east and west,
and to declare that Jesus Christ is the prince of peace. The
church is God's gift for such a time as this. This could be the
church's glorious hour. But a dream is only a dream until we
act. Will we act or will we run away? Will we share a witness
for peace or will we give excuses? The world waits to see. And
the King waits to see.

QUESTIONS

1. Are all moral issues of equal importance? Are there really moral pimples and cancer?
2. What are some other ways of running away from the issue of nuclear war besides those discussed in this chapter?
3. Which detours around the issue of nuclear war are most tempting to the church today?
4. How does the threat of nuclear war fit into biblical prophecies? Can biblical descriptions of destruction be literally related to a nuclear holocaust?
5. Is the issue really as simple as a choice between two roads?
6. Does the church have a special moral responsibility to blow the whistle in a democratic society?
7. Is the "me" question the most important one?
8. Would the church respond differently if a nuclear bomb exploded by accident and killed thousands?
9. Is there evidence of a peace witness among Christians in both eastern and western European countries?
10. What specific activities could the church do on an international basis to make its peace witness more visible?

NOTES

Chapter One: Why It's Urgent Now

1. Admiral Gene R. LaRocque, *The Defense Monitor*, 9, No.6 (1980), 3.

2. See for example George Kistiakowsky, *The Defense Monitor*, 10, No.2 (1981), 3; Herbert Scoville, Jr., *MX: Prescription for Disaster* (Cambridge, Mass.: MIT Press, 1981), pp.46-47; Harold Brown, *U.S. Department of Defense Annual Report, Fiscal Year 1981* (Washington, D.C.: U.S. Government Printing Office, 1981), p.67; The Palme Commission, *Common Security—A Blueprint for Survival.* Reported in the *New York Times*, June 2, 1982.

3. Scoville, p.67; Ruth Leger Sivard, *World Military and Social Expenditures 1981* (Leesburg, Va.: World Priorities, Inc., 1982), p.15.

4. Friedwardt Winterberg, *The Physical Properties of Thermonuclear Explosive Devices* (privately printed, 1981).

5. "George Kistiakowsky: Champion of Arms Control," *Chemical and Engineering News*, February 2, 1981, p.24.

6. Scoville, p.ix.

7. LaRocque, p.1.

8. Joseph Weizenbaum, quoted in "Scientists Preach Peace at MIT," *The Christian Century*, August 15-22, 1979, p.779.

9. "Nuclear War in Europe," *The Defense Monitor*, 10, No.7, (1981), 12; Nigel Calder, *Nuclear Nightmares: An Investigation of Possible Wars* (New York: Viking Press, 1980).

10. Desmond Ball in an *Adelphi Paper*, published by The International Institute for Strategic Studies. Reported in the *New York Times*, November 18, 1981.

11. "U.S. Nuclear Weapons Accidents: Danger in Our Midst," *The Defense Monitor*, 10, No.5, (1981).

12. Jack Anderson, "How Safe Are We From Our Own Nuclear

Weapons?" *Parade Magazine*, October 18, 1981.

13. "The Race to Nuclear War," *The Defense Monitor*, 9, No.6, (1980), 3.

14. John L. Kirkley, *Datamation*, September 1981, p.37.

15. Lloyd Dumas, "Systems Reliability and Accidental War," paper presented at the March 1982 meeting of the American Physical Society in Dallas, Tex.

16. James E. Muller, "On Accidental Nuclear War," in "My Turn," *Newsweek*, March 1, 1982.

Chapter Two: The Secrets

1. I highly recommend *Hiroshima-Nagasaki: A Pictorial Record of the Atomic Destruction* (Tokyo: Hiroshima-Nagasaki Publishing Committee, 1978); The Japanese Broadcasting Company, *Unforgettable Fire: Pictures Drawn By Atomic Bomb Survivors* (New York: Pantheon, 1981).

2. The statistical facts related to the Hiroshima destruction vary a great deal by sources. All the numbers reported here are taken from the recent compendium produced by the Committee for the Compilation of Materials on Damage entitled *Hiroshima and Nagasaki: The Physical, Medical and Social Effects of the Atomic Bombings* (New York: Basic Books, 1981).

3. Morton Sontheimer, "Memories of a Small Bomb," in "My Turn," *Newsweek*, June 29, 1981, p.9.

4. Henry Scott Stokes, "Children of the A-Bomb: Stunted Bodies and Lives," *New York Times*, August 10, 1981.

5. Robert Jay Lifton did the classic research in the study of psychological effects on the Hiroshima survivors. This section of my discussion is heavily based on Lifton's *Death in Life: Survivors of Hiroshima* (New York: Random House, 1967) and on his "In A Dark Time," in *The Final Epidemic*, ed. Ruth Adams and Susan Cullen (Chicago: Educational Foundation for Nuclear Science, 1981). The quotes in this section are from these two sources.

6. The Boston Study Group, *The Price of Defense* (New York: The New York Times Book Co., 1979), p.63.

7. E.I. Chazov, "A Clear and Present Danger—East," in *The Final Epidemic*, p.61.

8. Dale Aukerman, *Darkening Valley: A Biblical Perspective on Nuclear War* (New York: Seabury, 1981), pp.47-48. My theological analysis here and in many sections of the book is indebted to Aukerman's excellent work in *Darkening Valley*.

9. Daniel Ellsberg, "Call to Mutiny," in *Protest and Survive*, ed. E.P. Thompson and Dan Smith (New York: Monthly Review Press, 1981), p.v-vi.

10. Roger Fisher, "Preventing Nuclear War," in *The Final Epidemic*, p.234.

11. Robert Jungk, *Brighter than a Thousand Suns* (New York: Harcourt, Brace and Co., 1958), p. 201.

12. Sidney Lens, *The Day Before Doomsday: An Anatomy of the Nuclear Arms Race* (Boston: Beacon Press, 1977), p.33.

13. Aukerman, p.56.

Chapter Three: Why Nuclear Weapons Aren't Nice

1. Donald B. Kraybill and John P. Ranck, *Nuclear War and Lancaster County* (Lancaster, Pa.: Provident Bookstores, 1981). This is a technical description of a one megaton explosion over Lancaster City, which provides the basis for much of this chapter.

2. The following two standard sources were used to derive the calculations reported in this chapter. The U.S. Congressional Office of Technological Assessment (OTA), *The Effects of Nuclear War* (Washington, D.C.: U.S. Government Printing Office, 1979); Samuel Glasstone and Philip Dolan, *The Effects of Nuclear Weapons*, 3rd ed. (Washington, D.C.: U.S. Department of Defense and U.S. Department of Energy, 1977).

3. Federal Emergency Management Agency, *U.S. Crisis Relocation Planning* P&P7, (Washington, D.C., February 1981), p. 3.

4. U.S. Arms Control and Disarmament Agency, *Effects of Nuclear War* (Washington, D.C., April 1979), p. 20.

5. Glasstone and Dolan, pp.541-618.

6. Casualty estimates except for Leningrad are from U.S. Arms Control and Disarmament Agency, *U.S. Urban Population Vulnerability* (Washington, D.C., August 1979). Estimates for Leningrad casualties were obtained from OTA, *The Effects of Nuclear War*, p.37.

7. OTA, *The Effects of Nuclear War*, pp.63-108.

8. *The Final Epidemic*, pp.177-78.

9. The best scholarly study of the possible social chaos after a nuclear war is a book by Arthur M. Katz, *Life After Nuclear War: The Economic and Social Impacts of Nuclear Attacks on the United States* (Cambridge, Mass.: Ballinger Publishing Co., 1982).

10. Herbert L. Abrams, "Infection and Communicable Diseases," in *The Final Epidemic*, pp.192-222.

11. The American Medical Association meeting in Las Vegas in December 1981 passed a resolution calling on physicians to inform the members of Congress of the medical effects of a nuclear war. Physicians for Social Responsibility, a national organization of physicians, stresses the futility of civil defense preparations.

12. OTA, *The Effects of Nuclear War*, p.3.

13. Ernest J. Sternglass and William T. Land, "A Nuclear War's Devastating Effect on Climate," *New York Times*, May 28, 1982.

14. OTA, *The Effects of Nuclear War*, pp.111-12; *The Final Epidemic*, pp.117-50.

15. This is the imagery that Jonathan Schell employs in *The Fate of the Earth* (New York: Alfred A. Knopf, 1982).

16. John Sommerville, "Human Rights and Nuclear War," *The Churchman*, January 1982, p.10.

17. My contrast of the cross and the bomb is indebted to Aukerman's work in *Darkening Valley* and to Jim Wallis' analysis in *The Call to Conversion* (San Francisco: Harper and Row, 1981), p.88.

18. Wallis, p.88.

Chapter Four: Can We Trust the Giants?

1. For an excellent study of the relations between the superpowers, see Richard J. Barnet, *The Giants: Russia and America* (New York: Simon and Schuster, 1977).

2. The numbers of weapons in Figure 4.2 are reasonable estimates as of mid-1982. The estimates vary somewhat by source, but generally are similar to those reported in Figure 4.2. For comparisons see *The Military Balance 1980-81* (London: The International Institute for Strategic Studies, 1980); *World Armaments and Disarmament SIPRI Yearbook 1981* (Stockholm: International Peace Research Institute, 1981); *U.S. Department of Defense Annual Report, Fiscal Year 1981* (Washington, D.C.: U.S. Government Printing Office); Frank Blackaby, "World Arsenals 1982," *The Bulletin of the Atomic Scientists*, 38, No. 6 (June 1982), 21-26.

3. "Soviet Nuclear Superiority Disputed," *New York Times*, May 1, 1982. The *Department of Defense Annual Report 1982* (Washington, D.C.: U.S. Government Printing Office) describes the superpowers' nuclear arsenals as "equivalent."

4. "Rickover Versus Nuclear Arms and Corporate Power," *The Christian Science Monitor*, February 9, 1982, p.22.

5. Alan Wolfe, *The Rise and Fall of the Soviet Threat: Domestic Sources of the Cold War Consensus* (Washington, D.C.: Institute for Policy Studies, 1979).

6. Bernard Gwertzman, "Haig Attacks Soviet War By Proxy," *New York Times News Service*, April 25, 1981.

7. One of the most helpful discussions of the Soviet threat is *Questions and Answers on the Soviet Threat and National Security* (Philadelphia, Pa.: American Friends Disarmament Program, 1981).

8. U.S. Department of Defense, *Soviet Military Power* (Washington, D.C.: U.S. Government Printing Office, 1981).

9. National Science Foundation short course, "Arms Uncontrolled: Causes and Remedies of the Arms Race," Temple University, November 1980.

10. For a discussion of the decline of Soviet influence, see "So-

viet Geopolitical Momentum: Myth or Menace," *The Defense Monitor*, 9. No.1, (1980).

11. A profile of Soviet perceptions of the U.S. can be found in *Questions and Answers on the Soviet Threat and National Security*.

12. *U.S. Department of Defense Annual Report, Fiscal Year 1981* (Washington, D.C.: U.S. Government Printing Office, 1981).

13. "To the Brink and Back 330 Times," *Time*, January 17, 1977.

14. "Arming the World," *Time*, October 26, 1981.

15. "Some Defense Budget Considerations," *Journal of the Federation of American Scientists*, January 1982, p.6.

16. Jim Wallis in *The Call to Conversion*, p.93, proposes that instead of asking "What about the Russians?" Christians ought to ask "What about us?"

17. The political threat of Jesus is discussed by John Howard Yoder in *The Politics of Jesus* (Grand Rapids, Mich.: Eerdmans, 1972); see also Donald B. Kraybill, *The Upside-Down Kingdom* (Scottdale, Pa.: Herald Press, 1978).

18. *Congressional Record*, June 27, 1980, p.H5839.

19. *New York Times*, February 25, 1982.

Chapter Five: Why the Arms Race Doesn't Stop

1. George F. Kennan, *Albert Einstein Peace Prize Acceptance Remarks* (New York: Institute for World Order, 1981), p.1.

2. Kennan, p.2.

3. Sivard, pp.25-33.

4. Sam Day, ed., *Makers of the Nuclear Holocaust: A Guide to the Nuclear Weapons Complex and Citizen Action* (Nyack, N.Y.: Fellowship of Reconciliation, 1981), p.3.

5. "Builder of the B-1 Bomber," *New York Times*, October 11, 1981.

6. Michael Heylin, "Nuclear Arms Race Gearing for Speedup," *Chemistry and Engineering News*, March 16, 1981, p.34.

7. Gordon Adams, *The Iron Triangle: The Politics of Defense Contracting* (New York: Council on Economic Priorities, 1981).

8. Jerome Frank, *Sanity and Survival: Psychological Aspects of War and Peace* (New York: Random House, 1967).

9. Tom Wicker, syndicated column entitled "Beware of Military Gaposis," January 10, 1981.

10. Richard A. Stubbing, "The Imaginary Defense Gap: We Already Outspend Them," *Washington Post*, February 14, 1982.

11. U.S. Department of Defense, *Soviet Military Power*.

12. Scoville, pp.99-104.

13. Walter Wink, "Faith and Nuclear Paralysis," *The Christian*

Century, March 3, 1982, p.237.
    14. Wink, p.237.

Chapter Six: Rumors of Peace

    1. See for example the bibliography called The Christian Peace Shelf at the end of this book. In addition, I especially recommend for the serious reader John Howard Yoder's *The Politics of Jesus.*

    2. John Driver, *Community and Commitment* (Scottdale, Pa.: Herald Press, 1976), p.70.

    3. I describe the surprising social aspects of Jesus' ministry in several chapters of *The Upside-Down Kingdom.*

    4. The phrase "reverse fighting" is taken directly from Vernard Eller, *War and Peace from Genesis to Revelation* (Scottdale, Pa.: Herald Press, 1981).

    5. Marlin E. Miller, "The Gospel of Peace," *Mission-Focus,* 6, No.1, (September 1977), 2.

    6. An excellent historical record of early Christian pacifism can be found in Jean-Michel Hornus, *It Is Not Lawful for Me to Fight* (Scottdale, Pa.: Herald Press, 1980). See also Roland H. Bainton, *Christian Attitudes Toward War and Peace* (Nashville, Tenn.: Abingdon, 1960).

    7. Two helpful treatments of warfare in the Old Testament are Millard Lind's *Yaweh Is A Warrior* (Scottdale, Pa.: Herald Press, 1980) and Eller's *War and Peace from Genesis to Revelation.*

    8. Richard M. Sorley, S.J., in *New Testament Basis of Peacemaking* (Washington, D.C.: Center for Peace Studies, 1979), provides a detailed discussion of these and other related passages.

    9. Michael Walzer, *Just and Unjust Wars* (New York: Basic Books, 1977), p.282.

    10. For an extensive discussion of this passage in Romans, see Yoder, *The Politics of Jesus,* especially chapter 10.

Chapter Seven: Dare We Tolerate Nuclear Weapons?

    1. Ted Koontz in personal correspondence and by sharing draft copies of several papers in process has been extremely helpful to me in focusing the ethical issues surrounding nuclear deterrence. A provocative treatment of nuclear morality is J. Bryan Hehir's "The Just War and Catholic Theology: Dynamics of Change and Continuity," in *War or Peace,* ed. Thomas A. Shannon (Maryknoll, N.Y.: Orbis, 1980).

    2. Lloyd J. Averill, "Nuclear Morality," *The Christian Century,* April 14, 1982, p.438.

    3. New York's Terence Cardinal Cooke, in his December 7,

1981, letter to military chaplains, said that holding nuclear weapons is "morally tolerable; not satisfactory, but tolerable." Reported in the *New York Times*, December 15, 1981.

4. Wallis, p.93.

5. My critique of the deterrence concept relies heavily on Alan F. Geyer's excellent discussion of deterrence in *The Idea of Disarmament!* (Elgin, Ill.: The Brethren Press, 1982).

6. Geyer, p.59.

7. John E. Mack, "Psychosocial Trauma," in *The Final Epidemic*, p.22.

8. Michael J. Carey, "Psychological Fallout," *The Bulletin of the Atomic Scientists*, 38, No.1, (January 1982), 21.

9. Lester Thurow, "How to Wreck the Economy," *The New York Review*, May 14, 1981, and "Beware of Reagan's Military Spending," *New York Times*, May 31, 1981.

10. "Burning Up $1 Trillion," *Wall Street Journal*, January 22, 1980.

11. Robert DeGrasse, Jr., and David Gold, "Military Spending's Damage to the Economy," *New York Times*, December 30, 1981. See also "If U.S. Military Builds Up, Will Economy Be Held Down?" *Christian Science Monitor*, March 5, 1982.

12. Marion Anderson, *The Empty Pork Barrel 1982* (Lansing, Mich.: Employment Research Associates, 1982).

13. R.G. Kaiser, "Reagan's Defense Spending Could Turn Into Economic Nightmare," *Washington Post*, April 15, 1981.

14. James R. Anderson, *Bankrupting America, 1982* (Lansing, Mich.: Employment Research Associates, 1982).

15. Marion Anderson, *Converting the Work Force: Where the Jobs Would Be* (Lansing, Mich.: Employment Research Associates, 1980); Robert DeGrasse, Jr., et al., *Creating Solar Jobs* (Mountain View, Calif.: Mid Peninsula Conversion Project, 1978); David Gold, et al., *The Case for Economic Conversion* (Watertown, Mass.: Bay State Conversion Group, 1979).

16. "Poverty in the U.S. 1957-1980," *New York Times*, February 20, 1982.

17. These figures are adapted from several sources: Sivard, *World Military and Social Expenditures 1981*; "Haig Aide Says U.S. Opposes Sharing Wealth," *New York Times*, August 7, 1981; U.S. Department of State, "World Hunger," *Current Policy No. 299*, July 22, 1981; "A Survival Summit," *Newsweek*, October 26, 1981.

18. Geyer, p.164.

19. Edgar Metzler, "The Cross: Hidden by the Bomb," *Gospel Herald*, 74, No.31, (August 4, 1981), 593.

20. "State of the Union Address," January 1982.

21. "Pope Urges Abolishment of A-Arms," *New York Times*, December 24, 1981.

22. "Churchmen Vs. The Bomb," *Newsweek* magazine, January 11, 1982.

Chapter Eight: You Can Do Something
1. Wallis, p.104.
2. Geyer, p. 194.

Chapter Nine: Running Away from Nuclear War
1. "George Kistiakowsky: Champion of Arms Control," p.26.
2. Billy Graham, "A Change of Heart," *Sojourners* magazine, August 1979.
3. Graham, "A Change of Heart."
4. *New York Times*, November 18, 1981.
5. Aukerman, p.168.
6. John Stoner, in personal correspondence.
7. Graham, "A Change of Heart."

Appendix 1

HISTORICAL OVERVIEW OF THE NUCLEAR ARMS RACE

Both sides have had "firsts" in the nuclear arms race, but neither side has stayed ahead long. The U.S. has usually maintained a technological lead, which is eventually matched by the Soviets in a few years.

Atomic Bomb

U.S. 1945   **1949 USSR**

The nuclear age began with the explosion of a U.S. A-bomb over Hiroshima, Japan. Within four years the USSR conducted its first atomic test.

Intercontinental Bomber

U.S. 1948   **1955 USSR**

By 1948 the U.S. had begun to replace the propeller planes of World War II with long-range jets. In 1955 the U.S. began deployment of the all-jet intercontinental bomber, and the USSR soon followed suit.

Hydrogen Bomb

U.S. 1954   **1955 USSR**

The H-bomb multiplied the explosive force of the A-bomb 1,000 times.

Intercontinental Ballistic Missile (ICBM)

USSR 1957   **1958 U.S.**

A land-based missile to carry nuclear warheads intercontinental distances was successfully flight-tested by the USSR in 1957, and by the U.S. a year later. By 1962 both nations had ICBMs with a range of 6,000 miles.

Man-Made Satellite In Orbit

USSR 1957   **1958 U.S.**

The USSR's Sputnik I initiated a space race, which quickly took on military functions; the first U.S. satellite was launched into orbit the following year. Well over half the superpowers' satellites have been military—for surveillance, targeting, communications, etc.

Submarine-Launched Ballistic Missile (SLBM)

U.S. 1960   **1968 USSR**

A nuclear-powered submarine which could fire long-range missiles from a submerged position was the third means of strategic delivery to be developed.

Multiple Warhead (MRV)
U.S. 1966   **1968 USSR**
Missiles carrying several bombs increased the number of targets a U.S. missile could hit. The USSR had them two years later.

Anti-Ballistic Missile (ABM)
USSR 1968   **1972 U.S.**
Anti-ballistic missiles are defensive missiles designed to destroy attacking missiles. Considered ineffective, they were limited in a 1972 treaty. ABM research continues today, but neither side has an "effective" ABM force.

Multiple Independently-Targeted Warhead (MIRV)
U.S. 1970   **1975 USSR**
Further development of multiple warheads enabled one missile to target bombs on three to ten individually selected targets as far apart as 100 miles.

Long-Range Cruise Missile
U.S. 1982   **? USSR**
Launched from air, sea, and land, a new generation of missiles with a range up to 1,500 miles is in production. The cruise missile is small, relatively inexpensive, and highly accurate. Following the contours of the earth and flying under radar, it will be able to destroy its target without warning. The U.S. is reportedly seven to eight years in the lead in this technology.

Neutron Bomb
U.S. 1983   **? USSR**
This nuclear weapon releases more of its explosive energy in the form of an invisible, penetrating radiation than in heat and blast. The decision to produce the neutron bomb was announced by the U.S. in August 1981.

Anti-Satellite Weapons
U.S. 199?   **? USSR**
Because satellites play vital military roles, they have also inspired a search for weapons to destroy them. The USSR began testing interceptor satellites in 1968. Both superpowers are attempting to perfect lasers to destroy enemy satellites and nuclear missiles in the event of war.

SOURCE: Adapted from Ruth Leger Sivard, *World Military and Social Expenditures 1981,* (Leesburg, Va.: World Priorities, Inc., 1982), p. 14.

Appendix 2

WEAPON AND SOCIAL PROGRAM COST EQUIVALENTS

Weapons Cost in Fiscal 1982 Budget	Domestic Cuts in Fiscal 1982 Budget
One Trident Submarine 1.6 Billion	Child Nutrition 1.5 Billion
One KC-10A Cargo Plane 60 Million	Alcohol, Drug Abuse, and Mental Health 63 Million
MX Missile Development 2.9 Billion	Food Stamps 1.7 Billion
One CG-47 Aegis Cruiser 810 Million	Medicaid 914 Million
Two KC-10A Cargo Planes 120 Million	National Endowment for the Arts and Humanities 113 Million
One Trident Submarine 1.6 Billion	Unemployment Benefits 1.7 Billion
One SSN-688 Attack Submarine 650 Million	Education Aid for Poor Children 420 Million
Six Additional F-14A Fighter Planes 260 Million	Solar Energy Programs 249 Million

SOURCE: "What a Trillion and a Half Dollars Will Mean for You," Coalition for a New Foreign Policy and Physicians for Social Responsibility *Newsletter*, 2, No.3, (Fall 1981).

Appendix 3

THE WORLD'S NUCLEAR CLUB

Countries That Presently Have Nuclear Weapons

Britain	India
China	U.S.
France	USSR

Countries That Could Build Nuclear Weapons Now or in the Near Future

Canada	Argentina
Israel	South Africa
Italy	Switzerland
Japan	West Germany
Pakistan	

Countries That Could Build a Nuclear Weapon in the Next 10 Years

Brazil	Netherlands
Norway	Yugoslavia
Belgium	South Korea
Spain	Australia
Libya	Denmark
Egypt	Taiwan
Iraq	Austria
Finland	

Countries may not build a nuclear weapon even though they have the capacity.

SOURCE: U.S. Intelligence sources as reported in *New York Times*, July 14, 1981, and in *Newsweek*, June 22, 1981.

Appendix 4

SELECTED ORGANIZATIONS

A. Religious Organizations

American Friends Service Committee, an organization with regional offices which emphasizes education and nonviolent action against war and militarism. 1501 Cherry Street, Philadelphia, PA 19102. (215) 864-0204.

Center for Peace Studies. Department of Theology, Georgetown University, Washington, D.C. 20057. (202) 625-4240.

Church of the Brethren Peace Office, 1451 Dundee Avenue, Elgin, IL 60120.

Clergy and Laity Concerned, an interfaith organization which works for peace and justice. 198 Broadway, New York, NY 10038. (212) 964-6730.

Fellowship of Reconciliation, a religious pacifist organization committed to nonviolent methods of social change. Box 271, Nyack, NY 10960. (914) 358-4601.

Interfaith Center to Reverse the Arms Race. 132 North Euclid Avenue, Pasadena, CA 91101. (213) 449-9430.

Mennonite Central Committee, Peace Section, a center for education and coordination of Anabaptist peace witness. 21 South 12th Street, Akron, PA 17501. (717) 859-1151.

New Call to Peacemaking, a renewal movement within the historic peace churches (Mennonite, Brethren, and Quaker) committed to deepening their peace witness. Box 1245, Elkhart, IN 46515.

Pax Christi, the international Catholic peace organization. 3000 North Mango, Chicago, IL 60634. (312) 736-2113.

Peacemaking Project, coordinates United Presbyterian Church Peacemaking Efforts, 475 Riverside Drive, Room 1101, New York, NY 10115. (212) 870-3326.

Riverside Church Disarmament Program, provides speakers and resources for local disarmament education. 490 Riverside Drive, New York, NY 10027. (212) 222-5900.

Sojourners Peace Ministry. 1309 L Street NW, Washington, DC 20005. (202) 737-2780.

World Peacemakers, a mission group of the Church of the Saviour, which seeks to establish local groups in churches as well as across denominational lines. 2852 Ontario Road NW, Washington, DC 20009. (202) 265-7582.

B. General Organizations

Center for Defense Information, an excellent source for factual information and disarmament resources. 303 Capitol Gallery West, 600 Maryland Avenue SW, Washington, DC 20024. (202) 484-9490.

Coalition for a New Foreign and Military Policy, a coalition which researches, lobbies, and produces materials on disarmament and human rights issues. 120 Maryland Avenue NE, Washington, DC 20002. (202) 546-8400.

Council on Economic Priorities, a research organization which provides information about dependency on defense spending and economic conversion. 84 Fifth Avenue, New York, NY 10011. (212) 691-8550.

Ground Zero, coordinates public education on the arms race. 806 15th Street NW, Suite 421, Washington, DC, 20005. (202) 638-7402.

Institute for Policy Studies, a research and public education organization concerned with international issues. 1901 Q Street NW, Washington, DC 20009. (202) 234-9382.

NARMIC (National Action/Research on the Military Industrial Complex), a research and public education group on the defense industry. 1501 Cherry Street, Philadelphia, PA 19102. (215) 241-7175.

Nuclear Weapons Freeze Campaign. National Clearing House, 4144 Lindell Boulevard, 2nd Floor, St. Louis, MO 63108. (314) 533-1169.

Physicians for Social Responsibility, an organization of physicians, medical students, and other health professionals who provide information on the medical effects of nuclear war. P.O. Box 144, Watertown, MA 02172. (617) 924-3468.

War Resisters League. 339 Lafayette Street, New York, NY 10012.

Wilmington College Peace Resource Center. Wilmington, OH 45177. (513) 382-5338.

World Priorities, Inc.. Box 1003, Leesburg, VA 22075. (703) 777-6444.

Appendix 5

RESOURCES: BOOKS, FILMS, STUDY GUIDES
A. Selected Books

Adams, Ruth, and Susan Cullen, eds. *The Final Epidemic: Physicians and Scientists on Nuclear War.* Chicago: Education Foundation for Nuclear Science, 1981. Order from Physicians for Social Responsibility, listed in Appendix 4.

Aukerman, Dale. *Darkening Valley: A Biblical Perspective on Nuclear War.* New York: Seabury, 1981.

Barnet, Richard J. *Real Security.* New York: Simon and Schuster, 1981.

Ground Zero. *Nuclear War: What's In It For You.* New York: Simon and Schuster, 1982.

Rockman, Jane, ed. *Peace in Search of Makers.* Valley Forge, Pa.: Judson, 1979.

Sider, Ronald J., and Richard K. Taylor. *Nuclear Holocaust and Christian Hope.* Downers Grove, Ill.: InterVarsity Press, 1982.

Wallis, Jim. *The Call to Conversion: Rediscovering the Gospel for These Times.* New York: Harper and Row, 1981. Especially chapter 4, "The Peril."

_____, ed. *Waging Peace: A Handbook for the Struggle to Abolish Nuclear Weapons.* San Francisco: Harper and Row, 1982.

B. Study Guides and Resources
(See Appendix 4 for Full Addresses)

Boos-Koopman, Gayle, and Bill Price. *National Security and Christian Faith: A Study Guide on Real Security.* Washington, D.C.: World Peacemakers, 1982.

Center for Defense Information. *What Can I Do: Nuclear War Prevention Kit.* Washington, D.C.: Center for Defense Information. Excellent resource of ideas, organizations, films, addresses, and special suggestions for local action.

Cosby, Gordon, and Bill Price. *Handbook for World Peacemaker Groups.* Washington, D.C.: World Peacemakers.

Donaghy, John A. *Peacemaking and the Community of Faith: A Handbook for Congregations.* Nyack, N.Y.: Fellowship of Reconciliation.

Kownacki, Mary. ed. *A Race to Nowhere: An Arms Primer for Catholics.* Chicago: Pax Christi.

Sivard, Ruth Leger. *World Military and Social Expenditures.* Leesburg, Va.: World Priorities, Inc. Annual editions. Excellent resource for statistical information on nuclear arms.

Sojourners. *A Matter of Faith: A Study Guide for Churches on the Nuclear Arms Race.* Washington, D.C.: Sojourners Peace Ministry.

———. *My People I Am Your Security: Worship Resources in a Nuclear Age.* Washington, D.C.: Sojourners Peace Ministry.

Sojourners. *New Abolitionist Covenant.* A short guide for study and discussion. Distributed by Sojourners Peace Ministry.

United Presbyterian Church. *Nuclear Freeze Study and Action Guide.* New York: United Presbyterian Church).

C. Films and Graphics

The Last Epidemic: The Medical Consequences of Nuclear Weapons and Nuclear War. Contact Physicians for Social Responsibility.

Nuclear War Graphics Project, 100 Nevada Street, Northfield, MN 55057.

The War Game. Films Incorporated, 1144 Wilmette Avenue, Wilmette, IL 60091.

War/Peace Film Guide offers brief descriptions of 287 war/peace films and rental sources. World Without War Publications, 67 East Madison, Suite 1417, Chicago, IL 60603. (313) 236-7459.

War Without Winners. Contact Center for Defense Information.

For additional audiovisual suggestions, contact your denominational office or any of the peace organizations listed in Appendix 4.

Appendix 6

ACTIVITY RESOURCES

A. Nuclear Freeze Campaign

Nuclear Weapons Freeze Campaign
National Clearing House
4144 Lindell Boulevard
St. Louis, MO 63108

B. Studying the Local Effects of Nuclear War

1. Nuclear Mapping Kit distributed by The New Manhattan Project of American Friends Service Committee, 15 Rutherford Place, New York, NY 10003. (212) 777-4600.
2. *The Local Effects of Nuclear Weapons: A Guide to Studying Your Community*, distributed by Mennonite Central Committee, 21 South 12th Street, Akron, PA 17501. (717) 859-1151.

C. Researching Local Military Contractors

1. Contact NARMIC (National Action Research on the Military Complex), American Friends Service Committee, 1501 Cherry Street, Philadelphia, PA 19102. (215) 241-7175.
2. Contact the Washington Headquarters Services, The Pentagon, Room 3E843, Washington, DC 20301. (202) 295-6815. Ask for "Prime Contract Awards" by state and county.

D. General Activity Suggestions

"What Can I Do: Nuclear War Prevention Kit."
Order from Center for Defense Information. An excellent resource.

Appendix 7

TAX WITNESS RESOURCES

A. Books and Study Guides

Durland, William. *People Pay for Peace.* Colorado Springs, Colo.: Center Peace Publishers, 1982.

Kaufman, Donald D. *The Tax Dilemma: Praying for Peace, Paying for War.* Scottdale, Pa.: Herald Press, 1978.

_____. *What Belongs to Caesar?* Scottdale, Pa.: Herald Press, 1969.

Shelly, Maynard, and Ron Flickinger, eds. *Affirm Life: Pay for Peace.* Newton, Kan.: Historic Peace Church Task Force on Taxes, n.d.

War Resisters League. *Guide to War Tax Resistance.* New York, 1982.

B. Organizations

World Peace Fund
2111 Florida Avenue NW
Washington, DC 20008
(202) 483-3751

Promotes congressional legislation to allow conscientious objectors to designate part of their taxes for nonmilitary purposes.

The Center on Law and Pacifism
P.O. Box 1584
Colorado Springs, CO
(303) 635-0041

Publishes newsletter and provides legal services and counseling.

Appendix 8

SUGGESTIONS FOR DISCUSSION LEADERS

This book is designed for both personal and group study. The suggestions below may be helpful to leaders of groups that are using the book as a basis for discussion. Each chapter integrates technical material with theological issues and provides a framework for discussing nuclear war in Christian education settings. Chapters can be arranged in various formats if there are not enough discussion sessions to allot one per chapter. It would be ideal to have twelve sessions in order to allow time for outside speakers and/or special activities.

A. Twelve Tips

1. Encourage open discussion in the group by welcoming opinions that differ with the author's. The subject should stimulate a wide range of reactions. Try to create a setting where all the members feel free to express their ideas.
2. In addition to the questions at the end of each chapter, the author often asks questions in the text itself. These questions scattered throughout the text may also be helpful to stimulate discussion.
3. A film or a filmstrip might be used as a kickoff for the first session, as a pace-changing break between chapters, or as complementary material with a particular chapter.
4. Invite a physician to address the group on the medical effects of nuclear war. This would be especially appropriate with or after the material in chapter 3.
5. Invite a guest speaker to make a presentation in favor of maintaining military superiority with nuclear weapons.
6. Ask your local emergency management (civil defense) director to inform your group about local plans for responding to a nuclear attack.
7. As an introductory session you might ask someone to make a short presentation on the history of the arms race since 1945. Note the key events, issues, and overall trends. Such historical information should be readily available in a public library.
8. Write or call your denominational office, and ask for copies of any statements or position papers of your denomination on topics such as peace, disarmament, or the nuclear arms race.

Ask for a quantity of these to distribute to your group. Devote a session to discussing the statements.

9. If you plan to begin discussing this book at the first session, provide your participants with copies in advance so that they can read the first chapter(s) and come prepared for discussion.

10. Ask two teams of students (2 or 3 per team) to debate the question of nuclear disarmament. Ask the teams to take opposing sides and make a presentation of 10 to 15 minutes. Encourage the rest of the class to respond in discussion.

11. If the group has more than ten members, it may help to change pace and format by breaking down into smaller discussion groups occasionally.

12. It's important to devote some time in the course of this study to sharing and discussing specific plans for witness in response to the material. Encourage participants to commit themselves to small and specific acts of witness. Order a copy of *What Can I Do* from the Center for Defense Information (see Appendix 5 for address) at the beginning of the course.

B. Possible Format Arrangements by Number of Sessions

1. 12 sessions. Use some of the above suggestions for special activities in sessions one, six, and twelve. Assign a chapter for each of the other nine sessions.

2. 9 sessions. Assign a chapter for each session. Complement several of the sessions with some of the special activities above.

3. 6 sessions. The following chapter arrangements will fit together logically:

Session 1:	Chapter 1	Session 4:	Chapters 6,7
Session 2:	Chapters 2,3	Session 5:	Chapter 8
Session 3:	Chapters 4,5	Session 6:	Chapter 9

4. 4 sessions. The chapters may be ordered topically in the following fashion:

Session 1:	Chapters 1,2,3
Session 2:	Chapters 4,5
Session 3:	Chapters 6,7
Session 4:	Chapters 8,9

Scripture Index

General Index

Donald B. Kraybill is associate professor of sociology at Elizabethtown College, Pennsylvania. He served as a Mennonite pastor and church administrator for several years prior to graduate study at Temple University, where he received his PhD in 1975. He has taken postgraduate studies at Yale University and MIT.

Kraybill is an associate member of Physicians for Social Responsibility and has been active in peace education in a wide variety of church settings. In addition to numerous professional papers, he is the author of *The Upside-Down Kingdom* (Herald Press, 1978), which won the National Religious Book Award; coauthor of *Nuclear War and Lancaster County* (1981); and coeditor of *Perils of Professionalism* (Herald Press, 1982).

Married and the father of two daughters, Kraybill lives with his family in Elizabethtown, Pennsylvania, where they are members of the Elizabethtown Church of the Brethren.

The Christian Peace Shelf

The Christian Peace Shelf is a selection of Herald Press books and pamphlets devoted to the promotion of Christian peace principles and their applications. The editor (appointed by the Mennonite Central Committee Peace Section) and an editorial board from the Brethren in Christ Church, the General Conference Mennonite Church, the Mennonite Brethren Church, and the Mennonite Church, represent the historic concern for peace within these constituencies.

FOR SERIOUS STUDY

Durland, William R. *No King but Caesar?* (1975). A Catholic lawyer looks at Christian violence.

Enz, Jacob J. *The Christian and Warfare* (1972). The roots of pacifism in the Old Testament.

Hershberger, Guy F. *War, Peace, and Nonresistance* (Third Edition, 1969). A classic comprehensive work on nonresistance in faith and history.

Hornus, Jean-Michael. *It Is Not Lawful for Me to Fight* (1980). Early Christian attitudes toward war, violence, and the state.

Kaufman, Donald D. *What Belongs to Caesar?* (1969). Basic arguments against voluntary payment of war taxes.

Lasserre, Jean. *War and the Gospel* (1962). An analysis of Scriptures related to the ethical problem of war.

Lind, Millard C. *Yahweh Is a Warrior* (1980). The theology of warfare in ancient Israel.

Ramseyer, Robert L. *Mission and the Peace Witness* (1979). Implications of the biblical peace testimony for the evangelizing mission of the church.

Trocmé, André. *Jesus and the Nonviolent Revolution* (1975). The social and political relevance of Jesus.

Yoder, John H. *The Original Revolution* (1972). Essays on Christian pacifism.

————————. *Nevertheless* (1971). The varieties and shortcomings of Christian pacifism.

FOR EASY READING

Beachey, Duane. *Faith in a Nuclear Age* (1983). A Christian response to war.

Drescher, John M. *Why I Am a Conscientious Objector* (1982).

A personal summary of basic issues for every Christian facing military involvements.

Eller, Vernard. *War and Peace from Genesis to Revelation* (1981). Explores peace as a consistent theme developing throughout the Old and New Testaments.

Kaufman, Donald D. *The Tax Dilemma: Praying for Peace, Paying for War* (1978). Biblical, historical, and practical considerations on the war tax issue.

Kraybill, Donald B. *Facing Nuclear War* (1982). A plea for Christian witness.

_____. *The Upside-Down Kingdom* (1978). A study of the synoptic gospels on affluence, war-making, status-seeking, and religious exclusivism.

Miller, John W. *The Christian Way* (1969). A guide to the Christian life based on the Sermon on the Mount.

Miller, Melissa, and Phil M. Shenk. *The Path of Most Resistance* (1982). Stories of Mennonite conscientious objectors who did not cooperate with the Vietnam draft.

Sider, Ronald J. *Christ and Violence* (1979). A sweeping reappraisal of the church's teaching on violence.

Steiner, Susan Clemmer. *Joining the Army That Sheds No Blood* (1982). The case for biblical pacifism written for teens.

Wenger, J. C. *The Way of Peace* (1977). A brief treatment on Christ's teachings and the way of peace through the centuries.

FOR CHILDREN

Bauman, Elizabeth Hershberger. *Coals of Fire* (1954). Stories of people who returned good for evil.

Moore, Ruth Nulton. *Peace Treaty* (1977). A historical novel involving the efforts of Moravian missionary Christian Frederick Post to bring peace to the Ohio Valley in 1758.

Smucker, Barbara Claassen. *Henry's Red Sea* (1955). The dramatic escape of 1,000 Russian Mennonites from Berlin following World War II.